BEERHOUSES, BROTHELS AND BOBBIES

POLICING BY CONSENT IN HUDDERSFIELD AND THE HUDDERSFIELD DISTRICT IN THE MID-NINETEENTH CENTURY

DAVID TAYLOR

Published by University of Huddersfield Press

University of Huddersfield Press
The University of Huddersfield
Queensgate
Huddersfield HD1 3DH
Email enquiries university.press@hud.ac.uk

First published 2016

A CIP catalogue record for this book is available from the British Library.
ISBN 978-1-86218-139-7

Printed by The Amadeus Press,
Cleckheaton, West Yorkshire.

COVER IMAGE:
View of Huddersfield, William Cowen (1791–1864)
© Kirklees Image Archive

Contents

Tables

CHAPTER 1 1

Introduction: Themes, Sources and Context

WE LIVE – AND have lived for more than a century – in a policed society. We may be critical of the ways in which policing is organised and carried out but few would argue that we should not have uniformed, bureaucratically organized and accountable police forces. Yet (in historical terms) it is not that long ago that the introduction of such forces, the so-called 'new police', that replaced an older system based on parochial constables and night watchmen, was highly controversial. In the last fifty years police history has been a dynamic part of both academic and popular history. We now know so much more about the development of the 'new police' that few, if any, would subscribe to the comforting, 'Whiggish' narratives of the earliest police historians, such as Captain W L Melville Lee and Charles Reith.[1] But if we are all 'revisionists' now, there is considerable scope for disagreement, not least over the nature and extent of 'policing by consent', that supposedly distinctive feature of British policing. Further, despite the upsurge in publications our knowledge of the development of policing remains patchy, particularly in geographical terms. A considerable amount of attention has been devoted to the history of the police in London and the major cities but, with a few honourable exceptions, we know little about the policing of medium-sized towns and the counties. Given the importance of the West Riding to the socio-economic and political development of the country in the nineteenth century, it is surprising that so little research has been done on an area noted for its economic dynamism, social tensions and political agitation. This book goes some way to filling that gap by focussing on the advent of the 'new police' in Huddersfield and the Huddersfield district (that is, Upper Agbrigg) in the period c.1840 to 1868, which constituted the first generation of 'new policing' in the district. 1840 was a crucial year. The local magistrates had to decide whether or not to implement the recently-passed Rural Police Act. For reasons that will be discussed later, magistrates from urban and rural areas voted not to do so. So too, though coincidentally, was 1848. It was the year that saw the passing of the second Huddersfield Improvement Act, which paved the way for the creation of a 'new police' force in the town, and also saw the appointment of a superintending constable for the Huddersfield district, which led to an attempt to modernise parochial policing. 1868 is more of an arbitrary date but the incorporation of Huddersfield in that year had a significant impact on local policing. The town boundaries were extended, and the police force greatly enlarged, while there was a corresponding diminution in the Upper Agbrigg division of the West Riding County Constabulary (WRCC).

Association of British Counties Map of Yorkshire. Published under a Creative Commons Attribution-NonCommercial-NoDerivs 2.0 UK: England and Wales License.

Themes

There are three distinct strands to this book. The first is essentially institutional. Chapters two, three and eight consider in detail the way in which the 'new police' forces were created through an examination of the characteristics of the men who were recruited, their career outcomes and the developing structure of the forces as a whole. Although important in their own right, particularly chapter three which considers the fraught relationship between the Huddersfield Improvement Commissioners and successive superintendents of police, these chapters provide a framework for a broader social history of policing. This is the second strand, covered in chapters four, five, seven and eight, which consider the nature of police work and the experiences of policemen as individuals rather than as part of an overall statistical aggregate. The third strand comprises a social history of the district through the prism of policing. Chapters six, nine and ten focus on the communities and individuals who came into direct contact with the police on a day-to-day basis. The book falls into two distinct but complementary sections which approach the subject selectively. The beerhouse-brothels that figure so large in the discussion of Huddersfield do not appear in the consideration of Upper Agbrigg but this is not to suggest that the problem did not exist outside the town. Similarly, 'cruel' sports were not found solely in the countryside. Dogfights, for example, took place in Huddersfield as late as the 1860s. In both cases, repetition would not have added substantially to the overall arguments of the book. Likewise, embezzlement was a problem in Huddersfield but because less has been written about its rural manifestations it is discussed in detail only in part two. Even within the parameters of a local study certain topics have been omitted. Major offences, particularly the more spectacular and violent crimes, are touched on but briefly because they were few and far between and distract from the more mundane realities of crime and policing. There is, however, one omission that requires further explanation. The Huddersfield borough force was not unique in providing a fire-fighting capability. This had resource implications, even though the police fire brigade was but one of a number in the town. The provision of fire-fighting facilities in general was of considerable importance and deserves treatment in its own right. Policemen as firefighters are touched on briefly, not because their role was unimportant but because their role in Huddersfield needs fuller treatment at a later date.

There is an over-arching question that links the three strands – the notion, and more importantly, the realities of 'policing by consent' in the first generation of 'new policing', which is fully discussed in chapter eleven. The issues thus raised are central to much recent debate on the development of Victorian Britain but this is an unashamedly 'bottom-up' and local – but not parochial – study. By focussing on a relatively small geographical area (as well as a relatively brief time span), it is possible to tease out the complexities and contradictions in the development of 'new policing' that are necessarily lost in more general accounts. While it is important at times to generalise about regions and nations, it is equally important to ensure that such generalisations are based on an appropriate range of experiences and take into account particularities that are at the heart of the developing relationship between police and policed in these critical years. This is not to imply that the Huddersfield district is a microcosm of the country at large. While it is likely that the Huddersfield experience was not dissimilar from that of other medium-sized textile towns in the West Riding of Yorkshire and in south Lancashire, the emphasis here is on the distinctiveness of local circumstances and individuals and provides another building block from which broader conclusions can be drawn.

Sources

All histories are constrained by the availability and imperfections of source material and the reader needs to be aware of the problems associated with the primary sources that have been utilised. The minutes of the Huddersfield Improvement Commissioners and of their Watch Committee have been used extensively to create a picture of the emergence and development of the borough force between 1848 and 1868. They contain a wealth of valuable detail but there are important limitations. The commissioners did not think it appropriate or necessary to record the age, marital status and previous occupations of recruits to the force, nor did they systematically record the reasons for which men were dismissed. Occasionally, they tell why men resigned and the positions to which they moved but more often they do not. Discussions, at various levels, are recorded, sometimes in considerable detail, other times not. Indeed, some key events were not recorded at all even though other sources indicate that they were discussed. In contrast, the police registers of the WRCC contain considerable biographical details of the men who joined the force but they need to be treated with care. Place of birth, for example, is not the same as place of habitation at the time of joining. Similarly, the evidence of occupation can be misleading. No-one who served in the Upper Agbrigg division of the WRCC gave his occupation as 'policeman', even though several had been serving policemen when they applied to join the WRCC. The information on disciplinary records is patchy, in some cases giving reasons for dismissals in others not. There is also the vexed question of the honesty of the individuals. Edward Antrobus, who will figure large in the Honley riot of 1862, lied about his previous police experience and his official record is, quite simply, incorrect. Only later did the truth emerge and even then the police register was not amended. It is impossible to say how many other men were dishonest. Census material has been used to supplement information on individual officers. The general problems associated with the use of census enumerators' books are well known.[2] More specifically, many men served for only a brief period of time between censuses. Trying to identify which Joseph Baxter, for example, served as a policeman for three months in 1863 was highly time-consuming and ultimately fruitless. The most important source for this study has been the local and, to a lesser extent, the regional press. Again, the problems associated with such sources are well known. Two points deserve emphasis. First, coverage was selective as editors looked to circulation figures. The dramatic or the grotesque made good copy, the routine did not. Second, events were not reported objectively. Newspapers had overt political stances – the *Huddersfield Chronicle* was a conservative paper, the *Huddersfield Examiner* liberal – which influenced their coverage, including editorialising, on key events, such as the 1856 County and Borough Police Act. More subtly, the press reflected, often unconsciously and to varying degrees, prevailing assumptions about working-class men and women and the causes of criminality. While it is easier to determine what contemporaries believed to be the case, establishing the underlying 'realities' is more difficult not least because the voices of key players were not just distorted but often simply unheard. The voice of ordinary policemen is seldom heard. The evidence they gave in court was largely formulaic and gave little indication of their thinking about the job. There is virtually no direct evidence on why men joined the borough or county forces, what they thought of the job and why they left. There are also problems identifying the people who appeared in court. There are no surviving petty sessional records for these years. Furthermore, the individuals concerned rarely speak directly in the historical record. There are no memoirs or letters to explain their behaviour. In so far as they are heard, it is through the reports of their cases as they sought (in most cases) to exculpate themselves. Their words, when reported directly, were bowdlerised and regularised; often they were parodied. Even if they had been reported accurately, their words often reflected what they thought the magistrates wished to hear – that the offence was committed when the accused was "fresh" or "beerified" – rather than what they actually thought. Nonetheless, often through the unwitting testimony of the evidence, it is possible to piece together partial life-histories that help us understand the wider socio-economic context in which crimes were committed. The problems of source material are considerable and have to be confronted. There are times when the evidence seems akin to the images from a fairground hall of mirrors with some features grossly exaggerated, others diminished, some figures given exaggerated prominence and others glimpsed at the margins, if at all. Nonetheless, a picture can be constructed that is not simply caricature and this will be presented in the following pages. But, reader beware! Authorial confidence has to be judged in light of the frailties of the material from which the story has been constructed.

The central aim in writing this book has been to produce a thoroughly-researched but accessible account of critical developments –the advent of and response to the 'new police' – during an important period of time, the 'golden' years of Victorian Britain. So as not to disrupt the flow of the narrative, details of certain historiographical and methodological issues have been confined to the footnotes where full references are given. Finally, many of the issues discussed – the responsibilities and tactics of the police, the role of the law in criminalizing certain activities and the impact of wider socio-economic inequalities on both crime and policing – are not historical curiosities that can be safely labelled and put away like museum pieces but remain as relevant today as they were 150 years ago.

Context

Before moving to the main story, it is necessary to sketch in key aspects of the socio-economic context in which policing took place in Huddersfield and district in the middle decades of the nineteenth century. In 1837 White's *Directory* described Huddersfield as 'a populous, flourishing and handsome market town', a far cry from the early nineteenth century when it comprised an 'insignificant cluster of irregularly built lanes … [with] houses poor and scattered, the streets narrow, crooked and dirty.'[3] The growth of the fancy woollens trade* in the second quarter of the nineteenth century gave rise to an upsurge of new mill building, unmatched elsewhere in the West Riding. In 1851 the population of the township had risen to c.31,000 and reached c.70,000 by 1871. In 1851 roughly 80 per cent of the town's population lived within the limits of the improvement act, though this figure fell over the next twenty years. Since the 1820s there was a growing number of Irish people, living across the town but most particularly in and around Castlegate and Upperhead Row. Over the course of the 1850s and 1860s outlying villages, such as Lindley, Moldgreen and Paddock were gradually incorporated, both socially and economically, into Huddersfield. Incorporation gave formal recognition to this process of change. As in many other towns and cities, the middle classes moved away from the town centre, no longer wishing to live over their businesses. Huddersfield in 1871 was more socially segregated than in 1851 as the elites moved to Edgerton and Greenhead, the respectable lower middle classes to Primrose Hill and the Thornhill estate in Hillhouse and the respectable working classes to Rashcliffe and parts of Moldgreen.[4] The very poor, including many Irish, were confined to the courts and cellars in town but there remained large numbers of people still living in socially diverse districts in which relative prosperity and poverty coexisted cheek-by-jowl. Such changes increasingly led to the labelling of certain parts of the town as problematic, which in turn brought them more attention from the police and other authorities. Overall, Huddersfield was considered 'one of the prettiest and cleanest towns in the West Riding' and in comparisons with other industrial towns in the West Riding was relatively healthy. In the early 1840s the town's death rate was 18 per 1,000 compared to a West Riding average of 21. However, by the late 1860s, although still below the regional average, the death

* Fancy weaving, involving the use of various yarns – woollen, worsted, cotton and silk – to produce patterned cloths, was a feature of the Huddersfield district that can be traced back to the 1790s. Fancy waistcoats were a particular speciality. The third quarter of the nineteenth century saw the growth of the related novelty trade in which rabbit fur, feathers and even dog-hairs were incorporated into the cloth.

rate had increased by a third to 24 per 1,000.[5] The town had a problem with overcrowding in poorly built houses with limited access to water and even fewer sanitary provisions, and suffered periodic outbreaks of typhus, typhoid, diarrhoea and dysentery as well as influenza and even cholera. These problems were most acute in the closely-packed, poor working-class districts. 'Hell's Square' at the junction of Upperhead Row and Westgate was notorious for its recurrent outbreaks of epidemic disease.[6] Furthermore, physical squalor and moral decay were seen to go together.

Nonetheless, the town was seen to be prosperous in the third-quarter of the nineteenth century and its prosperity was firmly rooted in the burgeoning textile trades. The Great Exhibition of 1851 confirmed Huddersfield's standing as a major textiles centre. Six firms were awarded prize medals, including Armitage Brothers 'for excellence of manufacture, combined with economy' and J & T C Wrigley & Co. 'for general excellence of manufacture and ingenuity in new application of materials.'[7] In the mid-nineteenth century approximately 5,000 men and women (equivalent to 15 per cent of the population) were employed in the textile industries. The woollen trades predominated but cotton and silk became relatively more important in the third quarter of the nineteenth century. A number of factors contributed to this success: the continued growth of the fancy trade, notably the novelty trade; the development of the tweed trade; the introduction and improvement of the power loom; improved transport links (especially after the coming of the railway in 1848) and finally buoyant markets at home and abroad. Importantly, there was no dramatic or wholesale change from the old domestic production to the 'modern' integrated factory. Old and new coexisted. Handloom weavers – always the most vulnerable members of the textile fraternity – were an important element of the workforce in the 1860s even as factories and power looms became more common. There was never a repeat of the severe trade depression of 1837–43 but local trades, especially those dependent on exports, were subject to cyclical fluctuations that could throw once comfortably-off families into poverty as happened in 1865. There were also the unpredictable, random shocks – such as the Cotton Famine brought on by the American civil war – that could have dramatic social effects and important consequences in terms of criminal behaviour.

There was more to Huddersfield's success than spinning yarn and weaving cloth. Around these core industries developed a number of ancillary trades from dyeing to packaging and the demand generated had a knock-on effect that benefitted the town's growing 'shopocracy'. It is easy to understate the diversity of the local economy. There were butchers, bakers and tea-dealers; drapers, furriers, milliners and boot-makers; joiners, plumbers and painters; even an umbrella maker and a manufacturer of artificial legs, arms, hands and spring trusses! But there were also a large number of itinerant hawkers, peddlers, rag-and-bone men (and women) as well as unskilled labourers. In good times such people barely scraped a living; in bad times they struggled. Theirs was a 'makeshift economy' which comprised often intermittent, poorly-paid work, dependence upon charity or poor relief and recourse to crime. There were considerable inequalities in wealth (and its consequences in terms of ill-health and reduced life expectancy) and limited support for the losers in the economic life of the time. Mid-Victorian Huddersfield was more prosperous than ever before and the third-quarter of the nineteenth century saw striking improvement in the economic and social well-being of the town *in general terms*. But improvements in overall *per capita* income masked considerable variations. The town acquired yet more signifiers of progress and civilization – its Chamber of Commerce, its Philosophical Hall, its Collegiate Institute and its Literary & Scientific Society – but behind this facade there was an underside of insecurity, poverty and ill-health; of immorality and criminality that posed grave problems for the town's political elite. Indeed, as the march of civilization proceeded apace, so too did expectations of order and decorum, especially in public places. What might have been tolerated in the 1820s and 1830s was no longer acceptable in the 1850s and 1860s and the police had a central role to play, not just in fighting crime but in upholding new standards of behaviour.

Upper Agbrigg had its distinctive characteristics which gave rise to particular problems for the police. There was a sharp contrast between the compact geographical entity that was Huddersfield and the sprawling district that was Upper Agbrigg. Set in a diverse and dynamic region (the West Riding of Yorkshire) that played a critical part in the industrialisation of Britain, the district covered an area of almost 86,000 acres, including some bleak and inhospitable Pennine moorland, and contained a population of over 100,000. There were numerous villages and hamlets as well as some fourteen semi-industrial townships, varying in size from less than 2,000 people to over 10,000, to be found in the valleys of the Colne and the Holme rivers.[8] Old and new practices coexisted. Handloom weaving persisted in several villages (for example Kirkburton, Kirkheaton and Skelmanthorpe) while modern mills sprang up in others (such as Marsden and Meltham). Some communities (notably Golcar and Lockwood) prospered and grew as the result of modernization – the introduction of power looms – and proximity to Huddersfield while others (particularly Honley and Holmfirth) saw stagnation or decline. Social tensions created by economic change posed problems of order but they were compounded by a tradition of political radicalism and popular dissent, which manifested itself most notably in the Anti-Poor Law and Chartist movements of the 1830s and 1840s, which gave rise to fears that 'a vast number of the working classes ... are constantly aiming at the subversion of all social order'.[9] It also contributed to an ideological framework whereby police conduct was evaluated.

Some of the greatest problems stemmed from the geography of the region. The population was scattered and often in relatively inaccessible areas some distance from Huddersfield, where the office of the superintending constable (later district superintendent of police) was located. This was particularly true of places such as Marsden, Meltham, Holme, Saddleworth and Scammonden, seven or more miles from Huddersfield, located in the difficult to access hills of the Pennines. Much of the district around Marsden was 'uncultivated moorland'; the village of Holme was part of 'a mountainous moorland township'; and Scammonden was a 'wild and mountainous township'. Several of the villages closer to Huddersfield, such as Scholes and Shelley, were 'straggling' and 'scattered' while in the relatively compact village of Honley there were numerous small-scale (and independently-minded) landowners and artisans, who kept alive a radical tradition. Other townships, such as Holmfirth and Kirkheaton, had a reputation for lawlessness, especially cockfighting and brawling. However, proximity to Huddersfield did not guarantee an easier life for the police with upsurges of hostility towards them in adjacent villages such as Lindley, Birkby and Fartown. It was against this complex and evolving socio-economic and political background in which the superintending constable system and later the WRCC had to operate.

Endnotes

1 W L Melville Lee, *A History of Police in England*, London, Methuen, 1901 and C Reith, *A Short History of the British Police*, Oxford, Oxford University Press, 1948.

2 For an introduction see E Higgs, *A Clearer Sense of the Census*, London, HMSO, 1996.

3 G Phillips, 'Walks Around Huddersfield. No.1', *Bradford Observer*, [hereafter *B.Obs*], 2 September 1847.

4 There was also movement of the very poor, notably the 'low Irish' driven out to Johnny Moore's Hill, Paddock which was beyond the jurisdiction of the Improvement Commissioners. This section draws heavily on R Dennis, 'The Social geography of Victorian Huddersfield' in Hilary Haigh, ed., *Huddersfield: A Most Handsome Town*, Huddersfield, Kirklees Cultural Services, 1992, pp.423–48.

5 For further details, see H Marland, *Medicine and society in Wakefield and Huddersfield, 1780–1870*, Cambridge, Cambridge University press, 1987, esp. chapter two, section 3, pp.34–44.

6 *Ibid*, p.36. For continuing problems of insanitation, especially in unregulated lodging houses see *Huddersfield Chronicle*, [hereafter *HC*], 4 March 1865, 7 July, 1 & 8 September and 8 December 1866.

7 W B Crump & G Ghorbal, *History of the Huddersfield Woollen Industry*, Huddersfield, 1935, reprinted 1967, p.132.

8 D T Jenkins, 'Textiles and other industries, 1815–1914' in Haigh, *Huddersfield*, pp.241–74.

9 Captain Fenton to General Bouverie, 29 December 1832 quoted in J Hargreaves, '"A Metropolis of Discontent": Popular Protest in Huddersfield, c.1780–c.1850' in Haigh, *Huddersfield*, pp.208-9. See also N Pye, *The Home Office and the Chartists: Protest and Repression in the West Riding of Yorkshire*, Pontypool, Merlin, 2013.

The Development of the Huddersfield Borough Police Force: Continuity and Change

ON THE 6TH of November 1848 the Improvement Commissioners advertised for 'a number of persons to act as a constabulary force' within the limits of the Huddersfield Improvement Act, and the first men were sworn in in January 1849.[1] The creation of a 'new' police force marked an important stage in the development of policing in the town. The following years were to reveal major problems both in creating a disciplined and effective body of men and in developing a good working relationship with the town's commissioners. Nonetheless, in the last report before incorporation, Lieutenant-Colonel, John Woodford, Her Majesty's Inspector of Constabulary for the Northern District, judged the force to be 'an effective and well-selected body'.[2] This chapter will provide a largely statistical analysis of the development of the force that will be the backdrop to a consideration of the working lives of the men who patrolled the town and of the streets in which they operated. As in several other towns and cities, the transition from 'old' to 'new' policing was more gradual than once thought but, in adopting a recruitment policy in late 1848 that gave weight to experience, the new Improvement commissioners eased matters in the short-run while creating problems of inefficiency in the longer-term.

Policing Before 1848

Police reform in Huddersfield was a gradual process spread over several decades, though accelerating in the 1840s and 1850s. In the first decades of the nineteenth century, despite rapid population growth and bitter industrial and political struggles, there were but modest changes to the traditional institutions of law and order.[3] In 1812, in the wake of Luddite disturbances, the town vestry deemed it 'highly necessary' that 'a standing constable to act as a police officer' be elected. Reflecting contemporaries' beliefs regarding the cause of crime and disturbance, the constable was expected to visit on a regular basis public houses and lodging houses as well as examining hawkers, pedlars and the like for stolen goods. The post was made full-time in 1817 following 'the enormous burglaries and other depredations recently committed'.[4] Policing was further strengthened under the 1820 Huddersfield Improvement Act, which contained provisions for the appointment of 'such Number of able-bodied Men as they [the commissioners] shall judge proper to be employed as Watchmen and as a Patrol'.[5] Their wide-ranging responsibility was

> to apprehend and secure in some proper Place or Places of Security ... all Malefactors, Rogues, Vagabonds, idle and disorderly Persons, Disturbers of the Public Peace, Prostitutes and all Persons who shall be found wandering or misbehaving themselves during the Hours of keeping Watch.[6]

The new commissioners adopted a conservative approach when considering the establishment of the night watch, taking the advice of George Whitehead, the parochial assistant constable and manorial deputy constable, before establishing a watch of ten men under the oversight of a superintendent or captain of the watch. In 1822/3 Joseph Berry, who was already manorial deputy constable and probably parochial assistant constable as well, was appointed as captain of the watch. Cooperation with existing institutions continued for over a decade but in the mid-1830s the tripartite arrangement fell apart. Berry's successor, Francis Dalton, came in for criticism, particularly from the Radicals in the township vestry. In 1834 a challenge to his salary led to his resignation, which gave rise to a number of significant changes. In November 1834 the commissioners appointed as captain of watch Abraham Milnes with explicit instructions 'not to engage in any other business.' Although charged with the responsibility of reporting and arresting thieves, Milnes' role was more supervisory, checking nightly on the watchmen, reporting neglect and misconduct, as well as ensuring that the town's gas lamps were kept clean and functioning properly. Not long after, an attempt by the town vestry to establish a day-patrol was thwarted by the manorial Court Leet. Seizing upon the opportunity, in 1836 the commissioners appointed William Dukes as patrolman and governor of the lock-up in Bull and Mouth Street. Within months two more patrolmen were appointed, thereby unifying control of day and night policing, though this did not immediately translate into coordinated action.

It was in this context that the permissive Rural Police Act of 1839 was considered in the town. There was strong opposition, not least from the radical linen draper and one-time chief constable, William Stocks, to a proposal that was seen to threaten the autonomy of the township. Huddersfield, like many other towns both small and large, was jealous of its powers. There was no desire to relinquish them to a county police force. The town's leading political figures agreed that policing arrangements were adequate, without putting an undue burden on the ratepayer. There was some high-flown rhetoric about the beauty of the British Constitution and the principles of common law going back to Magna Carta, and beyond, but one of the most telling arguments was that the proposed rural police force would be under the 'Influence and Direction of a power over whom the Inhabitants have no influence or control'.[7] The other key consideration was expense: a rural police force, it was argued, would put an unfair burden on local ratepayers.[8]

The situation changed in the mid-1840s. In 1845, for reasons which remain unclear, the commissioners did not re-appoint two of their three patrolmen. John Danson remained, primarily responsible for the lock-up. This provided an opportunity for the town vestry to fill the gap by appointing two paid constables under the provision of the 1842 Parish Constable Act.[9] The Chartist Joshua Hobson had spoken out vehemently against the appointment of paid constables, denouncing them as spies, but other Radicals, notably John Leech and Lawrence Pitkethly, were key figures in persuading the vestry meeting of 13th of February 1845 to appoint two paid constables. This was an attempt by the Radicals to seize the initiative by putting forward their own nominees, William Townend and John Wood. The move was only partially successful. The magistrates refused to ratify both men and a further meeting took place to find two 'proper persons' to act as constables in place of the two men previously nominated. Wood's name was withdrawn but Townend's was put forward again, this time with that of Abraham Sedgwick. They were appointed and after 1846 worked under the purview of a standing committee and later under the Watch Committee of the Huddersfield Improvement Commission.

Townend and Sedgwick were conscientious and active officers. They were praised by the magistrates for their 'vigilant search' following a highway robbery near Huddersfield and their prosecution of 'the notorious "Bill Weetman" whose house in Castlegate had been used for prostitution. Through their diligence 'such characters as [Weetman] will now have very little rest for the soles of the feet in Huddersfield.'[10] In January 1845, following the arrest of a thief in Huddersfield, the *Bradford Observer* was fully of praise, opining that police in 'the whole West Riding could not match ... the Huddersfield constables.'[11] Notwithstanding organizational changes and some successes by the new Huddersfield constables, policing arrangements prior to 1848 had been heavily criticized, particularly in the pages of the *Leeds Mercury*. In September 1846 it highlighted 'the defective state of the Huddersfield police' which it claimed 'has long been a matter of surprise and regret to the inhabitants'.[12] The most sustained criticism came from certain witnesses, giving evidence to the preliminary inquiry on the Huddersfield Improvement bill. Systemic failure, the result of fragmentation and the lack of an over-arching authority was the central argument. The night watch, comprising a dozen men under a captain of watch, was appointed by the Commissioners for Lighting, Watching and Cleansing; a patrolman, largely responsible for the town prison, was also appointed by the Commissioners; additionally, two paid parochial officers, operating during the day, were appointed by the town vestry under the 1842 Parochial Constable Act; and there was an honorary Chief Constable appointed annually by the Court Leet.[13] There were also more specific criticisms. The inefficiency of the poorly-paid night watch, which had not been augmented since the mid-1830s, led to the employment of private watchmen; the effectiveness of the paid constables was severely constrained by 'the caprice of a Town Meeting' and the pernicious influence of beerhouse keepers in 'disorderly parts of the town'; and in the absence of 'united management', not only was there no coordination between night-watchmen and day constables, but worse there were quarrels between them.[14] As a consequence of these shortcomings, it was argued, the level of criminality in the town was much higher than in neighbouring Halifax or Wakefield. Twice as many people from Huddersfield appeared at the assizes in 1847 than from Halifax; a fact which, for contemporaries, could only be explained by the weak police institutions in the former.[15] Conventional wisdom at the time believed that criminals migrated from well-policed areas to weakly-policed areas. In hindsight, these figures might point to the opposite conclusion, namely that the Huddersfield police were more efficient in capturing criminals than their counterparts in Halifax! However, it was the case for the prosecution that carried the day. There was much force in the arguments – notably the concern with fragmented authority – but it is important to recognize the political purpose to discredit the old order. Milnes, the captain of the night watch, was scarcely given a hearing as he tried to defend the quality of the men under his command.

The New Borough Force: Size and Structure

The 1848 Improvement Act marked a new era in which the town would have a unified and full-time police force, with its own superintendent constable and under the control of the Watch Committee.[16] This was emphasized in the rather rudimentary seven-point conditions of service approved by the Improvement Commission in December, 1848.[17] There would be 'no conflicting jurisdictions, no rivalry on account of different masters, no keeping back of information for sake of pocketing perquisites'.[18] Rather, 'the whole force will form but one combination ready to be brought to bear at any one point in time of emergency or danger'.[19] Furthermore, the commissioners made every effort 'to select efficient officers and to introduce a system of strict discipline and subordination'.[20] Members of the force were to be aged between twenty-five and forty on recruitment and expected to live within the boundaries of the act, though dispensation not to do so could be sought from the Watch Committee. All men were expected to be available night and day, with the day constables expected to be in 'complete uniform at all times.' Further, all men were made aware that they could be suspended from duty or dismissed 'for unfitness, negligence or misconduct'. This was a clear statement of intent, implicitly rejecting a flawed past and promising an improved future; but the realities of creating an efficient force proved to be considerable.

In practical terms there was less of a break with the past. Advertisements had been placed locally and in 'several Towns in Yorkshire and Lancashire where there is a good organized Police force' and a total of just over 200 applications were received.[21] The commissioners adopted a three-point recruitment strategy. First, men not linked to previous policing in the town were appointed to the three senior posts. Of these only one was a local man. John Cheeseborough, previously the town magistrates' bailiff, was appointed superintendent constable.[22] The inspector of the night constables, John Thomas, came from Ripon recommended by 'the Earl of Ripon and by the mayor and several Aldermen and Town Councillors of Ripon', while the sergeant of the night constables, John Brown, an ex-army man, and a serving officer in the Manchester force was commended by Inspector Mullen of the Manchester Detective force. The major victim of the reorganization was Abraham Milnes, the captain of the old night-watch, still in post for the interim, who was interviewed in person but not appointed to the new force. The second part of the strategy was to identify men of proven ability already serving as law enforcement officers. All members of the night-watch and the two parochial officers were interviewed and six of the old night-watch were appointed as night constables, both paid parochial officers (Townend and Sedgwick) became day constables and the previous patrolman, responsible for the town gaol, John Danson, was also appointed as day constable.[23] The third element of the strategy was to appoint men new to the town to the remaining eight night-constable posts. This pattern of recruitment contrasted with the 'clean sweep' approach adopted in Hull and nearby Halifax but had more in common with two other nearby West Riding forces, Leeds and Sheffield, though in neither of those cities was there the same degree of concern with 'old' policing arrangements as in Huddersfield.[24] In addition to the continuity in personnel, the new force in Huddersfield was not significantly larger than its predecessor.[25] On the eve of the 1848 Improvement Act there were twelve night-watchmen and three day constables; immediately afterwards, there were fifteen night constables, including a sergeant, and overseen by an inspector, and three day constables. However, crucially there was no fragmentation of authority. From 1848 at the head of the police hierarchy stood the superintendent constable; and the town force, in turn, was responsible to the newly-appointed Watch Committee.

One of the main criticisms levelled at the old commissioners was their failure to increase the size of the night watch, notwithstanding the growth of the town. This was not the case after 1848. During the mid-1850s, with legislative change moving haltingly through parliament, numbers were increased initially to twenty-five and later to thirty-two. This enlargement was not without its critics. At least one commissioner (Mr. J Turner) claimed that police numbers could be reduced because they were 'idle and inefficient'.[26] A more sustained attack was made in the early 1860s by the 'economical' faction. Turner, a long-time critic of expenditure on the police, returned to the fray in the summer of 1861, reiterating his opinion that the town 'could do with fewer police' but this time supported by the influential figure of the chair of the commissioners, William Keighley, who made clear that 'considering the population of the town and the limits of their area' police numbers were 'beyond what was needful' and that there was no case for 'keeping so large a staff in times of peace'.[27] Two months later Keighley returned to the subject, declaring that there was now 'an opportunity for retrenchment'.[28] Information relating to the size and cost of various forces in Yorkshire and Lancashire was presented to the October meeting of the commissioners. Although costs per man were not out of line with other forces, Keighley made much of the fact that Huddersfield was 'at the head of the list both as to the number of policemen and as to the area and population over which they had to exercise duties'.[29] Turner, unsurprisingly, argued that the force could be cut by three or four men, but not all agreed. Commissioner John Sykes received vocal support when he argued that property was better protected and crime lessened by the presence of the force as presently constituted. Natural wastage took the force down to thirty in the summer of 1862 but the following year it stood at thirty-one, at which level it remained until 1867.[30] On the eve of incorporation the strength of the force was back to thirty-two men.[31]

The favourable position of the town and its force is clear from the annual returns made by Her Majesty's Inspector of Constabulary. The area policed by the Huddersfield force was relatively small, amounting to twenty-three acres per constable from 1857 onwards, though in the early 1850s the figure was about thirty-five acres. These were the lowest figures in the West Riding and only Halifax and Wakefield had a similar ratio. The annual report for 1862, using the most recent census figures, gave a ratio of population to police in Huddersfield of 738:1, the most favourable in the West Riding.[32] Moreover, this represented a significant improvement on the position in the early 1850s when, with a smaller force, the ratio had been approximately 1250:1. The Huddersfield police/population ratio was strikingly low. Generally speaking, the larger cities were more heavily policed but Bradford, Leeds and Sheffield all had ratios 20 to 30 per cent higher; while towns more comparable in size, such as Halifax, Wakefield and York had ratios 25 to 35 per cent higher. Thus, members of the Huddersfield police force enjoyed a double advantage: both the *per capita* area and population to be policed were appreciably less than in other West Riding towns and cities.

Table 2.1: Persons per constable & acres per constable: West Riding of Yorkshire, 1862

	PERSONS/CONSTABLE	ACRES/CONSTABLE
Bradford	*892*	*55*
Doncaster	*1264*	*145*
Halifax	*1000*	*27*
Huddersfield	*738*	*23*
Leeds	*908*	*84*
Pontefract	*1068*	*372*
Ripon	*3086*	*723*
Sheffield	*969*	*120*
Wakefield	*927*	*25*
York	*1009*	*68*
West Riding	*1485*	*2858*

Source: *Parliamentary Papers*, 1863 (20), Reports of Inspectors of Constabulary for Year Ending Sept. 1862

There were a number of distinctive features of the town police. Unlike many towns, Huddersfield had a separate day and night force until 1863 when, following a suggestion by Colonel Woodford, and encouraged by the new superintendent of police, William Hannan, the Watch Committee resolved to abolish the distinction between day and night constables. The decision met with considerable opposition from the four day constables, three of whom had seven years' service to their names and no record of misconduct. They argued that promotion to day constable 'has always been looked upon as a reward for good and meritorious conduct' and, as a consequence, 'a compulsory return is looked upon … as in some degree a degradation, or at any rate as a punishment for improper conduct.'[33] The dispute reached crisis point in early June when the four men were suspended and they then handed in their resignations. In early July a compromise was agreed. The men were reinstated and paid for the two weeks' suspension but on condition that they would accept the proposed change. At the subsequent meeting of the commissioners, Keighley talked emolliently of misunderstandings and a desire to act in the best interest of the men, while reaffirming the decision to abolish the distinction between day and night men, but the fact remained that the day constables had been forced to back down.[34] The Watch Committee also had a policy of approving men as supernumerary constables, from whose ranks full-time constables were recruited. Finally, the new commissioners continued a policy, dating back to the 1830s, of appointing additional night constables for the winter months, some of whom became full-time constables.

As the force grew in size and its duties expanded it became clear that a more sophisticated structure was needed. By the mid-1850s it was recognised that a single class for all constables was unsatisfactory and a source of grievance. As a consequence, a three-class structure evolved. In 1856 night constables were divided into two classes, with day constables a separate category.[35] Following the amalgamation of the day and night forces in 1865 there were three classes of constable. On appointment all constables were in the lowest class, where, to all intents and purposes, they served their apprenticeship, learning on the job. Promotion to the second class was almost automatic but further progress was not guaranteed. In contrast, the first class comprised the more able men, often in the early years of the career, but showing promise and a determination to move up the police hierarchy. The first and third classes were relatively unproblematic but the same could not be said of the second class, in which several long-serving men found themselves stranded, their careers (and their pay prospects) stagnating. It is no coincidence that a 6*d* (2½ p) per week increase for good conduct was introduced in 1861 and a merit class (effectively a reward for long service) in 1864. Finally, after a period in the mid-1850s when detective responsibilities were shared by the sergeants in the force, a detective officer was officially designated in 1858 and this area of work was expanded in subsequent years.[36] Thus, over the course of two decades a larger, more complex force came into being.

The minutes of the Improvement Commission carry little information on the ages, places of birth and occupations of the men recruited to the town's police force. No conduct registers have survived (if they were ever kept) so recourse has to be made to census returns, which provide a good guide to the age structure of the force.[37] The average age of the men who comprised the initial force in 1849 was thirty-five. This reflected the commissioners' policy of retaining men of proven ability. The average age of such experienced men was forty years, though this figure is skewed by the surprising presence of sixty-year-old James Hirst. The 'new' men had a lower average age but the presence of two men in their forties pushed it up to thirty-two. In terms of experience, the commissioners' recruitment policy made sense but, given the physical demands of the job, there was a trade-off between experience and efficiency. By the end of the 1850s it was apparent that some of the older men were less efficient and not always fully fit for all police duties. In contrast to the initial force, the men subsequently appointed tended to be younger, with an average age of twenty-seven years. Two-thirds of recruits in the 1850s and 1860s were in their twenties and the remainder (with one exception) in their low to mid-thirties.

Evidence relating to places of birth and previous occupations is less complete. A large majority of Huddersfield police men were local men. Just over 40 per cent were born in Huddersfield or nearby townships such as Almondbury and Lockwood, and a further 35 per cent in other parts of the West Riding. Contrary to experience elsewhere, there was but one Irish-born policemen in the first generation of new policing in the town.[38] In terms of occupational background the striking feature of the census information is the absence of previous police experience. Predictably many were drawn from the local woollen trade, though there were also tailors, shoemakers, cordwainers and cloggers. A small percentage were general or agricultural labourers. Although recruitment reflected the wider economic structure of the region and the fluctuating fortunes of various trades, there is no evidence to suggest a meaningful link between either long-term or short-term unemployment.[39] Nonetheless, the decision to become and remain a policeman depended in no small measure on the financial rewards of the job.

The New Borough Force: Pay, Perquisites and Promotion

One of the great financial advantages of police work was its regularity – there were none of the seasonal variations experienced in many trades – but this in itself was not sufficient to attract and retain capable men. The old (pre-1848) commissioners had been criticised for the low pay of their night-watchmen but the new commissioners were also concerned to keep to a minimum the 'burden' on local rate payers. Police pay rates were determined by the Watch Committee. There was no automatic review process and pay increases were commonly granted in response to pressure from the force. Memorials containing the demands of men of all rank were presented to the Watch Committee on an irregular basis throughout the 1850s and 1860s. It was commonplace to seek comparison with pay rates in other forces before coming to a decision; and the continuing presence of an 'economical' faction among the commissioners ensured that any pay increases were subject to rigorous scrutiny. The initial wage rates agreed in December 1848 were as follows:

Table 2.2: Huddersfield borough police: rates of pay

RANK	WEEKLY PAY	OTHER BENEFITS
Superintendent	*£1-10-0*	*House at lock-up*
Inspector – night	*£1-3-0*	*Great coat & oilskin*
Sergeant – night	*£1-0-0*	*Great coat & oilskin*
Day constable	*18s*	*Uniform*
Night constable	*17s*	*Uniform*

Source: Huddersfield Improvement Commission Minutes, KMT 18/2/2/1, 1 December 1848

To put these figures in perspective, in terms of wages, local operatives, according to the *Morning Chronicle*, were 'very fairly situated'. Slubbers, carders, spinners, dyers, fullers, raisers and finishers 'may average about 18*s* (90p) a week' but the inclusion of male weavers – especially woollen handloom weavers – dragged down the average to 14*s* (70p) or 15*s* (75p).* Furthermore, labourers working in the local construction industry earned only 14*s* (70p) a week and their employment was far from regular.[40] For these more vulnerable members of the local economy policing may well have

* The present-day equivalent of £1 in 1850, using the retail price index, would be c.£95. However, using average earnings, £1 a week in 1850 would be equivalent to c.£700 a week in the present. For details, including a discussion of the methodological issues involved, see www.measuringworth.com.

been financially attractive but it is less obvious that the wages of a constable were sufficient to attract (or retain) 'good' men from an artisanal background. The high rate of turnover lends support to this proposition. Nevertheless, police wage rates remained largely unchanged for almost a decade. The forthcoming creation of the WRCC created a problem for the town force. In August 1856 the commissioners expressed concern that men were leaving to join the better-paid county force and in January 1857 the chief constable of the WRCC, Colonel Cobbe, wrote to the commissioners, commenting on the number of Huddersfield policemen who were applying 'to better their condition' in the county force.[41] As a consequence modest increases were approved for all ranks, except sergeant. Despite pressure from the 'economical' faction on the commission, further increases were approved in the early and mid-1860s, in part in response to the observation by the inspector of constabulary that low wages were making it difficult to recruit and retain good men. The position is summarised in table 2:3.

Table 2.3: Huddersfield borough police: pay increases 1856 & 1865

RANK	WEEKLY PAY: 1856	RANK	WEEKLY PAY: 1865
Superintendent			
Inspector	*£1-3-0 to £1-4-0*	*Inspector*	*£1-8-0 to £1-10-0*
Sergeant	*£1-2-0*	*Sergeant*	*£1-4-0 to £1-5-0*
Day constable	*18s to £1*	*Detective Constable*	*£1-5-0 to £1-7-0*
1st Class night constable	*17s to 19s*	*Merit Class*	*£1 to £1-1-0*
2nd Class night constable	*17s to 18s*	*1st Class constable*	*£1 to £1-1-0*
		2nd Class constable	*19s to £1*
		3rd Class constable	*18s to 19s*

Source: Watch Committee Minutes KMT 18/2/3/14/1, 28 July 1856 and KMT 18/2/3/14/2, 27 November 1865

The average weekly pay for constables in the West Riding in 1857 varied from a low of 18*s* (90p) to a high of £1-2-0 (£1-10) and in the late-1860s from a low of £1 to a high of £1-3-0 (£1.15). Huddersfield policemen were paid at the lower end of the range in 1857 and at the lowest level in 1865.[42]

Basic police pay was augmented in two ways. The first was an annual discretionary payment, agreed by the Watch Committee from 'a general fund for meritorious conduct etc.' made up of fees, allowances, rewards and so forth. From 1850 all men received an annual payment that reflected their performance during the past year. The scheme was not without its critics. It was suspended in 1856 and, though reinstated the following year, was criticised by Superintendent Beaumont, who wanted it to be 'done away with altogether'.[43] The commissioners thought otherwise. As William Keighley explained 'the Commissioners did not begrudge them having [it] because they considered that their office was not in many respects an enviable one, and that they were occasionally exposed to danger and personal violence'.[44] Only with the belated introduction of a superannuation scheme in 1864 was the perquisite fund allocation finally abolished.

The criteria for allocation are not set out in the Watch Committee minutes. Initially decisions appear to have been based partly on length of service and partly on the disciplinary performance of the individual. By the late-1850s and early-1860s the number of cases brought before the town's magistrates were considered. There was a clear hierarchical dimension to the awards. In every year for which detailed records survive, the superintendent of police received the largest sum of money, followed by other senior officers. In 1850 the newly-promoted Superintendent Thomas received £2-10-0 (£2.50), substantially more than the £1-10-0 (£1.50) awarded to seven other men.[45] In 1857 Superintendent Beaumont was awarded a gentlemanly four guineas (£4-4-0 or £4.20), five long-serving inspectors and sergeants received £3 while the remaining men were awarded sums varying from 5*s* (25p) to £1-17-6 (£1.87½). Newly-appointed men received least, a reflection of the fact that they had brought few, if any, cases before the town's magistrates. Although the Watch Committee did not record the reasons for its decisions, it is clear that effectiveness (measured by the number of cases brought) was usually a key consideration. In 1857, for example, Jonathan Sheffield, despite being in the force for just over a year, had brought fifty cases (the third highest total) and was rewarded with a payment of £1-17-6 (£1.85½). Benjamin Marsden, a longer-serving man with a similar record of cases received the same sum, despite having been reported for assaulting drill-sergeant Mellor during the past year. In contrast other long-serving men, but with significantly fewer cases to their names, received only £1-12-6 (£1.62½) while two others with a single disciplinary report against their names received £1-10-0 (£1.50). Recently appointed men were not totally ignored and even one supernumerary constable received 5*s* (25p). Only one man received nothing. John Field had been in the force for only six months and had no cases to his name. However, the fact that he was reportedly intending 'to leave immediately on receiving his expected perquisite' scuppered his chances! A similar pattern emerges from the most detailed information which relates to the 1862 distribution. The superintendent (Priday) was awarded three guineas (£3-3-0 or £3-15), the two inspectors (Townend and White) and the detective constable (Partridge) two guineas (£2-2-0 or £2.10) and the three sergeants £2 each. In terms of effectiveness detective Partridge clearly (and unexpectedly) led the field with ninety-one cases but the other men combined their responsibilities as senior officers with an above average number of arrests.[46] Among the ordinary constables, hierarchy continued to play an important role. First-class constables Hutchinson and Irving were deemed worthy of a payment of £1-5-0 (£1.25) whereas second-class class constables Eli Nutton and Hugh Moore only of £1-2-6 (£1.10½). Indeed, Moore might well have felt badly treated as his tally of forty cases was exceeded only by that of the force's detective. The most common payment was of £1, which was paid to men with fewer cases to their name, irrespective of length of service. There were some variations. Constables Lee and Sykes had a solid record in terms of cases but appear to have been penalized for having received money from the sick fund during the past year. More baffling is the case of first-class constable William Redfearn who, despite five-and-a-half years in the force and over thirty cases in the previous year, was awarded the same sum as James Gledhill, an original member of the force with only eight cases to his name that year. A small number of men received a mere 10*s* (50p). Two were supernumerary constables but three ordinary constables were penalized for their disciplinary record – two had been found drunk on duty and the third in the harness room when he should have been working his beat.

The allocation of the perquisite fund has been considered in detail for two reasons.[47] First, it was a supplement to the regular income of the police. For most men in the early 1860s their award was roughly equivalent to a week's wages, though somewhat more in the case of senior men. Put another way, for constables with a good disciplinary record, it was worth approximately an additional 6*d* (2½p) per week. However, it was a discretionary award, which leads to the second point. The annual allocation was another opportunity for successive

Watch Committees to exercise their control over the town's police force, rewarding the worthy but not those who had transgressed.[48] This in turn reflects upon the management approach of the Watch Committee and the Improvement Commissioners more generally. They saw it as their responsibility to be involved in a hands-on manner in the running of the police. Such micro-management, which contrasts for example with the approach adopted in Leeds and particularly Hull – though not dissimilar to Halifax – was to have significant repercussions regarding working relationships, not least with senior officers of the force.

The second way of augmenting income was via promotion from within the ranks. Until 1863 the most common career progression was from supernumerary constable to night constable and then to day constable. A much smaller number of men were more successful, progressing from day constable to night sergeant to day sergeants and maybe to inspector or superintendent.[49] Overall, meaningful progression through the ranks was restricted to a small minority. Prior to the amalgamation of the day and night force, thirty-three men (including one man re-appointed) were appointed as night constables and served for at least five years.[50] Sixteen (c.50 per cent) made the transition from night to day constable and would have seen their weekly wage increased by 1*s* (5p). Of these men eight (50 per cent) went on to become sergeants with a further 2*s* (10p) per week pay increase but only one gained further promotion under the Improvement Commission. In contrast, all three men who were appointed as day constables in 1848/9 became inspectors. While it would be wrong to dismiss the importance of a pay increase of 1*s* (5p) or 2*s* (10p) per week, it remains the case that Huddersfield policemen were relatively poorly paid in comparison with fellow officers in Yorkshire, and internal promotion prospects, except for the first generation of men appointed in 1848/9, were limited. A discretionary perquisite scheme that offered the equivalent of just over a week's wages, or 6*d* (2½p) increase per week), made some difference but was offset by the fact that there was no guaranteed superannuation scheme until 1864.

Recruitment, Retention and Discipline

Despite the modest growth in wages and limited promotion opportunities, the town force grew in size and complexity, stabilizing around a total of thirty-one men in the 1860s. Closer examination, however, reveals a more diverse and problematic picture. Beneath the headline figure of the overall police establishment there was considerable movement in and out of the town force. In the twenty-year history of policing under the 1848 Improvement Commission almost 200 men were recruited. There was a cluster of problems (experienced in most towns and cities) relating to recruitment and retention and the creation of an efficient body of men.[51] However, as will be discussed in chapter three, the situation was further complicated by the high turnover of senior officers and ongoing tensions between police superintendents and successive watch committees. In this respect Huddersfield was highly unusual.

Recruitment, in quantitative terms, was not as great a problem in Huddersfield as in, for example, Middlesbrough where, in times of economic boom, high-paid local industries reduced the flow of recruits and even attracted men away from the force.[52] A steady number of men presented themselves to the Watch Committee whenever advertisements were placed.[53] In total some 184 men were appointed between late-1848 and late-1868, though actual recruitment levels fluctuated from year to year: eighteen in 1849, fourteen in 1854 and thirteen in 1865.[54] In qualitative terms, matters were less positive. Retention of newly appointed recruits was a problem in all new police forces. In Huddersfield, taking the period as a whole, 56 per cent of recruits left within their first year and a further 28 per cent served between one and four years. Only 15 per cent served for more than five years. Unusually, the percentage of recruits serving less than one year was noticeably higher in the second half of the period (that is after the passing of the 1856 County and Borough Police Act) than the first.[55] Even allowing for the distorting effect of a higher number of incomplete careers among the second cohort, the fact remains: only a small minority of men made a career of policing, even though their impact was out of proportion to their number. Inexperience and limited experience were striking features of the first generation of 'new police' in the town.

In comparison with other towns, Huddersfield's retention record was poor. The contrast with Halifax is striking. Of its original force, only 20 per cent left within the first year while 40 per cent served for five years or more and 25 per cent for over twenty years. However, looking more generally at the period 1851–72, 43 per cent of Halifax policemen served less than one year and only 17 per cent serving more than five years. These figures are not significantly different from those for the atypical town of Middlesbrough, where the percentage of recruits leaving within their first year dropped from 50 per cent to just over 40 per cent from the mid-1850s to the late-1860s while approximately 20 percent served for more than 5 years in the 1860s.[56] The Huddersfield experience (which excludes men in post at incorporation) is summarised in Table 2.4.

Table 2.4: Huddersfield borough police length of completed career service, 1848–68

RECRUITMENT PERIOD	1848–68 NOS.	1848–68 %	1848–56 NOS.	1848–56 %	1857–68 NOS.	1857–68 %
Length of service						
Less than 1 year	*83*	*56*	*43*	*52*	*40*	*62*
1 year or more but less than 5	*42*	*28*	*20*	*24*	*22*	*34*
5 years or more but less than 10	*17*	*11*	*14*	*17*	*3*	*5*
10 years and above	*6*	*4*	*6*	*7*	*0*	*0*
Total	*148*		*83*		*65*	

Source: Huddersfield Improvement Commission Minutes, KMT 18/2/2/1 & 2; Watch Committee Minutes 18/ 2/3/13/1; 18/ 2/3/14/1 & 2

The scale of the challenge becomes even more apparent when the service figures are examined in greater detail. Table 2.5 summarizes the career outcomes for the men who joined the town's police force. Significant numbers either left voluntarily (resigned) or were dismissed. Only a very small number served through to retirement or died while in employment, a reflection, in no small measure, of the belated introduction of a superannuation scheme. The figure for those retiring is slightly misleading as a small number of men (probably no more than four or five in total) were required to resign and then given some form of allowance.

At least of 28 per cent of Huddersfield police recruits resigned and a staggering 46 per cent were dismissed.[57] In comparison, in Halifax between 1851 and 1872 just over a third of recruits were dismissed, in Hull between 1836 and 1866 almost a quarter of recruits were dismissed, while in Sheffield, between 1845 and 1879, the figure was less than 10 per cent. In Leeds in the 1850s the wastage rate averaged 33 per cent (18.5 per cent resignations and 14.5 percent

Table 2.5: Huddersfield borough police force: completed career outcomes, 1848–68

RECRUITMENT PERIOD	1848–68	1848–68	1848–56	1848–56	1857–68	1857–68
2.5 (I): ALL	CAREERS	INCLUDING	UNKNOWN	OUTCOME		
Career outcome	*No.*	*%*	*No.*	*%*	*No.*	*%*
Resigned	*42*	*28*	*23*	*28*	*19*	*29*
Dismissed	*68*	*46*	*35*	*42*	*33*	*51*
Retired or died	*3*	*2*	*2*	*2*	*1*	*1*
Not known	*35*	*24*	*23*	*28*	*12*	*18*
Total	*148*		*83*		*65*	
2.5 (II):	KNOWN	CAREER	OUTCOMES	ONLY		
Resigned	*42*	*37*	*23*	*38*	*19*	*36*
Dismissed	*68*	*60*	*35*	*58*	*33*	*62*
Retired or died	*4*	*4*	*2*	*3*	*1*	*2*
Total	*114*		*60*		*54*	

Source: See Table 2.4

dismissals) and falling to 29 per cent (16 per cent resignations and 13 per cent dismissals) in the following decade. Even in the more volatile Middlesbrough force the dismissal rate stood at 36 per cent, significantly lower than the Huddersfield figure.

There was an even greater degree of 'churning' taking place on an annual basis. High levels of dismissals and resignations were disruptive at least, demoralizing at worst. In 1849, the worst year for the Huddersfield force, eight men were dismissed and a further three resigned out of a force of eighteen men. The situation eased in the early 1850s but, in the years 1857–59, twenty-one men resigned or were dismissed. This was, in part at least, a reflection of the enlargement of the force to meet governmental expectations as enshrined in the 1856 County and Borough Police Act and the loss of some men to the better-paid West Riding County Constabulary, but the situation was exacerbated by the appointment of an acerbic and controversial new police superintendent, George Beaumont. Similar short-term upheavals, usually associated with significant expansion, were experienced elsewhere. In Hull in 1836, the first year of the new force, the wastage rate was almost 20 per cent and exceeded 30 per cent in 1857 as the force was expanded following the 1856 County and Borough Police Act. In the Leeds force two periods of rapid expansion in numbers, 1838–9 and 1859–60, saw turnover rates of 46 per cent and 43 per cent respectively. However, there is not a simple explanation for such variations. Some watch committees took a firm disciplinary line, others not. A sacking offence in one force would be dealt with by a reprimand or fine in another. Some watch committees adopted rigorous selection procedures, others not; some were more judicious in their appointments than others. Other factors played a part. The quality of leadership, training and support similarly varied from force to force as did the quality of the recruits. At present insufficient is known about the experiences and practices of individual forces to offer anything but the broadest conclusions. The approaches adopted in Huddersfield will be explored later in this chapter but, whatever the precise causes of such high turnover rates, the upshot was that local watch committees and police chiefs faced considerable difficulties in creating effective forces.

Table 2.6: Huddersfield borough police: resignations and dismissals, 1848–68

LENGTH OF SERVICE	LESS THAN 1 YEAR	%	1 YEAR BUT LESS THAN 2	%	2 YEARS BUT LESS THAN 5	%	5 YEARS OR MORE	%	TOTAL
Recruitment period									
1848–68									
Resignation	*22*	*52*	*3*	*7*	*5*	*12*	*12*	*29*	*42*
Dismissal	*40*	*58*	*15*	*22*	*4*	*6*	*10*	*14*	*69*
1848–56									
Resignation	*12*	*52*	*2*	*9*	*1*	*4*	*8*	*35*	*23*
Dismissal	*20*	*56*	*6*	*17*	*1*	*3*	*9*	*39*	*36*
1857–68									
Resignation	*10*	*53*	*1*	*5*	*4*	*21*	*4*	*21*	*19*
Dismissal	*20*	*61*	*9*	*27*	*3*	*9*	*1*	*3*	*33*

Source: See Table 2.4

The figures for resignations and dismissals need to be broken down according to length of service. This is done in table 2.6. As in Halifax, Hull, Leeds, Middlesbrough and Sheffield, those unsuited to policing soon found their shortcomings exposed. 58 per cent of all dismissals in Huddersfield took place in the first twelve months (often within the first few weeks, even days) and a further 22 per cent in the following year. Long-serving men were far less likely to be dismissed. Similarly, half of those who found the demands of policing too onerous (or the pay too little) resigned from the force within a year. Of those who remained, many made a career of policing, serving for ten years or more, but a significant minority resigned after five or more years' service. From the outset, senior police figures and members of the Watch Committee were well aware of the problems of retention in the early months but only later realised that there was a different retention problem among men who appeared to have adapted to the demands of police work.

Table 2.7: Huddersfield borough police: disciplinary record, 1848-1868

NO. RECORDED OFFENCES	0	%	1	%	2-4	%	5 OR MORE	%
All recruits	*65*	*35*	*56*	*30*	*45*	*29*	*8*	*5*
Dismissed	*0*	*0*	*32*	*44*	*34*	*47*	*4*	*6*
Resigned	*20*	*49*	*8*	*20*	*13*	*32*	*0*	*0*

Source: See Table 2.4

Finally, resignations and dismissals need to be set into a broader context of discipline. Table 2.7 summarizes this position. Discipline was a problem for the majority of recruits. Incidents of neglect of duty, drunkenness on duty, absence without leave, frequenting beer houses and brothels, insubordination and even assaults on fellow officers are scattered through the Watch Committee minutes. Little more than one-third of the men recruited in the town force had an unblemished career record. A further 30 per cent had one disciplinary offences against their names but the remainder were multiple offenders, in one case accumulating a total of nine offences. Those men who were dismissed unsurprisingly had committed an above average number of offences. In contrast almost half of the men who resigned had no record of misconduct, though a minority (a third of this sub-group) were multiple offenders. Acts of indiscipline were very much the prerogative of men in the early months or years as policemen. Almost 50 per cent of offences were committed by men who had served less than a year but length of service was not a guarantor of good discipline. A quarter of all recorded acts of indiscipline were committed by men who were established members of the force. In the majority of cases acts of indiscipline were penultimate steps in a career that was about to end in resignation or dismissal. However, it is important to note that a poor disciplinary record was not necessarily a barrier to a successful police career. William Townend, for example, had a poor record in his early years but became a stalwart of the force, twice serving as temporary superintendent of police and serving for some forty years while Nathaniel Partridge became a successful detective, albeit one who fell foul of the authorities.

Leaving aside the small number of men who retired on grounds of ill-health and an equally small number who retired for personal reasons (such as caring for a sick relative), resignation was essentially an individual's negative judgment on the force. Over half the men who resigned did so within their first twelve months, some after little more than a few weeks, even days. This pattern remained constant throughout the period. However, there was a second, though smaller upsurge of resignations among men who had served for more than five years and who, on the surface at least, appeared to have made the transition to career policemen. Overall almost 30 per cent of resignations fell into this category but there appears to be a significant difference between early recruits (in the years 1848–56), for whom the figure is 35 per cent, and later recruits (in the years 1857–68), for whom the figure is 21 per cent. With a larger number of incomplete careers among the latter group, this figure is almost certainly an underestimate but it might suggest a greater awareness of the demands of policing among later recruits. Unfortunately, the reasons that drove men to resign have rarely been recorded. Clearly the demands of the job were considerable. Strict discipline, long hours on the beat, especially at night, the physical risks associated with the job – from flat feet and rheumatism to injuries inflicted by runaway horses or irate members of the public – made it a more demanding occupation than many local jobs. Policing undoubtedly held out the prospect of regular pay but, as the recurring demands for higher wages bear witness, many policemen felt that the material rewards were not sufficient to offset the trials of the job. Such problems pressed most heavily in the early days and months of transition from civilian life, but never entirely disappeared. A man who had served five years but found promotion beyond his reach faced a future in which the disadvantages grew as the advantages faded. Some (albeit a very small number) resigned for more positive reasons – three or four to set up businesses – but these were very much the exceptions.[58] Those who resigned were, for the most part, expressing a negative judgment about their experience of policing. Some jumped before they were pushed and a small number were instructed to resign.[59]

The decision to dismiss was made by the Watch Committee, usually on the advice of the police superintendent. The pattern of dismissals is similar to that of resignations. Overall, 58 per cent of dismissals took place in the first twelve months but with a further 22 per cent within the next year. As with resignations, there was a second, later upsurge with 14 per cent of dismissals among men who had served more than five years. More so than with resignations, there was a contrast between recruits in the years 1848–56 and those in the years 1857–68. Dismissals in the first two years of service rose from 73 per cent in the first period to 88 in the second. However, whereas a significant percentage of dismissals for the first period were among men with over five years' service, there were few in this category for the second period, though this figure is distorted by the large number of incomplete careers among this second group of men. Nonetheless, this evidence suggests that the commissioners were struggling to find suitable new recruits, especially in the 1860s.

The reasons for dismissal – for both newly appointed men and those with a longer period of service – are more fully recorded and are utterly predictable: neglect of duty, drunkenness, insubordination and, to a much lesser extent, immoral or criminal behaviour. 43 per cent of dismissals (for which reasons are recorded) were for drunkenness on duty and another 43 per cent for various forms of neglect of duty (including being asleep on duty or otherwise absent) while the remainder were evenly divided between insubordination and immorality, the latter most commonly being found in a brothel.[60]

Drink was the undoing of many constables. James Watkins had already been reported for loitering on his beat when he went absent for half an hour. When found by the night inspector and sergeant he was drunk and 'his coat was all over mud, as if he had been laid in the street'.[61] Alfred Crowther, George Woodhead and Henry Newsome were all found 'drunk on their respective beats and utterly unfit for duty'.[62] Newsome might have saved his career had he not lied to the Watch Committee. For Crowther and Woodhead, it was a second offence. All three were dismissed. Even worse was William Hollingrake, found drunk on duty, his behaviour 'so outrageous that he had to be confined in the Lock-up cell all night'.[63] More mundanely, Allen Wood, another night constable, was found 'asleep in his bed and the worse for liquor' when he should have been on duty.[64] Thomas Schofield was also dismissed 'for absenting himself from duty without leave on three occasions and for drinking in a notorious Beerhouse in Castle Gate'.[65] This was a long-standing problem that dated back to the earliest days of the force. Following the dismissal of night-constable Butler, found drinking in the *Crescent Hotel* in the High Street at 3 a.m., while on duty, the Watch Committee lamented 'the practice adopted by some publicans of giving the police drink to prevent them reporting their houses'.[66] A similar complaint was aired in 1864 as the Watch Committee noted ruefully that '[s]everal Licensed Victuallers in the town have been in the habit of entertaining Police Constables or suffering them to linger in their Houses and have liquor during the time of their being on duty'.[67] However, not all incidents of neglect of duty were associated with drunkenness. Henry Sedgwick lost his position having been found simply asleep in an omnibus, as did John Drury who was similarly discovered 'asleep in a yard in Cross Church Street'.[68]

Given the hierarchical nature of the police force, challenges to the authority of senior officers were treated severely. Incidences of neglect of duty which might have led to a reprimand resulted in dismissal when compounded by insubordination. For example, John Lee was charged with neglect of duty and being under the influence of liquor but responded angrily, throwing his lamp into the road when spoken to by the night inspector and showing at the Watch House a 'spirit of insubordination' which resulted in his dismissal.[69] Similarly, Charles Cliffe was not only guilty of drinking in a public house while on duty but sealed his dismissal by 'shewing a spirit of insubordination'.[70]

A small number of men lost their position for behaviour that was immoral or criminal, even though no formal legal action was taken. Some combined more routine offences of drunkenness and neglect with immoral behaviour. Few men could equal the disciplinary record of John Brown, the highly recommended sergeant from Manchester. In a single week in 1849 he managed to be absent from duty, to be found asleep on duty, to abandon his beat because of drunkenness (and requiring PC Megson to 'show him the way home', thereby abandoning his beat) and finally to be found in a brothel. A further complaint that Brown demanded alcohol and women seems almost superfluous in the circumstances.[71] In fact, Reuben Megson was almost as bad. Having been drunk on duty and absent from his beat on a number of occasions, he brought his brief police career to an end when 'he and two others of the Night Constabulary ... left their beats to accompany two Prostitutes to a Brothel at Marsh Cliffe'.[72] Others were clearly criminal, even though no formal charges were made. Thomas Jansen and Joseph Baxter are a case in point. Jansen found a gold bracelet which he sold to Baxter. Baxter, for his part, not only bought the bracelet, knowing how it had been obtained, but then took a 10*s* (50p) reward, which he shared with Jansen, and lied about how it came into its possession.[73]

The Watch Committee and Police Discipline

High rates of turnover, very short lengths of service and an ongoing disciplinary problem were the distinctive features of the Huddersfield 'new' police. Why this should be so – and why Huddersfield should compare unfavourably with towns such as Halifax and Middlesbrough – is not easy to explain. It is unlikely that the quality of recruits was significantly different than elsewhere in Yorkshire and the comments of the inspector of police in his annual reports do not indicate that he was aware of a particular problem in the town, though some local commentators complained that the men who joined did not view policing as a career but 'imagined they could suit themselves and leave the force when they pleased'.[74] The broader problem was poor management. The *Chronicle* captured a recurring public mood when it expressed its concerns with 'the continual reports of drunkenness against the privates in the night force' and concluded that 'there must either very little care exercised in the choosing of men to fill the office; or that the force must be in a very defective state of supervision'.[75]

Successive Watch Committees clearly played an active role in recruitment and discipline. Applications were considered, though only one man was not appointed – and that following a poor reference from Leeds city police – and each case reported by the superintendent of police was considered individually. The range of punishments handed out suggests the Watch Committee tried to respond sensitively, evaluating the strength of the charge brought against the constable, distinguishing between different levels of seriousness of offences and assessing the potential of the individual officer, rather than impose a blanket policy. Ill-disciplined constables were variously admonished, cautioned, reprimanded and severely reprimanded as well as being fined, demoted, suspended and dismissed. On some occasions the Watch Committee accepted a constable's explanation and threw out the charge. Night constables Heywood, Gledhill, Beevers (S), Marsden and Wilson, for example, were all found in the *Horse Shoe Inn* in June 1850. The Watch Committee, however, accepted their explanation that they, 'wet and exhausted' after attending a fire in Hillbank Lane had 'repaired to the Public House … to procure refreshment which had been taken in only moderate quantity'.[76] More often they found in favour of the senior officers who brought the charges. In many cases, the Watch Committee did not adopt a hard-line policy but gave men a second opportunity, particularly if they saw evidence of potential. The situation was further complicated by the fact that the commissioners did not automatically accept the recommendations for dismissal from their Watch Committee.

Judgement on the success of the Watch Committee's policy is complicated by the incompleteness of the record, but an analysis of 100 disciplinary cases, for which full information is available, yields the following figures. In 35 per cent of the cases dismissal was for a first offence. No leniency was shown, for example, to Paul Bray for his (unspecified) 'gross neglect of duty' in 1856, or for Allen Wood, found drunk and asleep in 1849 and certainly not for Clayton Connard, found ratting in a local beerhouse and stripped to the waist challenging all and sundry to fight in 1866. Even long-serving men like Edward Morton (found drunk in the *Ramsden Arms*) and Joseph Haigh, who allowed 'improper characters' to meet in his house, were not given a second chance. However, for every man dismissed for his first disciplinary offence, two were given a second chance, or more. Of this group, comprising sixty-five men, almost exactly 50 per cent (thirty-two men) were subsequently dismissed and a further 20 per cent (thirteen men) subsequently resigned, most commonly in the immediate aftermath of disciplinary action. The remaining 30 per cent (twenty men) went on to complete a successful career in the town's police force. These figures reveal that the approach, which does not appear to have varied significantly over the period was, more often than not, unsuccessful.

Looking at the men who were subsequently dismissed, it is difficult to escape the conclusion that judgments were faulty and optimism misplaced. In February 1849 Inspector Sedgwick and Sergeant Townend reported James Watkins for being drunk on duty for a second time and also for being absent from his beat on a number of occasions. The Watch Committee decided to reprimand rather than dismiss Watkins as they believed he was 'in every way likely to make a good officer if he could be induced to refrain from drink'.[77] The following month he was found 'loitering on his beat' in a state of inebriation. This time he was dismissed. Similarly, Alfred Crowther was charged with being 'the worse for liquor', barely a month after he had been reprimanded for having been found drunk, asleep in a stable, while on duty. Deemed to be 'otherwise an efficient officer' he was merely admonished but in July of the same year he was once again charged with being 'the worse for liquor and unfit for duty' but he pleaded with the Watch Committee for a further chance, claiming that he had renounced alcohol. In addition, there was 'testimony to his general intelligence, activity and subordination'. Duly reprimanded, he was allowed to continue in the force but his conversion to teetotalism was a failure and in December 1849, having been found drunk on duty once again, he was finally dismissed.[78] The commissioners persisted with their lenient approach, notably in the case of Hamor Sedgwick. Appointed a night constable in February 1853 he was promoted to day constable in May 1854. In 1856 he was a first-class night constable but in November of that year he was reprimanded for being absent from duty and given a final warning. In February 1859 he was reprimanded again for being 'slightly under the influence of alcohol' and in October 1860 he was severely reprimanded for being absent without leave. No reason is recorded for his continued presence in the force. In December 1861 his good fortune seemed to have run out as the Watch Committee recommended that he be dismissed for being (once again) absent without leave. Sedgwick successfully appealed to the commissioners, pointing out in a memorial both his record as a good policeman and the 'effect of starving my children who are innocent' that would follow from his dismissal. Sedgwick was suspended for two weeks.[79] In 1862 he was finally dismissed, having been, yet again, absent from his beat. But not all cases were as extreme as this. Benjamin Marsden, for example, appointed in 1849, worked his way up to the rank of sergeant and, on a number of occasions, displayed considerable courage in dealing with violent individuals, but he had a drink problem. In June 1852 he was reprimanded for it; in October 1854 he received a severe reprimand and, finally, in August 1858 the Watch Committee decided to dismiss him for being drunk and neglecting his duty.

However, in a significant minority of cases the decision of the Watch Committee (or the commissioners) was vindicated. Nowhere was this clearer than in the case of William Townend. Townend, the one-time parochial constable, became a senior and much-venerated figure both before and after incorporation and yet his early police career was far from unblemished. He was twice severely reprimanded in October 1851 for being drunk in the street and for insubordination after a drunken fight in the police office. In July 1852 the Watch Committee recommended his dismissal for being drunk and absent from duty. For reasons that were never recorded, the commissioners decided merely to suspend him for one month. Nor was that the end of the matter. In January 1856 he was severely reprimanded for attending a masquerade ball when he should have been on duty. Fortunately, for both the individual and the force as a whole, Townend was extremely fortunate to survive but went on to give sterling service. Nor was he alone. Hugh Moore and Ramsden White were a further two men who justified the faith held in them (see chapter four).

Conclusion

After the 1856 County & Borough Police Act, the continuing approval of Her Majesty's Inspector of Constabulary was undoubtedly important, not least because of its financial implications. Woodford declared himself satisfied with the 'smart, active … and thoroughly effective' men he inspected but he was aware of the day-to-day realities of the Huddersfield police force that were not captured in the once-a-year annual inspection. However, it would be wrong to dismiss totally Woodford's comments as superficial or wholly inaccurate. They contained an important germ of truth. A core of experienced men came into being over the course of the 1850s and 1860s that provided stability to the force and offset the problem of drunken constables and sexually-incontinent senior officers. A snap-shot from 1860 makes the point.

Table 2.8: Huddersfield borough police: length of service, 1860

LENGTH OF SERVICE	10 YEARS OR MORE	5 TO 9 YEARS	1 TO 4 YEARS	LESS THAN 1 YEAR
Rank				
Inspector	2			
Sergeant	2		1	
1st Class PC			3	
2nd Class PC	2		1	
3rd Class PC	3	3	7	7
Total	9	3	12	7
As % of total force	29	10	39	22

Source: Watch Committee Minutes, KMT 18/2/3/14/1, 23 January 1860

Furthermore, the development of policing was ongoing. The force became larger, more complex and better organised over time, particularly under the guidance of the experienced William Hannan. The process continued under the final superintendent appointed by the Improvement Commissioners, James Withers. Given 'the full charge and superintendence of the whole Police Force' and being 'responsible for the general conduct and management thereof', he informed the Watch Committee that he wished to bring Huddersfield more in line with 'the Metropolitan System'.[80] Withers was tactful enough to recognize that improvements had been made but his comments were an implied criticism not only of his predecessors but also of previous Watch Committees for not improving the quality of the force. The details of Withers' plan of reform is summarized below.

Table 2.9: Huddersfield borough police: Supt. Withers' reorganisation, 1868

HOW EMPLOYED	HEAD CONSTABLE	INSPECTOR	DETECTIVE INSPECTOR	SUB-INSPECTOR	SERGEANTS	ACTING SERGEANTS	PCS	TOTAL
Day Duty		*1*				*1*	*4*	*6*
Night Duty					*2*	*1*	*15*	*18*
Office Duty					*1*		*2*	*3*
Specially Employed	*1*		*1*				*1*	*3*
Total	*1*	*1*	*1*		*3*	*2*	*22*	*30*

Source: Watch Committee Minutes, KMT 18/2/3/14/2, 30 December 1867 Reorganisation, 1868

During the daytime, the first relief of two men, always wearing white gloves but not permitted to carry sticks, patrolled the town from 6 a.m. to 9 a.m. and again from 2 p.m. to 9 p.m. while the second relief (also of two similarly attired men) were on duty from 9 a.m., to 2 p.m. and again from 6 p.m. to 9 p.m. Thus day duty was arranged so that there were four constables, an acting sergeant and an inspector on duty between 6 p.m. and 9 p.m. 'when the operatives are returning from their work and moving about'.[81] During the night two sections patrolled the town from 9 p.m. to 6 a.m., thereby ensuring that 'the town is never left without Constables'. Inspectors and sergeants were clearly instructed to 'visit the men on their beats at their usual points and also at uncertain times at different places on their beats' and to ensure that full records of such visits were kept. Finally, arrangements were made to improve the running of the police office and cells. The range and scale of these improvements provides an eloquent commentary on what had *not* been achieved under the 1848 Improvement Commission. Nonetheless, this was the 'effective and well selected body of men' from which the enlarged borough force would be developed after 1868, but there was clearly scope for improvement. At the annual borough police dinner, held at the *Ramsden Arms* in May 1868, Joel Denham, chair of the Watch Committee, spoke of the harmony and good feeling which prevailed between the commissioners and the force but stressed that commissioners were determined to continue 'to raise the standard of discipline and the efficiency of the [men of the] force' as well as 'to elevate them socially'.[82] The rough diamonds still required further polishing.

Endnotes

1 The 1848 Act retain the geographical limits laid down in the 1820 Improvement Act, namely an area which extended 'Twelve hundred Yards each Way from the Spot where the old Cross stood in the Centre of the Market Place in *Huddersfield*'. This meant that certain areas, which were commonly thought of as being part of Huddersfield and which were so included for census purposes actually fell outside the act. In the late 1840s, when it was estimated that the population of Huddersfield was in the region of 25,000 people, only 20,000 fell under the 1848 Act.

2 Her Majesty's Inspector of Constabulary, Year Ending Sept. 1868, *Parliamentary Papers*, 1868–9 (22), p.104.

3 This section draws heavily upon D Griffiths, *Pioneers or Partisans? Governing Huddersfield 1820–48*, Huddersfield, 2008.

4 Quoted in Griffiths, *Pioneers or Partisans,* p.21.

5 *An Act for lighting, watching, and cleansing the Town of Huddersfield*, 1 George IV, cap. xlviii, §xviii.

6 *Ibid*, §xix.

7 *Halifax Guardian*, 10 Sept. 1840.

8 Even more striking was the hostility in Sheffield to the proposed creation of a county force. The *Sheffield Independent* (hereafter *Sheff. I*), waxed eloquently against the 'indignity' of Sheffield being put on a par with 'petty places' such as 'Penistone, Holmfirth and Delph' (12 December 1840) and the 'despotic' threat to 'free local government' posed by the proposed police force (17 October 1841). Within little more than two years Sheffield became an incorporated borough. Paradoxically cost considerations played an important part in derailing the incorporation movement in Huddersfield at this time.

9 The 1842 Parish Constable Act has been largely overlooked by police historians but was to be an important piece of legislation in the West Riding as is detailed in Part 2 especially chapter seven.

10 *Leeds Mercury, [*hereafter *LM]*, 20 September 1845. See also 9 & 16 August 1845, 14 November 1846.

11 *B.Obs,* 13 January 1848. See *LM* 9 March, 20 September & 13 December 1845; 21 March, 15 August & 14 November 1846; and 22 May & 30 October 1848 for examples of Townend and Sedgwick successfully apprehending both major and petty criminals.

12 *LM,* 1 May 1841 and 12 September 1846. Earlier in the year the paper referred to 'a great deal of drunkenness and profligacy' among the Huddersfield watchmen. *LM,* 13 June 1846. See also *LM* 1 January 1848 on the use of private constable to supplement the town's night watch.

13 For further details of policing arrangements before the 1848 Improvement Act, see Griffiths, *Pioneers or Partisans?* esp. pp.22–26.

14 *Minutes of Proceedings on a Preliminary Inquiry on the Huddersfield Improvement Bill*, held February 1848 but published 1851, West Yorkshire Archive Service, Kirklees, KMT 18/2/1/1, esp. pp.17-19. See also QQ, 39, 613-4, 739, & 747. Parochial constable William Townend commented on the threats made to him at the annual vestry meeting (Q.1348) and bemoaned the absence of 'a properly regulated police force' (Q.1342).

15 See for example, Townend's evidence given to the Preliminary Enquiry on the Huddersfield Improvement Bill in February 1848, KMT, 18/2/1/1, p.10.

16 The geographical coverage of the 1848 Improvement Act remained the same as under the 1820 Act. However, the township had grown considerably and important districts, such as Lindley, Marsh and Paddock fell outside the act. Responsibility for policing these areas fell to the West Riding County Constabulary and its predecessors. See Part 2.

17 Huddersfield Improvement Commission [hereafter HIC] Minutes, KMT18/2/2/1, p.86.

18 *Ibid*, p.62.

19 *Ibid*.

20 *LM*, 25 August 1849.

21 HIC Minutes, KMT18/2/2/1, p.84–5.

22 Little is known of Cheeseborough's background but his period of office was brief and terminated by an incapacitating illness. As magistrates' bailiff he helped prove the case against John Sutcliffe, who was charged with permitting dicing in his beer house. *LM*, 15 July 1848

23 Danson was an experienced man, having been appointed in 1837, but his appointment owed something to sentiment. He had been seriously injured in 1840 in an incident which saw the brutal murder of head constable Dukes. The injuries there sustained and a subsequent decline in his health reduced his physical efficiency and the new Commissioners paid him less than the other two day constables in 1848. Danson resigned because of ill-health in March 1849. HIC Minutes, KMT 18/2/2/1, pp.88–9.

24 In Hull, such was the dissatisfaction with the old police that the new force established in 1836 contained no men with previous experience of policing the city. D R Walsh, The Reform of Urban Policing in Victorian England: A Study of Kingston upon Hull from 1836 to 1866, unpublished PhD, University of Hull, 1997. For Halifax see J Posner, The Establishment and Development of the New Police in Halifax, 1848-1914, unpublished PhD, University of Huddersfield, 2015. For Sheffield see C A Williams, Police and Crime in Sheffield, 1818-1874, unpublished PhD, Sheffield University, 1998 and for Leeds see D C Churchill, Crime, Policing and Control in Leeds, c. 1830–1890, unpublished PhD, University of Leeds, 2012.

25 Unusually the new police force in Halifax was smaller than the earlier watch. The success of a large number of Radicals and four Chartists in the first elections is an important factor, though policing does not appear to have been a major issue in the incorporation campaign in Halifax. Posner, Establishment and Development, pp. 37, 39 & 42.

26 *HC*, 5 January 1856. At the same meeting of the commissioners Mr Moore put down this criticism with the observation that if 'Mr Turner lived at Seed Hill and saw the congregation of Castlegate vagabonds so frequently

assembled ... he would not think the police too numerous.' In fact, Turner, self-styled defender of the rate-payer, appears to have believed the day police numbered six men – in fact, there were three.

27 HIC monthly meeting, 3 July 1861, *HC*, 6 July 1861.

28 HIC monthly meeting, 4 September 1861, *HC*, 7 September 1861.

29 HIC monthly meeting, 2 October 1861, *HC*, 5 October 1861.

30 Contrast this with Leeds where the local watch committee, constrained by the economical faction on the council in the late 1850s was forced by HMIC to increase the size of the city force. Churchill chapter three.

31 In the following year the town's boundaries were significantly extended and the town's force expanded accordingly.

32 The annual returns show that police population ratio constant at 1:711 but, as this was based on an unchanging (1861) population figure, in reality the ratio worsened over the decade.

33 HIC monthly meeting, *HC*, 13 June 1863.

34 HIC monthly meeting *HC*, 4 July 1863. This contrasts with the more serious police pay strike in Hull in 1853.

35 The HIC minutes refer to the re-introduction of the second-class category in 1861 but not to the year in which it was abolished.

36 This contrasts with the approach adopted in Halifax where a detective was part of the initial force established in 1848. Posner, Establishment and Development, p.42.

37 The approach adopted was to identify all town policemen in the censuses of 1851 and 1861 and to trace then back and forward thereby covering the five censuses from 1841 to 1881.

38 C Emsley & M Clapson, 'Recruiting the English Policeman, c.1840–1940', *Policing and Society*, 3 (1994), pp.269–86.

39 Compare this to recruitment to the Buckinghamshire County Constabulary where the long-term decline of the furniture trade yielded many police recruits or to Middlesbrough where short-term, cyclical fluctuations in the iron and steel trade impacted on police recruitment.

40 *Morning Chronicle, The Manufacturing Districts. The Cloth Districts of Yorkshire – The Huddersfield Fancy Goods, and the Dewsbury "Shoddy Mills"*, Letter XIV, 18 January 1850.

41 HIC monthly meeting, *HC*, 9 August 1856 and 10 January 1857. In fact, the WRCC police registers suggest that this was less of a problem.

42 The figures come from the annual returns of the inspector of constabulary for the northern region. Huddersfield police were below the median wage figures for the country at large in 1857 but at the median in 1865. See C Steedman, *Policing the Victorian Community: The formation of English provincial police forces, 1856–80*, London, Routledge & Kegan Paul, 1984, p.109.

43 HIC monthly meeting *HC*, 6 September 1856 and 17 & 24 June 1857

44 HIC monthly meeting, *HC*, 21 June 1862.

45 Watch Committee Minutes, KMT 18/2/3/13/1, 14 & 28 January 1850. In addition, sums of £1-5-0 (£1.25), £1 and 15*s* (0.75p) were handed out to other men.

46 Townend and White were responsible for twenty-two and twenty-eight cases

respectively, Ramsden thirty-seven and Mellor and Morton thirty-five each. Only one other officer exceeded these totals.

47 The details of the superannuation scheme have not been considered, primarily because the impact was not felt until the 1870s by which time Huddersfield was no longer run by the Improvement Commissioners.

48 The Watch Committee also made a small number of discretionary awards for various forms of commendable behaviour, but these were less important than the annual payment from the perquisite fund.

49 See chapter four for a fuller discussion of career outcomes.

50 There were, of course, more men appointed as night constables whose careers were extremely short-lived (i.e. less than one year). Only one man served more than one year but less than five as a night constable.

51 Although there was much talk of improving police efficiency and effectiveness in the 1850s and 1860s, the main criterion used to determine efficiency was the ratio of population to police.

52 D Taylor, *Policing the Victorian Town: the development of the police in Middlesbrough, c.1840–1914*, Palgrave, Basingstoke, 2002, esp. chapter three. Middlesbrough, despite its distinctive pattern of industrial growth, was not unique. On several occasions HMIC complained that industrial prosperity was making recruitment difficult for many forces in northern and central England and south Wales.

53 In December 1853 there were twenty-two applications for four new night constables; in May 1857 twenty-four applications for three permanent posts as night constable; and twenty for another three posts as night constable in 1859. Watch Committee Minutes, KMT 18/2/3/13/1 19 December 1853, KMT 18/2/3/14/1 30 May 1857 and 24 January 1859.

54 The precise number of men recruited into the Huddersfield police is difficult to calculate. In the absence of a police register or conduct book, the minutes of the Watch Committee and of the Improvement Commission are the principle sources of information. However, published accounts of Commissioners' meetings in the town's two newspapers the *Chronicle* and the *Examiner* throw up a few names not found elsewhere. Unsurprisingly, it is not always possible to establish the career records of all recruits. Nonetheless, the broad patterns that emerge from this data are unlikely to have been significantly distorted by the missing information.

55 The precise figures are as follows: 52% of recruits served less than one year in the period 1848-56 compared with 62% in the period 1857-68.

56 Posner, Establishment and Development, p.93 and Taylor, *Policing the Victorian Town*, p.42.

57 The minutes of the Watch Committee and of the Improvement Commission do not contain full information on the town's police. The figure in the text is based on returns for a total of 148 men known to have been appointed. For only 111 men are reasons given for leaving. If this figure is used the percentage retiring rises to 35 per cent and 61 per cent for resignations and dismissals respectively.

58 Strikingly, only one Huddersfield policeman sought promotion in another force – and he was unsuccessful.

59 For the purposes of analysis those required to resign have been included with those dismissed on the grounds that the Watch Committee was making a negative judgment on these men. From an individual point of view being able to say that he resigned rather than having been dismissed could be important for future job prospects.
60 There were also a small number of supernumerary constables, dismissed for their inadequacies as would-be policemen, who have been excluded from this analysis.
61 Watch Committee Minutes, KMT 2/3/13/1, 12 March 1849.
62 Watch Committee Minutes, KMT 2/3/13/1, 9 July 1849.
63 Watch Committee Minutes, KMT 2/3/13/1, 1 December 1851. See also Sam Beavers KMT 2/3/13/1, 30 December 1850 & 28 December 1853; Thomas Wright KMT 2/1/13/1 1 September 1851 & Henry Beevers 2 June 1855; John Spivey KMT 18/2/3/14/1 24 May 1858; James Lodge KMT 18/2/3/14/2 13 November 1862 & John Drury 28 December 1858; James Buckley, KMT 18/2/3/14/2, 23 July 1866.
64 Watch Committee Minutes, KMT 2/3/13/1, 9 July 1849.
65 Watch Committee Minutes, KMT 18/2/3/14/2, 29 December 1862
66 *HC*, 9 July 1859.
67 Watch Committee Minutes, KMT 18/2/3/14/2, 24 October 1864.
68 Watch Committee Minutes, KMT 18/2/3/14/2, 25 November 1861, 28 July 1862 and 25 April 1864.
69 Watch Committee Minutes, KMT 18/2/3/14/1, 23 February 1857.
70 Watch Committee Minutes, KMT 2/3/14/1, 24 January 1859.
71 Watch Committee Minutes, KMT 2/3/13/1, 15 January 1849.
72 KMT 2/3/13/1, 15 January 1849.
73 KMT 18/2/3/14/2, 9 August 1865.
74 *HC*, 16 December 1865. There were other contemporary critics of the quality of local police recruits but, as they looked for a force comprised entirely of teetotallers, their views can be discounted as unrealistic.
75 *HC*, 2 November 1850.
76 Watch Committee Minutes KMT 18/2/3/13/1, 24 June 1850.
77 Watch Committee Minutes KMT 18/2/3/13/1, 12 February 1849.
78 Watch Committee Minutes, KMT 18/2/3/13/1, 9 July & 3 December 1849.
79 Watch Committee Minutes, KMT 18/2/3/14/2, 24 December 1860 & KMT 18/2/2/2, 4 December 1861.
80 Watch Committee Minutes, KMT 18/2/3/14/2 23 December and 30 December 1857.
81 The two reliefs changed duty 'every alternate day' to balance the workload.
82 *HC*, 23 May 1868.

The Watch Committee, Her Majesty's Inspector of Constabulary and the Management of the Huddersfield Police Force

THE MAIN FOCUS of this book is on day-to-day police work but it is necessary to locate the town's force in its broader political context and to consider, specifically, the relationship with those who were responsible for its overall management. Some of the work of the Watch Committee has already been discussed but this chapter will concentrate on the relationship between local elected politicians and successive superintendents of police before looking briefly at the relationship with the inspectorate of constabulary set up by the 1856 County & Borough Police Act. Huddersfield was unusual in having a high rate of turnover of police superintendents but its experience highlights problems in establishing a working relationship between local politicians and their paid servants that were common to many boroughs in the first generation of 'new' policing.[1]

Huddersfield Politics under the 1848 Improvement Act

Under the 1848 Improvement Act (11 & 12Vic. cap. cxl), Huddersfield – more accurately 'such Parts of the several Hamlets of *Huddersfield, Bradley, Deighton-with-Sheepridge, Fartown* and *Marsh-with-Paddock* … as are within a Radius of Twelve hundred Yards in every Direction from the Spot where the Old Cross formerly stood, in the Centre of the Market Place in *Huddersfield*' – was to be governed by twenty-one commissioners, three nominated by the Lord of the Manor (John William Ramsden), the remainder to be elected by male rate-payers duly registered.[2] The commissioners were drawn from a predictable range of trades and professions – manufacturers, merchants, shop-keepers and so forth. Unsurprisingly in a nonconformist stronghold, many were Wesleyans and Congregationalists with a smaller number of Baptists. Contrary to earlier views, there was also a significant Church of England presence. The town was also a Liberal stronghold, though there were divisions between more conservative Whigs and Radicals but, despite earlier support for Chartism, there was no Chartist presence to compare with nearby Halifax. There was, however, an easily-overlooked Tory presence. A full history of the politics of Huddersfield under the Improvement Act has yet to be written but the broad contours can be identified.[3]

1848 was a pivotal year in the politics of the town – a clear 'repudiation of the 1820 settlement and a fresh start for the town's governance'.[4] The old system – the oligarchic Commission for Lighting, Watching and Cleansing the Town established under the 1820 Improvement Act – had been found wanting and was replaced by a system based on a property-based franchise. There were clear winners – notably Joshua Hobson, a driving force behind the 1848 Act and subsequently full-time clerk to the Board of Works – but also losers. For some, unreconciled to the new order and convinced (irrespective of many facts to the contrary) that the town had been run more effectively and less expensively before 1848, it was the end of the road. There was, however, an important element of continuity, personified by Joseph Brook, one of the first commissioners appointed in 1820 but also the first chair of the new Improvement Commission, and by John Jarrett, inspector of scavengers, first appointed in 1838. More importantly, post-1848 politics created new alliances which involved some strange bedfellows. In broad terms, there were two groupings: improvers and economists. The former group, the self-styled 'friends of progress' included former political foes. The two leading figures were Joseph Brook, a man of 'conservative principles', and Joshua Hobson, one of the leading Chartists of the early 1840s but now committed to sanitary reform.[5] The latter group, railing against the alleged extravagance of the improvers, included disgruntled members of the town's petty bourgeoisie, as much angered by their loss of political influence as by a desire to reduce rates, and Radicals who felt both cheated by the complex property franchise that was less democratic than the old town vestry and betrayed by their erstwhile colleague, Hobson. The local politics of the first decade of the Improvement Commission were fractious and often highly personalised but the underlying concern with economy was long-lived, flaring up in the early 1860s, when attempts were made to reduce the size of the town's police force, and in the early 1870s, when the pay of borough officials was a major electoral issue and contributed to the departure of the well-regarded and efficient superintendent Withers.

Particularly in the early and mid-1850s local politics was polarised. The Woolpack committee – named after the inn in New Street where its members met – ran 'economical' slates which were particularly successful in 1853. Nonetheless, there were overlaps between the two factions with the same names appearing on both lists. Further, while there may have been differences within the wider electorate, there was comparatively little difference in socio-economic terms between commissioners belonging to the two groupings. There were more petty-bourgeois figures in the 'economical' faction and they tended to be younger in age. There were also a significant number of Congregationalists in their ranks and, with few exceptions, they voted Liberal rather than Whig. In contrast, members of the 'reformist' faction were more likely to be Church of England or Wesleyan Methodist and to have voted Whig or Conservative. The importance of differences in religious background can easily be overstated. C H Jones, the leading advocate of 'economy' in the 1850s was most loyally supported by three fellow-Congregationalists (Joseph Bottomley, Titus Thewlis and Wright Mellor), two Wesleyan Methodists (Benjamin Robinson and Josephus Jagger Roebuck) and an Anglican (Foster Shaw). It is important to recognise the extent to which the town's politicians were drawn from a relatively narrow socio-economic and intellectual spectrum, which resulted in commonalities of thought and unspoken assumptions that united competing politicians on a number of major issues, not least the management of the police.

Politicians and The Police

The 1848 Improvement Act incorporated the 1847 Town Police Clauses Act which gave the commissioners the power to appoint 'a Superintendent Constable and also such Number of Constables as they judge necessary for the Protection of the Inhabitants and Property' and also to determine their rates of pay. Paragraph VI also provided 'for the Commissioners from Time to Time to remove any such Superintendent Constable, Constables, and Officers as they think fit'. The commissioners were proud and jealous of their police force. This was seen most clearly in 1855 when they fought tenaciously to preserve the independence of the borough force. More importantly, for day-to-day policing, the commissioners were agreed that they – particularly through their Watch Committee – had clear responsibility for the policing of the town, agreeing the appointment (and re-appointment) of constables and their dismissals; issuing instructions about police responsibilities – from checking warehouses to seizing dangerous dogs – through to reviewing beats and considering ancillary support through improved lighting. In that regard, the commissioners clearly saw themselves as masters and the police as their servants. However, there were two key problems regarding the implementation of this relationship. First, even for a medium-sized force, the scale of activities and the likelihood of unforeseen emergencies meant that the police superintendent (and indeed constables) needed – and acquired *de facto* – a degree of operational independence. This must not be overstated but, as several commissioners recognised, it was impractical to have every decision of the superintendent of police approved by members of the Watch Committee. Second, there was scope for disagreement as to the appropriate model of policing for the town's force and of the appropriate personal qualities of its superintendent. Close scrutiny of a town's police force was common – not least in nearby Halifax – but the micro-management style adopted, particularly but not exclusively in the mid-1850s, and the recurring emphasis on individual morality created, rather than solved, problems of management.

The responsibility for law enforcement in the boroughs of nineteenth-century England rested on local watch committees and justices, both of whom had statutory powers, and chief constables, who retained the common-law powers of constables. The relationship between these three elements was not spelt out in detail and, therefore, was a matter of local negotiation and compromise, often involving trial and error. This gave rise to considerable variations in practice across forces, from close supervision by a watch committee (as in Huddersfield and Halifax) to more of a free hand for a chief constable (as in Hull).[6] Much discussion has focussed on the notion of police independence and the enforcement of specific policies. The clashes between the chief constables of Birmingham and Liverpool with their local watch committees, in 1880 and 1890, dominate the literature. Despite some vigorous arguments by Brogden and Jefferson & Grimshaw, the present consensus is that there was general agreement that watch committees had the power to instruct their chief police officers on matters of law enforcement policy.[7] However, the power to instruct did not, in itself, resolve the question of the appropriate day-to-day relationship between watch committees and their senior officials. Further, such questions could not be divorced from wider financial considerations, which in some boroughs led to reductions in force size. Demands for 'economy' were important – and the town force was reduced by one for a brief period in the early 1860s – but of greater importance in Huddersfield were considerations about the appropriate management model for policing in the town and on the necessary qualities of a superintendent of police.

The hiring and firing of ordinary constables was clearly an important function of the Watch Committee but there was a greater responsibility: appointing an efficient superintendent of police and developing an effective working relationship with him. In this the Watch Committee failed, almost without qualification. If Huddersfield had 'an unenviable notoriety in regard to its police and their irregularities', nowhere was this more apparent than at the very top of the force.[8] During the existence of the Improvement Commission there were five superintendents of police, all but one of whom left unwillingly following friction with the town's political leaders. The disputes, particularly those that took place in 1854/5, raised important questions regarding the qualities of a head constable, his role and responsibilities and his relationship with the Watch Committee and the Improvement Commission. Finding the right man was problematic enough but matters were exacerbated by political conflict and personal animosity. The importance of strong leadership was clearly recognised and the members of the Watch Committee, not unreasonably, looked outside the town for men of proven ability and experience in an established urban police force. Unfortunately, on more than one occasion, their judgement was lacking, both in terms of the individuals selected and, more importantly, in their determination to be involved in day-to-day police matters.

The 1850s: Superintendents Thomas and Beaumont

Problems emerged at a very early stage, though the untimely enforced resignation through ill-health of Superintendent Cheeseborough was unfortunate and unforeseeable. The other senior appointments (Sergeant Brown and Inspector Thomas) were more problematic.

Brown's staggering indiscipline has been noted in chapter two but Thomas's early months were little better in disciplinary terms. In August 1849 he was in trouble on three separate occasions. One evening he failed to visit his men on duty between the hours of 10.30 p.m. and 2.40 a.m., spending the time in various local beerhouses. 'Worse for liquor' he then verbally abused Sergeant Sedgwick in the street. Later that month he was accused of immorality by two of his fellow officers. PC Mellor gave evidence that he 'had seen Inspector Thomas in the *Unicorn Inn* ... with a female'. Sergeant Sedgwick was more explicit, alleging that Thomas 'had had improper connections with a woman that had been taken to the Watch-house for shelter ... [and] improper intimacy with another man's wife in Castlegate'.[9] Amidst criticisms of 'gross neglect' and 'gross impropriety', the Watch Committee recommended his dismissal for being drunk, unfit for duty and abusing a fellow officer. The commissioners decided to override the decision of their Watch Committee, for reasons that were not recorded in the minutes but which were probably influenced by the incapacitation of Cheeseborough.[10]

On the enforced resignation of John Cheeseborough, Thomas took over as superintendent of police. For three years there were no serious problems. Indeed, Thomas proved himself to be a determined senior officer, playing an active role in quelling disturbances in Castlegate and tackling the problems of immorality, disorderly houses and cruel sports. In May 1850 the commissioners praised him and fellow-officer, Townend, for 'exerting themselves in the most praiseworthy manner ... to check this great and growing evil [of] these plague spots ... brothels'.[11] In January 1851 he brought to court nine men charged with organising a dogfight in the cellar of a house in Bradley Street, while a year later he showed his personal courage in quelling, albeit with some difficulty, a major disturbance in Castlegate.[12] 1852 was a very successful year for Thomas. He made a number of high-profile arrests – including a thief arrested in a Dewsbury singing-room and a forger tracked down and apprehended in Manchester – while his conduct in the aftermath of the Holmfirth disaster highlighted another positive aspect of policing.[13] However, his very hands-on approach was to be a source of contention under the new political grouping, led by C H Jones (later to become the first mayor of the newly-incorporated Huddersfield), which was elected to power in 1853.[14]

The early years of the Improvement Commission had seen significant reforms in the town and, while this was a source of considerable local pride, it also gave rise to concern among some rate-payers. In the run-up to the 1853 election of commissioners 'economy' became a central issue. Addressing a public meeting in August 1853, a local solicitor, J I Freeman, was unequivocal: 'many offices might be abolished; many salaries curtailed; and the whole affair [of local government] carried on upon a much more economical scale'.[15] The election was a triumph for the faction headed by Jones and his right-hand man, Joseph Boothroyd. Their impact was immediate and dramatic. An Enquiry Committee was set up and chaired by Jones, who was determined to root out lax book-keeping by the earlier commissioners. Hobson, a major figure behind many of the reforms in the town after 1848, having been attacked in the pre-election campaign, found himself heavily criticised for negligence; John Jarrett, superintendent of scavengers, was brought to court and found guilty of embezzlement in the spring of 1854 – an incident which precipitated Hobson's resignation; and in July of the same year Jones explicitly stated his belief that 'sufficient supervision was not exercised in the departments occupied by Superintendent Thomas'.[16]

Jones was clearly determined to exercise tighter control over financial matters but this was part of a wider vision of the role of the commissioners in relation to their officials. He and his supporters adopted a business model of local government, likening their role to that of a company's board of directors.[17] Jones had no doubt that it was his responsibility to keep a close eye on all aspects of the work undertaken by the Improvement Commissioners and to intervene if necessary. He informed the Watch Committee at its meeting on the 4th of August 1855:

> [h]e considered it the duty of the chairman to watch what was going on; and if he apprehended that any officer was liable to be damaged, or an office was likely to be damaged by the conduct of an officer, he was bound to look on and prevent the injury.[18]

In general terms, this meant asserting repeatedly the authority of the commissioners over the town's police force, including its senior officer. More particularly, it translated into taking an active role in the investigation of charges of improper behaviour and the disciplinary action that might be required.

As early as June 1854 Jones raised the question of the relationship between the officials sworn in at the Court Leet and policing within the limits of the Improvement Act. Jones' argument that the swearing in of Thomas as an officer of the manorial Court Leet was 'a dangerous precedent' owed more to his experience of policing in Manchester and revealed an ignorance (genuine or feigned) of the honorific nature of the post and the benign relationship between the Court Leet and the town police authorities that had developed since the mid-1840s. He also overlooked the fact that it had been sanctioned by the commissioners themselves.[19] Of greater significance was his decision to 'originate a conversation' on the seemingly technical issue of 'the necessity of keeping the efforts of the town police within the limits of the Improvement Act'.[20] This was not a straightforward matter. As the town's magistrates had observed, it was folly for the borough police to stop their enquiries or halt a pursuit simply because a suspect moved out of the area defined by the Improvement Act. The situation was further complicated by the relationship with the superintending constable for the Upper Agbrigg district, Thomas Heaton, whose salary was paid in part by the ratepayers of Huddersfield, which meant that Thomas could call upon Heaton for assistance but not *vice versa*. In practice, Heaton had developed a good working relationship with Thomas and other town officers, notably Townend and Sedgwick, which resulted in mutually advantageous reciprocal action. Further, as the Holmfirth tragedy clearly demonstrated, it was important to leave 'some discretionary power ... in the hands of Superintendent Thomas [because] many emergencies happened where there was neither time or [*sic*] opportunity for running after commissioners to grant permission'.[21] Initially no others had joined the conversation but Jones, undeterred, spurred on the Improvement Commissioners to instruct Thomas, in January 1855, 'not to allow the night or the day police to act beyond the limits of the act without the previous joint sanction of two members of the [watch] committee'.[22] This decision had more to do with the politics than the practicalities of policing. Jones was determined to assert his authority and curb the independence that Thomas had shown on a number of occasions.[23]

The clash between the two men undoubtedly had a strong personal element. Jones, a gentleman and Congregationalist, 'a sturdy Nonconformist of the old-fashioned type,' had little in common with a man who had a reputation for drinking and gambling.[24] Neither did he approve of Thomas's 'hands-on', thief-taker style of policing. Matters took an unexpected but significant turn in the spring of 1855 when Thomas was attacked by Henry Lord in the *Zetland Hotel*.[25] Lord, no lover of the local police, was part of the wider 'economical' faction headed by Jones. Later the same month Lord wrote to the Watch Committee alleging two counts of misconduct by Thomas, which set off a long running clash that culminated in Thomas's dismissal.[26] The first charge, relating to the incident at the *Zetland*, was dismissed and it was noted that 'the person bringing the charge [i.e. Lord] had been subject to penal consequences for an assault upon the superintendent and two out of the four witnesses were relatives of the complaining party'.[27] The second allegation, that Thomas had been at a fancy-dress ball and subsequently drinking at the *Cross Keys*, High Street, from the evening of Easter Monday through to seven the following morning, was also dismissed, though Thomas was criticised for being in a public house for such a length of time when his professional presence was not required. Lord then made a third accusation that Thomas had been drinking and gambling at the *Golden Lion Inn*, Pontefract, when he (and another officer) had accompanied a prisoner to the quarter sessions. The Watch Committee enquired into the allegation, upheld the charge and recommended the dismissal of Thomas for misconduct.

A special meeting of the commissioners was called to consider this recommendation, by which time news had spread round the town and memorials were delivered to the Improvement Commissioners from the magistrates of the Huddersfield bench, the Superintending Constable of the Upper Agbrigg district, '166 of the principal inhabitants of the town' and the town's pawnbrokers. Each of them 'spoke warmly of the excellent qualities of Superintendent Thomas, and of his great efficiency as a police officer'.[28] The ensuing debate was more than a dispute about the fitness of the police superintendent. The politics were often murky but it is clear that political factionalism fuelled an often ill-tempered series of exchanges. Dirty linen was washed in public as earlier allegations of Thomas's drunk and disorderly behaviour were aired. There was a widespread acceptance that Thomas was 'an officer of great talent… fully alive to all his duties [who] had served them efficiently for five years'.[29] His defenders conceded that he had 'little venial peccadilos' [*sic*] but argued that it was 'sometimes necessary for a policeman to appear to be fit company for the bad characters they might have to associate with. Some had to get liquor in order to get others in a similar state'.[30] Indeed, as Commissioner Thornton asserted, it was not possible to get 'the most pious and moral men to become policemen'.[31] Such arguments cut no ice with the chairman, Jones and his leading supporter Boothroyd. They conceded that Thomas had been an effective officer, but the central issue in their eyes was one of morality and fitness for position. Boothroyd in particular dwelt upon the details of Thomas's behaviour at Pontefract and argued that not only had this charge been proved beyond 'the shadow of a doubt' but also that this proof of his present drinking and domino-playing (albeit while off duty) 'quite removed the doubt entertained respecting former charges'.[32] To complete his case he resurrected charges against Thomas dating from 1849. In a similar vein commissioner Shaw argued that 'they ought to have an upright and honest man' as police superintendent.[33] The attempt to save Thomas failed. A motion to suspend him for a month was defeated by nine votes to five.[34]

Then matters became somewhat farcical. A new police superintendent was needed; advertisements were placed; a shortlist drawn up; candidates interviewed and a decision made by the Watch Committee – that the best man for the post was none other than John Thomas![35] The decision provoked a crisis in local politics. There were questions about the constitutionality of reappointing a man who had been dismissed by the commissioners; further clashes between pragmatists and moralists; and heightened personal feeling. The first special meeting of the commissioners took place in mid-July. Thomas's enemies were accused of prior collusion in mounting their attack and Jones was specifically accused of 'vindictiveness and persecution'. Despite strong support from Benjamin Thornton, who claimed that Thomas was 'a most useful, vigilant and excellent officer [who] was very popular with the ratepayers ...[and] liked by every body except thieves, rogues and vagabonds', there remained a powerful group who were totally opposed to Thomas. When it came to the vote the commissioners were evenly split (eight votes for dismissal, eight votes against), leaving the chair, none other than Jones, with the casting vote. This he refused to use, notwithstanding the fact that he told the meeting that he could 'never act with him [Thomas] again [as] all my confidence in that officer is forfeited' and that should Thomas be appointed 'he [Jones] should feel obliged to resign his office as chairman'.[36]

The local press was unimpressed with the behaviour of the commissioners. The question had become 'the occasion of a series of party moves as unprincipled as they are contemptible [that were] waged with an intemperance and virulence ... [that was] not very creditable to those concerned'.[37] Instead of debate there was 'a long and irregular conversation' conducted in 'a regular babel of sound'.[38] The *Examiner* made a veiled criticism of Hobson and 'his puppets' who were 'disgracing and degrading' the commission and was scathing in condemning the 'Jonathan Wilde' defence that 'it is necessary for a police superintendent to be a rogue and vagabond, a drunkard and gambler' to catch criminals.[39] However, if the first special meeting showed the commissioners in a bad light, the second was worse. Held in early August, it was even more heated. Jones's resignation prior to the meeting further heightened personal animosity. In a lengthy and often vituperative speech, explaining his decision to resign, Jones became increasingly shrill as he defended himself. He listed all those who had made major errors of judgment: the magistrates who had 'decided wrongly' in the original case involving Lord and Thomas; the Watch Committee, with whom 'he entirely differed' regarding the *Cross Keys* incident and even the commissioners who 'now were in a wrong position'.[40] Jones continued his excoriating personal attacks on Thomas, accusing him of 'encouraging gambling and drunkenness' and condemning him as 'a violent worthless character'. Boothroyd was little less intemperate. Thomas was 'utterly incompetent'. 'The simple question', he asserted, 'was whether Thomas was morally qualified for the post'. Commissioner Shaw supplied the answer for the 'moralist' faction. 'How could [he] properly carry out his duties?' he asked rhetorically. 'Would he not feel it necessary to wink at the faults of others or feel that he was acting unjustly towards them?' It was clear: Thomas was not 'a fit man to be at the head of the police'.[41]

Jones condemned Thomas for his 'improper conduct, including drunkenness [which] would be an encouragement to crime' whereas he should be 'superior to the vices he was employed to check'.[42] However, there was a further concern. Jones argued that 'the chief constable ought to act as a head constable not as a thief taker [and] ought to be the director of the thief takers'.[43] Passions were inflamed on both sides. Hobson (himself subject to much criticism from Jones and his clique) saw Thomas as a victim of 'rancorous and vindictive feeling' and condemned the 'system of espionage' that had been resorted to by Jones and his supporters. Thomas, they argued, had been 'tracked down from street to street, from house to house, and all his faults observed'.[44] Tempers flared as Boothroyd was denounced as a man 'who assumed the tone of a person who thought himself purer and better than others'; Jones was attacked for attempting to brow beat the Watch Committee and pursuing Thomas malevolently. Once again the commissioners were evenly divided (nine men on each side) but this time the new chair, John Firth, voted in favour of not reappointing Thomas.[45]

This was the end of Thomas's police career but not the end of story. A month after his dismissal Thomas met Jones in Market Street. Words were exchanged, Thomas tweaked Jones's nose and found himself indicted on a charge of assault and actual bodily harm. The case was heard at the Wakefield Quarter Sessions and Jones's evidence was ridiculed in the local press. 'We fancy,' opined the *Chronicle*, 'that some of the many who saw Mr. Jones passing up and down the street so prominently after the encounter will be surprised to learn that "his life was greatly despaired of" in consequence of the "bodily harm" which the nose-wringer inflicted'.[46] After two hours' deliberation the jury found Thomas 'guilty of a very slight assault under very aggravated circumstances; and ... therefore recommend[ed] the defendant to the merciful consideration of the court'.[47] Jones' behaviour in court did little to enhance his reputation. He told the magistrates that he was not pressing for imprisonment, an 'effort at magnanimity [which] excited derision and merriment among the spectators at court'.[48] In fact Thomas was fined £5 and had to find sureties for good behaviour for six months of £100 and an additional two of £50 from others, a sentence which 'created considerable surprise'.[49]

The Jones/Thomas conflict made good copy because of the clash of personalities but it is important not to lose sight of the principles involved. Jones was arguing for a model of policing in which ultimate responsibility rested unequivocally with the Improvement Commissioners, who would exercise detailed oversight of police practice. The decision not to appoint Thomas delighted Jones as it presented him with an opportunity to introduce his alternative, 'a new system, [with] new discipline, new orders [and] new men'.[50] Indeed, steps had already been taken before the decision of the 4th August not to appoint Thomas. Boothroyd had already written to 'Mr. Crossley of Halifax' but jumped the gun by proposing

of the Huddersfield Watch Committee not only believed in (and exercised) their right to be involved in disciplinary matters – notwithstanding the mixed success of such an approach as explored in chapter two – but also they showed no willingness to acknowledge the expertise of their senior police officer. Worse, they failed to appreciate how their interventions in disciplinary matters undermined the authority of this man.

Priday left in September 1862 but his reputation was further tarnished by another sexual scandal as he faced a bastardy charge. The complainant, Martha Hilton, fell outside mid-Victorian definitions of respectability, getting 'her living by cleaning and charring and other domestic occupations and also by hawking oranges in public houses at night'.[65] In the face of Hilton's revelations about an incident in the Police-office and references to twice-weekly visits to the superintendent, Priday agreed to make a weekly payment of 2*s* (10p) towards the upkeep of the child. It was not the most dignified way to be remembered in the town.

For the next new broom, the commissioners looked to the boom town of Middlesbrough and its superintendent, William Hannan, notwithstanding the presence of the strong, experienced local candidate, William Townend. Hannan was very much the founding father of 'new policing' in Middlesbrough and, initially, he made a positive impact in Huddersfield. The day and night police were amalgamated, record-keeping improved and new regulations introduced. He persuaded the commissioners to introduce a superannuation scheme and, most importantly, took a strong and successful line against the scandal of beerhouse-brothels. The high-profile and successful prosecution of two husband and wife beerhouse keepers for procuring young girls and keeping them as prostitutes (see chapter five) brought considerable praise. His monthly reports in the mid-1860s were increasingly positive and the evidence he presented of improved police efficiency led to some improvement in relations with the Watch Committee. Nonetheless, there were complaints of police brutality under Hannan and his own personal conduct came in for criticism. The first sign of major trouble came following the 1865 Huddersfield election won, unusually, by the Tories. Election day itself had been something of a triumph as Hannan and Cobbe acted together but the aftermath proved problematic. Complaints of intimidation by the losing candidate (Leatham) led to a parliamentary enquiry to which Hannan was called to give evidence. His performance before the Select Committee gave rise to criticism on the Improvement Commission where he was accused of acting for 'party purposes' and giving false evidence of violence by the Leathamites. Joel Denham, in particular, argued that the matter reflected on 'the character of one of the servants of the town'.[66] Although Hannan survived, when he appeared before the Watch Committee he ruefully noted that 'not one Superintendent had left Huddersfield to go to a better situation but had left in disgrace'.[67] Matters worsened in 1867, following the addition of a 'godly leaven of the Puritan element' in the Improvement Commission.[68] Hannan found himself under attack but this time on matters of morality rather than politics. The first issue was the question of drunkenness in the town. Hannan was a long-time critic of beerhouses and had played an active role in prosecuting the proprietors of beerhouse-brothels but in the late-summer of 1867 matters flared up, following the appearance of a report that purported to show that Huddersfield had one of the worst rates of drunkenness in the country. Hannan was asked to provide the Watch Committee with an explanation. His report was highly critical of the 'places of low amusement where obscene song, filthy comedy and degrading conversation ... excite the worst passions', bemoaned the 'non-existence of any public park, or any place of public recreation' and made a plea for 'better educated [working-class] people'.[69] He also drew attention to the marked differences of recording from force to force. Unlike in many towns, in Huddersfield all known cases of drunkenness were recorded thereby creating an exaggerated impression of the scale of the problem. As commissioner Clough conceded: 'Huddersfield was not such an abominable place as has been represented'.[70] This was not good enough for those who believed that a solution could be found through the enforcement of the existing law and the passing of new. Denham, again, was scathing in his criticism of Hannan's failure to improve the moral condition of the town. Hannan, not least with his knowledge of the extent of the problem in Middlesbrough, felt, not unreasonably, that he was being unfairly criticised.

The second issue also had to do with popular recreation. This time in the form of Guy Fawkes night celebrations. Earlier in the century Huddersfield had had a reputation for being one of the most riotous towns on the 5th of November. Attempts to clear the Market Square in the late 1840s had led to the humiliation of the police, notably the newly-appointed superintending constable, Thomas Heaton, (see chapter seven) but there had been relatively little trouble for over a decade. Hannan's approach was low-key not least because arrests were likely 'to result in conflict with the police, if not in riot'.[71] In terms of 'policing by consent', this was a sensible stance on the part of the police but it was insufficient for the recently-elected 'Puritans' under a chairman, who was a man 'who advocates the making of drunkards sober by Act of Parliament and the force of authority.'[72] The new Watch Committee rejected Hannan's advice not to change existing policy. As well as instructing the police to take firm action, members of the Watch Committee also took to the streets of the town, particularly St. George's Square, to arrest revellers, letting off squibs. The outcome was predictable. Bonfires were lit, fireworks set off and the 'over-zeal and frog-swelling pride of "authority" ... [made them] the butts of fun, frolic and scorn of the assembled crowd'.[73] The events also proved to be the final straw for Hannan, whose health was also deteriorating. In late October he had intimated that he was considering resignation but when he did so the Watch Committee themselves had recommended that the commissioners should not accept his resignation. There was but a brief delay. Rumours swept the town that Hannan was about to resign and take over the *Bull and Mouth Inn* and on the 6th of November the Watch Committee resolved that 'the conduct of many of the Police Force ... was very inefficient and deserving of the censure of the Commissioners'.[74] That was the end of Hannan's career as superintendent of police; he resigned to become a publican. Given his track record, as much in Middlesbrough as Huddersfield, it is difficult to escape the conclusion that, once again, personality and local politics as well as the practicalities of policing, played a crucial role.

By this time the days of the Improvement Commission were coming to an end and the next new broom, James Withers from Preston, was brought in with an eye to the needs of the new, enlarged borough. His success is part of another story.[75] However, there was evidence of a new outlook on the part of the commissioners. The Watch Committee resolved that Withers would 'have the full charge and superintendence of the whole Police Force'.[76] This time words were backed up by deeds. Withers introduced a new system of policing, closely based on that of the Metropolitan police and set about tightening up discipline. There was no evidence of friction between the superintendent of police and his masters, among whom was the influential figure of the town's first mayor, C H Jones, the same man who had fought literally and metaphorically with a former superintendent of police in the mid-1850s! Despite his success, Withers left in 1874 when his request for an increased salary was rejected. Once again, the question of the salaries of public servants was controversial and Jones was unable to convince his colleagues of rewarding a man with a proven track record. Withers moved to nearby Bradford where he served as Chief Constable with distinction for twenty years.

Conclusion: the Role of the Watch Committee

As for Huddersfield under the 1848 Improvement Act, it bowed out with 'an unenviable notoriety' – a somewhat inglorious but not unjustified epitaph. Successive Watch Committees seemed singularly inept in choosing men to be superintendents of police. This was very much the case with regard to George Beaumont but it was not obvious that John Thomas and William Hannan, for all their rough-and-ready ways, lacked the ability to head up a relatively small borough force. A significant part of the problem rested with the Watch Committees (or certain of its members) who not only had a particularly moral view of what a police superintendent should be but also, on many occasions, felt that they should keep the force, including its senior officers, under close scrutiny and intervene in matters that were of a more day-to-day management nature. There is a striking contrast between Huddersfield and Hull in this regard. While it is undoubtedly the case that Hull's chief constable, Alexander MacManus, was a very able officer, it is also the case that successive Watch Committees viewed the police as competent professionals, who could be entrusted with the operational responsibility to police Hull and whom they would support in times of criticism.[77] Similarly, the first generation of 'new policing' in Halifax was characterised by a positive relationship between the Watch Committee and the town police, notwithstanding the close scrutiny exercised by its Watch Committee.[78] Hull might have been exceptional but so too, in a very different way, was Huddersfield.[79] The relationship between any borough chief constable or superintendent of police and his Watch Committee was one that had to be negotiated. The Watch Committee might 'hire and fire' and determine local policy priorities but there was a degree of day-to-day operational control that had to reside with senior police officers. Drawing the line was not easy but, as more forces came into being and time passed, some chief constables were able to carve out a degree of autonomy, not least as their watch committees acknowledged their experience and developing expertise. There could still be problems – not least the spectacular clash between the Head Constable of Liverpool and the local Watch Committee – but in most boroughs a *modus vivendi* was established relatively smoothly in the first decade or so of a new force being established.[80] This was not the case in Huddersfield where several commissioners held strong views about the police, their conduct and the extent to which local politicians should be directly involved in the management of the police. To think in terms of master and servants was commonplace but operationalising that relationship, while difficult, was not necessarily insoluble. However, in Huddersfield successive Watch Committees acted like the head of a household, who not only employed a cook and told her what he expected for dinner, but also told her what ingredients to use and how to cook them! Culinary metaphors apart, this interventionism led to repeated confrontations between key figures which, exacerbated by personality clashes, hindered the development of an efficient force.

The Borough Police Force, The Government and Her Majesty's Inspector of Constabulary

Policing in Huddersfield (as elsewhere) operated within a broader framework created by government legislation. That framework was to be changed significantly in the mid-1850s as proposals for police reform were discussed in parliament. Palmer's detailed analysis of the legislative battle that led to the defeat of Palmerston's first police bill in 1854 and the subsequent success of Grey's bill in 1856 rightly makes much of the opposition from the incorporated boroughs, led by the mayors and aldermen of cities such as Leeds and York.[81] However, the predicament faced by a town such as Huddersfield, policed under an Improvement Commission, was often ignored at the time and has been neglected by later historians.

There was a strong and broad-based sense of local pride in Huddersfield, manifesting itself in a variety of ways. Opposition to the subsuming of the town's police into a larger, more distant county force was one example.[82] The permissive Rural Police Act of 1839 had provoked considerable concern, but this paled into insignificance as the implications of the later reform proposals were grasped by the town's politicians. In March 1856 the Improvement Commissioners decided to petition parliament, opposing Grey's bill. An indignant C H Jones bemoaned the fact that 'members of parliament seemed almost ignorant of Improvement Commissioners' and, as a consequence, their failure to recognise the town as a borough within the meaning of the bill would result in Huddersfield 'being treated in the same manner as the humblest village'.[83] Local differences were overlooked as the commissioners stressed the efficiency of the town's force in glowing terms.

> [T]he police force ... has been fully adequate to the requirements of the ... town; and its efficiency has been seen not only in the detection and suppression of crime, but also the removal of those haunts of infamy and the correction of debasing practices once so numerous and so prevalent in [Huddersfield].

Such efficiency, they argued, was based on local control.

> [T]he general efficiency of the police arrangements is attributable to the fact that the ... police force has been governed and conducted by a local board intimately acquainted with the requirements of the ... town, and the practices of its inhabitants.[84]

Success was far from guaranteed. Grey was strongly opposed to further modifications to the police bill, fearing that a concession for one town would open the floodgates and delay or even derail the bill in its passage through parliament. Despite some sympathy for Huddersfield's position from the under-secretary at the Home Department, Massey, the absence of support from other similarly placed towns weakened the argument.[85] Fortunately for the commissioners, the town's Liberal MP, Viscount Goderich, lobbied Grey at considerable length, stressing the existence of 'a perfectly efficient police'. Indeed, this became his central argument: if the present police system 'is done away with it will be impossible to carry out effectively the Improvement Act of 1848'.[86] The effect of this behind-the-scene lobbying became apparent towards the end of a long debate in the House of Commons during the committee stage of the bill. Goderich rose to ask Grey what would be the impact of the bill on Huddersfield. Grey reassured him that 'Huddersfield would continue under the power of the existing [i.e.1848] act'.[87]

This was not entirely the end of the matter. Colonel Cobbe, chief constable of the WRCC, made it clear in meetings with Grey and Her Majesty's Inspector of Constabulary for the northern counties,

Colonel Woodford, that he wished to see the Huddersfield police incorporated into the county force. Grey was unsympathetic unless there was evidence of inefficiency in the town's force.[88] Woodford's first inspection, scheduled for the 10th of March, was critical. He judged the twenty-six constables 'with one exception ... to be smart, active men and thoroughly effective.'[89] Later that month he wrote to the Watch Committee, requesting them to consider appointing additional men, because of the length of certain beats, but stressing that this was 'with a view to the greater efficiency of the establishment with which I had in all other respects reason to be well satisfied'.[90] In fact, the matter was largely a foregone conclusion. Prior to the official inspection, Woodford had met with members of the Watch Committee and expressed himself 'highly pleased with the character and efficiency of the force at Huddersfield', noting that at a recent meeting of magistrates at Wakefield the town's force had been held up as a model. Indeed, he also let it be known that Huddersfield 'would not be as efficiently watched during the night under the arrangements of the county constabulary' as it was under the Improvement Commissioners.[91]

Relations with the inspectorate remained good during the next decade. The force was deemed to be 'efficient' from 1857 to 1868 and was not singled out for particular criticism. The cells, it was true, were criticised in 1858 and again in 1864 when 'their isolation and faulty construction' was identified; while in 1861 'the inaccurate and very careless manner in which some of the books had been kept' was noted.[92] The attempts to reduce police numbers in the early 1860s was a potential source of conflict with potentially negative financial implications. The 'economical' faction was challenged on precisely this point. In the event the slight reduction in numbers passed with little comment: Woodford noted that it 'did not appear ... to have impaired the general efficiency of the establishment'.[93] However, when Keighley broached the subject of further reductions, Woodford made it clear that 'he did not think it advisable, under existing circumstances, to reduce the force' further.[94] Notwithstanding such shortcomings the 'general efficiency of the establishment' was noted on a regular basis.[95] Thus, despite the problems between Watch Committees and superintendents, the Huddersfield police force in the 1850s and 1860s developed into an efficient force in the judgement of Her Majesty's Inspector of Constabulary. In no small measure this was due to the emergence of a core of 'long-term' policemen, to whose careers we now turn.

Endnotes

1 A brief survey of northern forces (Cheshire, Derbyshire, Durham, Lancashire and Yorkshire) shows that only Birkenhead, Oldham and Rochdale experienced a number of short-serving head constables. In contrast Bradford had only three head constables between 1847 and 1894, all of whom served twelve years or more; in Halifax head constable served for twenty-one years between 1851 and 1872; in Hull head constable MacManus, thirty years (and dying in post); in Middlesbrough Hannan served for eight years and his successor Saggerson for twenty-three in Sheffield Rayner served for fourteen years, his successor, Jackson, twenty-nine; in Hartlepool head constable Waters served seventeen years; and in Wakefield the first head constable served twenty years from 1848 to 1868. More research is needed on several of these forces. The problems in Birkenhead, for example, were not necessarily the same as those in Huddersfield. Finally, the assumption that longevity of service guaranteed police efficiency should be resisted. M Stallion & D S Wall, *The British Police: Police Forces and Chief Officers, 1829–2000*, Police History Society, Gateshead, Athenaeum Press, 1999.

2 Para.XIV named the first eighteen commissioners: Joseph Armitage Esq., George Armitage Esq., James Booth, Joseph Beaumont junior, John Brook, Thomas Pearson Crossland, Thomas Firth (Tea Dealer), Thomas Atkinson Heaps, Abraham Hirst, William Kaye, Jere Kaye, Thomas Mallinson, William Moore, John Newhouse, Samuel Routledge, John Sutcliffe Esq. and Joseph Shaw.

3 D Griffiths, *Joseph Brook of Greenhead: 'Father of the Town'*, Huddersfield Local History Society, 2013 contains some clear and succinct observations on the politics of the town in the 1840s and 1850s.

4 D Griffith, *Pioneers or Partisans? Governing Huddersfield, 1820–1848,* Huddersfield Local History Society, 2008, p.57.

5 George Loch, the agent of the Ramsden estate from 1844, was another key figure in the drive for improvement.

6 See M Brogden, *The Police: Autonomy and Consent, London,* Academic Press, 1982, T Jefferson & R Grimshaw, Controlling the Constable, London, Frederick Muller/Cobden Trust, 1984, L Lustgarten, *The Governance of Police,* London, Sweet & Maxwell, 1986 and R Reiner, *Chief Constables,* Oxford University Press, 1992.

7 Reiner, *Chief Constables*, p.13.

8 *HC,* 16 October 1858.

9 Watch Committee Minutes, KMT 2/3/13/1, 13 August 1849.

10 In the absence of detailed information in the minutes of the Improvement Commission and the Watch Committee (and the absence of a local newspaper) one cannot say with confidence why this happened. However, the evidence of the early 1850s suggests that Thomas was an active officer, enforcing many of the commissioners' policies regarding beerhouses and brothels, and well-regarded by some, if not all of the commissioners. See for,

example, *HC*, 18 May, 14 September 1850, 18 January, 1 February, 17 April, 26 June 1851, 9 September & 4 November 1854.

11 *HC,* 11 & 18 May, 1850.

12 *HC,* 18 January 1851 and 17 April 1852.

13 *HC,* 7 February, 13 March & 2 October 1852.

14 The concern with policing was one part of a wider campaign to improve the efficiency and economy of local government, which falls beyond the scope of this book.

15 *HC,* 13 August 1853.

16 *HC,* 4 March, 8 April & 15 July 1854.

17 For example, see Commissioner Shaw's comparison of the members Watch Committee to company directors, *Huddersfield Examiner, [*hereafter *HEx],* 4 August 1855.

18 *HC,* 4 August 1855.

19 As the clerk to the commissioners informed members regarding the decision to swear-in Thomas as deputy-constable at the Court Leet. *HC,* 6 January, 1855.

20 *HC,* 9 December 1854.

21 Commissioner Thornton. *HC,* 4 November 1854. Jones also objected to Thomas's decision to allow two officers to assist the Hull police during the Queen's visit to that city, claiming erroneously that the Hull request had not been considered.

22 *HC,* 6 January, 1855.

23 At times Jones played fast and loose with the truth. He accused Thomas, on one occasion, of permitting two constables to assist the Hull force during the visit of the queen, without the permission of the commissioners. In fact, the Watch Committee had discussed and approved Thomas's proposal in response to a request from the authorities in Hull. *HC,* 4 November 1854.

24 A W Sykes, *Ramsden Street Independent Church, Huddersfield. Notes and Records of a Hundred Years, 1825–1925,* Huddersfield, 1925, p. 99–100 cited in E A H Haigh, ed., *Huddersfield: A Most Handsome Town,* Huddersfield, 1992, p.128.

25 Henry Lord is a somewhat enigmatic figure who had a chequered career and aroused strong feelings. A painter and decorator, living in Zetland Street, he was found guilty of assault on a number of occasions but also accused the police of assaulting him. In August 1852 he had written to the commissioners complaining about Inspector Sedgwick, though this was not upheld. He was also accused of receiving 'a large job of work without a contract' in 1853 and stood surety for the disgraced John Jarrett in the following year. More generally, he was prominent in local matters, alleging favouritism among local officials (at a public meeting regarding the Huddersfield cemetery in April 1852), questioning alleged police perquisites (at the Improvement Commission's annual meeting in June 1853) and asserting that police "added nought" for the £1,257 spent on them in the previous year. He was also a member of the Working Men's Committee and a supporter of the Huddersfield Temperance Drum and Fife Band.

26 *HC,* 19 & 28 May 1855; KMT, 2/2/1, 6 June, 13 July & 1 August 1855.

27 *HC,* 28 May 1855.

28 *HC & HEx,* 9 June 1855.

29 Messrs. Dransfield and J Brook, *HC,* 9 June 1855.
30 *HC,* 9 June 1855.
31 *Ibid.*
32 *Ibid.*
33 *HEx,* 14 July 1855.
34 Watch Committee Minutes, KMT 18/2/2/1, 6 June 1855.
35 *HC,* 30 June 1855.
36 Watch Committee Minutes, KMT 18/2/2/1, 13 July 1855 & *HC,* 14 July 1855.
37 HEx, 28 July 1855.
38 *HC,* 14 July 1855.
39 *HEx,* 28 July 1855.
40 *HC,* 4 August 1855.
41 *HC,* 4 August 1855.
42 Watch Committee Minutes, KMT, 18/2/2/1, 6 June, 4 & 13 July & 1 August, 1855.
43 *HC,* 4 August 1855.
44 *HC,* 4 August 1855.
45 HIC Minutes, KMT, 18/2/2/1, 1 August 1855.
46 *HC,* 29 December 1855.
47 *HC,* 5 January 1856.
48 *LM,* 3 January 1856.
49 *LM,* 3 January 1856.
50 *LM,* 3 January 1856.
51 Boothroyd defended his action on the ground that it was 'only a private communication' but it is highly unlikely that Jones was unaware of the letter. The evidence, though incomplete, points to careful planning to bring in a favoured candidate.
52 *HC,* 7 November 1857. The Watch Committee minutes are silent on the matter.
53 *HC,* 14 August & 4 September, 1858.
54 *HC,* 16 October 1858.
55 *Ibid.*
56 HIC Minutes, KMT 18/2/2/1, 27 October & 4 November 1857.
57 HIC Minutes, KMT 18/2/2/1, 4 November 1857.
58 *HC,* 6 November 1858.
59 *HC,* 3 March 1859. It is not known how or why Priday's speech was leaked but it is probable that whoever was responsible was confident that the *Chronicle,* whose editor was Joshua Hobson, would be sympathetic to anti-Jones sentiments, however indirectly expressed.
60 Watch Committee Minutes, KMT 18/2/3/14/1, 25 August 1862.
61 *HC,* 11 October 1862. The letter was dated 25 August.
62 *Ibid.* Letter dated 30 August 1862.
63 *Ibid.* Letter dated 2 September.
64 *Ibid.*
65 *HC,* 20 June 1863. Hilton had a criminal record, having been found guilty of foul and abusive language when arrested by Detective Partridge as she hawked oranges at the railway station. She is not to be confused with Mary Ann Hilton, discussed in chapter six.

66 *HC,* 7 July 1866.
67 *Ibid,* 7 July 1866. See also *HC,* 1 September 1866.
68 *HC,* 9 November 1867.
69 *HC,* 7 September 1867.
70 *Ibid.*
71 *HC,* 9 November 1867.
72 *Ibid.*
73 *Ibid.*
74 Watch Committee Minutes, KMT 18/2/3/14/2, 6 November 1867.
75 See D Taylor, 'A fit man to be at the head of the police'. Head constables and watch committees in the first generation of 'new policing: a Yorkshire perspective, c.1840-1870' in K Stevenson, *et. al., eds., Leading the Police: A History of Chief Constables*, London, Routledge, 2017, forthcoming. The author is also working on policing in the last quarter of the nineteenth century as part of a collection of essays to be published by the Huddersfield Local History Society to celebrate the 150th anniversary of incorporation.
76 Watch Committee Minutes, KMT 18/2/3//14/2, 26 December 1867.
77 See particularly the robust defence by the Watch Committee of the town's police following accusations of misconduct made regarding the 1857 Blanket Row fire. D R Walsh, The Reform of Urban Policing in Victorian England: A Study of Kingston upon Hull from 1836 to 1866, unpublished PhD, University of Hull, 1997, pp338ff.
78 There were problems in Halifax in the early 1870s. The emergence of an increasingly powerful temperance movement and accusations that the superintendent of police was too close to the local drinks trade led to the dramatic resignation of Superintendent Pearson in 1872. J Posner, The Establishment and Development of the New Police in Halifax, 1848–1914, unpublished PhD, University of Huddersfield, 2015, p.107ff.
79 More research is needed on the relationship between watch committees and police superintendents in the first generation of 'new policing', especially in the medium-sized boroughs.
80 The central issue was the prosecution of brothels. The police adopted a pragmatic approach, prosecuting problematic and notorious brothels but turning a blind eye to 'respectable' ones. The Watch Committee ordered that all brothels be prosecuted contrary to the judgement of the chief constable, William Nott-Bower. One of the unforeseen consequences was the relocation of city-centre brothels to more respectable suburbs. The policy of indiscriminate prosecutions of brothels was quickly abandoned even though the Watch Committee had asserted its authority over its chief constable. W Nott-Bower, *Fifty Two Years a Policeman,* London, Edward Arnold, 1926, pp.139–46.
81 S H Palmer, *Police and Protest in England and Wales, 1780–1850,* Cambridge University Press, 1990, chapter twelve, section II, esp. pp.504–516.
82 There were some who supported amalgamation. The *Chronicle,* continued to argue for it on grounds of economy, see 14 March 1857.
83 *HC, 8* March 1856. Such sentiments were not unique to Huddersfield.
84 HIC Minutes, KMT 2/2/1, 5 March 1856 and *HC, 8 March 1856.*
85 Belated a similarly case was made for exempting Barnsley.

86 Report of Jones's meeting with Goderich and subsequent letter to Grey, reported to Huddersfield Improvement Commissioners. *HC,* 10 May 1856. For details of Goderich see www.oxforddnb.com/article/35792 accessed 19 May 2015.
87 *Hansard, House of Commons debate,* 25 April 1856.
88 HIC Minutes, KMT 18/2/2/1, 4 March 1857.
89 Reports of Inspectors of Constabulary to Secretary of State, 1856–7, *Parliamentary Papers,* 1857/8 (20), p.71.
90 Letter dated 31 March 1857 read to commissioners meeting of 25 April 1857, *HC,* 9 May 1857.
91 HIC Minutes, KMT 18/2/2/1, 4 March 1857 and *HC,* 7 March 1857.
92 Reports of Inspectors of Constabulary to Secretary of State, 1857/8, *Parliamentary Papers,* 1859 (17), p.74 and 1865 (32), p.96 for cells. *Reports of Inspectors of Constabulary to Secretary of State, 1860/1, Parliamentary Papers,* 1862 (28) p.67 for books. A year later the inspector found the 'same want of care and accuracy'. *Parliamentary Papers,* 1863 (20), p.75. Beaumont's financial irregularities in 1858/9 were not picked up.
93 Reports of Inspectors of Constabulary for the year ending 29th September 1862, Parliamentary Papers, 1863 (20).
94 *HC,* 12 July 1862.
95 The term 'efficiency' needs to be understood in terms of contemporary expectations. The newly-appointed Inspectors of Constabulary did not have a sophisticated measure of efficiency. To the contrary they applied a rough-and-ready criterion of one constable per 1,000 population to determine 'efficiency' and Huddersfield had a police/population ratio of 1:900 (or better) throughout the late 1850s and 1860s.

The Men of the Borough Force

DESPITE BEING A relatively small borough force, the Huddersfield police under the 1848 Improvement Act was an evolving and complex entity. While it is important to be aware of the broad contours of the force in the 1850s and 1860s – the length of service, the disciplinary record, the resignations, the dismissals and the like – behind the statistical abstractions were men, of varying ability and commitment, who, for varying lengths of time, were responsible for the policing of the town. These are the men who appear occasionally in faded Victorian photographs but whose voices are seldom heard directly in the historical record. Much about them is unknown and unknowable. However, it is possible to reconstruct something of their public life and their experiences as policemen. Unsurprisingly, there is more information relating to the successful and long-serving men but there is also material that casts some light on the less successful and more transient figures who donned the police uniform. No two police careers were the same but, for the purpose of analysis, it is useful to distinguish between five broad categories of men: first, the short-stay men, who rarely served more than a year or two and never made a career of policing; second, the longer-serving men, often serving for a decade or more but who never moved on from the rank of constable; third, another, smaller group of career policemen, who only managed to gain promotion to sergeant; fourth, an even smaller group, the high-fliers who achieved two or more promotions; and finally, the men at the top – the superintendents, who were at the interface between the local politicians and the men of the force. The first group, by definition, falls outside the scope of this chapter

– the peccadillos that led to their dismissal and, to a much lesser extent, their reasons for resigning have been discussed in chapter two – while the last group has been discussed in chapter three.[1] The remaining groups will be examined here in as much detail as the historical record allows. The emergence of a core of experienced men, many of whom never moved beyond the rank of constable, was significant in the creation of a policed society in Huddersfield but it was the small number of high-fliers who provided leadership, as well as experience, in a force beset by ongoing tensions between Watch Committees and superintendents.

Promotion was determined by the interplay of three broad factors: ambition, ability and opportunity. Although promotion had obvious attractions – not least, better pay and enhanced status – not all long-serving constables either wished to take on additional responsibilities or had the ability to do so. Capable men such as John Boler and James Gledhill, whose records are comparable with colleagues who were promoted, seem to have been satisfied with life as a constable. Others simply lacked the physical or mental wherewithal to be considered for promotion. The long-serving James Hirst had a dismal performance record and limited physical fitness. John Dodson was little better as his 'blissful ignorance' while a robbery took place on his beat in 1854 bears witness. Others such as Henry Beevers and Hamor Sedgwick clearly showed both some ambition and ability but lacked the discipline required. However, ambition and ability alone did not guarantee promotion. Opportunity was critical. The expansion of numbers and the growth in complexity of the force in the early 1850s created opportunities for promotion but with able men in post and a stabilization in the size of the force, thereafter opportunities dried up. As a consequence, a number of men, for example John Nutton and Noah Worsnip, had to wait many years, not gaining promotion until after incorporation when the town force was significantly expanded.

All of the men whose careers are analysed here started their police careers in the lowest rank before gaining promotion and, as a consequence of their experience on the beat, there were certain important commonalities, irrespective of their different career trajectories.[2] Policing in Huddersfield, as in other boroughs, was arduous but often mundane and tedious. Tramping the streets of the town throughout the year and in all weathers was physically demanding. Consequently, greater experience was bought at the price of decreasing physical efficiency. In addition to such routine hazards, there were less predictable dangers – runaway horses, and dangerous dogs, floods and fires and, last but not least angry men, women and even children.[3] As the briefest perusal of the town's crime statistics reveals, the bulk of police time was devoted to low-level crime and regulatory offences. Maintaining 'order and decorum' in public places, containing anti-social behaviour – especially where it impinged upon 'respectable' rate-payers and the town's elites was at the heart of policing. Much of every constable's time was given over to dealing with beggars and vagrants, with gamblers in beerhouses or in the streets and back lanes, with drunk and disorderly men and lewd and disorderly women. The bulk of the crime prosecuted in the town was dealt with summarily by the local magistrates. Drink-related offences, particularly assaults, were commonplace as were petty thefts from shops and lodging houses or from the person, often in a public house or beershop.[4] There were relatively few serious crimes that led to a trial at the local quarter sessions and even fewer that were serious enough to warrant trial at assize. Furthermore, the more serious crimes were predictably but disproportionately dealt with by the abler and experienced (usually higher ranking) men and also by the specialist detectives appointed from the mid-1850s onwards. For some men the routines and realities of the beat was but a phase in a career that brought promotion and more responsibility but also more pay and some escape from basic policing. For others, this was the totality of their police careers and it is to this group that we first turn.

Long-serving Constables

There were eighteen long-serving men in the Huddersfield police force who never rose beyond the rank of constable.[5] All were appointed to the lowest rank – night constable before the 1863 reorganization, third-class constable thereafter – and (with one partial exception) progressed no further than first-class constable. These men were very much the workhorses of the force, familiar figures patrolling the streets of the town, day and night, for several years. Of the eleven who completed their careers before incorporation, two were forced to retire because of ill-health, one died in service while three resigned and five were dismissed. In contrast, of the seven men in post on the eve of incorporation, only one of whom had been appointed before 1856, six were subsequently superannuated and one retired. In part, this contrast between early-appointees and late-appointees reflected the belated introduction of a superannuation scheme in Huddersfield. Men joining in the late-1840s and early-1850s had no prospect of a pension. Consequently, some worked until their health failed; others resigned or were dismissed as frustration at their lack of progress and concern at the lack of security about their future kicked in. However, there was a more significant division that owed less to the date of appointment. 50 per cent of this group had an exemplary (or near exemplary) disciplinary record whereas the remainder did not. Indeed, three men were dismissed, re-appointed and subsequently dismissed a second time. The former were solid, reliable men but demonstrating little potential for more senior roles; the latter were often men of some ability, which often compensated for their poor discipline. A closer examination of individual careers brings out the variations within this group of men.

Henry Beevers was appointed a supernumerary constable in January 1849 and a month later made a permanent night constable. His record (in terms of arrest, at least) was modest.[6] Most of the cases he brought before the local magistrates involved breaches of licensing laws and gambling, though he was involved in the arrest of notorious local criminal 'Slasher' Wilson in December 1854. Reprimanded for being drunk and unfit for duty in 1850, he was fortunate not to be dismissed in 1855 when he (and a fellow officer, William Redfearn) were found drunk on duty in the *Wheatsheaf* in Upperhead Row. His career appeared to take off in the following year. In February 1856 he was appointed a day constable and in the November, as part of a general restructuring, he was appointed night-sergeant. Progress was undermined by his weakness for drink. In March 1857 he was severely reprimanded and demoted from sergeant to day constable and in October 1858 he was further reduced to third-class constable for being drunk and unfit for duty. His last years were plagued by ill-health. In March 1860 he was incapacitated by 'a paralytic stroke' which led to his retirement from the force.[7]

Beevers was the only man in this group to be (albeit briefly) promoted but there were several others whose competence as policemen was undermined by ill-discipline. William Redfearn started his police career as an additional winter constable in 1853/4 but soon became a first-class night constable (1856) and a first-class day constable (1859). His arrest record in the years 1857 to 1859 show him to be one of the most efficient men in the force. Many of his cases were (unsurprisingly) mundane. In October 1858 he brought charges against 'two of the frail sisterhood' for theft from the person of weaver, Benjamin Bottom, with whom they had been drinking in the *White Horse* beerhouse in Castlegate. Others were more dramatic: a pickpocket operating at a funeral at the parish church was chased and arrested in Bull and Mouth Street but there were also more serious cases. In August 1857 the Great Northern Railway Company was the victim of a major embezzlement and it was PC Redfearn who finally arrested Edward Thorpe in Hull. After five years in the force and on the brink of a promising police career, and in circumstances that were never made clear, in July 1859 he was found guilty of insubordination to a senior officer and reprimanded. Worse, one month later he was demoted to the third class, allegedly for 'gossiping with a civilian unnecessarily for fifteen minutes when on duty'. That proved to be the final straw. Redfearn handed in his resignation immediately. Likewise, David Hutchinson served successfully for six years (even taking on additional responsibilities) before a clash with a senior officer and a charge of insubordination led to his resignation.

Other cases were more problematic and raise questions about the judgment of the Watch Committee. Hamor Sedgwick's chequered career has already been considered (see chapter two) but his was not an isolated case. Joseph Graham, in a career that spanned twenty years, was disciplined on more than a dozen occasions for neglect of duty and being under the influence of alcohol. Other than displaying bravery in the flood at Aspley in October 1857, there was nothing in his record that stood out. His promotion to first-class constable in 1867 was very much a reward for diligent, long service and in less than a year another drink-related incident saw him demoted to the third class. John Spivey was another reappointed after dismissal only to be dismissed for a second time. Although praised for his actions during a flood, this time at Folly Hall in 1858, his performance record was barely average and he was a repeat offender, appearing before the Watch Committee on charges of neglect of duty and insubordination. The reasons behind the Watch Committee's decision were not recorded. It is impossible to say whether it was a case of over-optimism and misplaced faith or a reflection of the poor quality of applicants. Whatever the reasons, one conclusion is clear: several long-term policemen were of limited effectiveness as well as being problematic for their superiors.

There were, however, several men who, while lacking the ability to progress rapidly up the police hierarchy, did not exhibit such lack of discipline or frustration but were held back by lack of opportunity. None exemplified this more than John Boler, Noah Worsnip and John Nutton. Boler was appointed in 1861 and with his large, flowing beard was a well-known figure in the town. A conscientious policeman, a frequent figure in the local courts and with only a couple of minor blemishes on his record, he was a reliable and effective man but was still a constable when he was superannuated in 1876. Worsnip's career was very similar. He was first appointed in 1857. Seven years later he became a first-class constable and in March 1868 he was awarded a merit badge for his long service. The praise accorded him by the magistrates at the West Riding Sessions in January 1868 summed up his career: 'very prudent and very proper'. He was the epitome of the exemplary constable. Only after incorporation, and some fifteen years into his police career, was he promoted to sergeant. John Nutton, appointed in 1859, was another slow-burner whose career only took off after incorporation and at the end of a long career. Despite an above-average record in terms of arrests in the early 1860s his career appears to have been held back by some disciplinary problems, including a conviction by the local magistrates for an assault that he made during an 'Irish row' in 1863. However, by the time sciatica forced his retirement in 1890 he had made the rank of inspector.

What was the work of these stalwarts of the town police? In so far as they were crime fighters, they dealt mainly with petty thefts. Maidservants stole shawls and sheets; workmen stole materials from their masters and tools from their mates; and men and women stole from their neighbours. Many of the cases were so blatant that the thief was caught in the act and brought to the police by the victim. Many others were 'solved' when the appropriated goods were presented to one of the many of the pawnbrokers in town, who in turn (and for obvious reasons) duly informed the police. Rarely was much 'detection' required and rarely were the police required to pursue their enquiries and activities outside the town. More importantly, crime fighting was but a small part of police work. More often the constable was a 'domestic missionary', maintaining 'order and decorum' in public places through the imposition of laws and values that were not always shared by the public at large. Much police effort was directed at the disorderly and disruptive but also the destitute.[8]

A substantial amount of time was devoted to keeping under surveillance the numerous public houses and beerhouses in the town. There was a shared perception among the local magistrates, senior police officers and members of the local elites that such establishments, through their encouragement of drinking and gambling, were breeding grounds of vice and crime.[9] There was not a single officer, unless he left within days or months, who had not brought a charge against some pub landlord or beerhouse keeper. Over the years the local magistrates heard literally hundreds of cases of breaches of the licensing laws. There were prosecutions for selling liquor before or after permitted hours and particularly for sales made during the hours of divine service on Sundays. There were prosecutions for permitting gambling on the premises, for not maintaining order, for harbouring known thieves and prostitutes and other suspicious characters. The police, usually but not exclusively singly, were regular visitors and when they were refused admittance prosecution followed. Furthermore, it was in such drinking establishments that numerous thefts from the person were perpetrated.

Drunk and disorderly behaviour in the streets of the town was the most common problem facing the police. Many incidents were relatively low-key. Some verbose but not obstreperous drunks were guided home; others, less capable, were taken to the cells to sleep off their excesses. When PC Graham found Susanna Gibson in a drunken stupor in Kirkgate in April 1855 'she was so drunk that he was obliged to wheel her to the lock-up on a cart' whereas John Delaney, once woken from his drunken slumber in a pigsty in Boulder's Yard, was able to stumble to the cells in the company of the same officer.[10] Not all arrests of drunks were so uneventful. The public were more likely to be unhelpful, if not outrightly hostile, when drunks were dragged along the streets or handcuffed and carted to the lock-up and there were parts of town where there was limited respect for the officers of the law.[11] The journey to the lock-up could be hazardous, particularly for an officer on his own. While handcuffs helped restrain the prisoner they also limited the action of the officer. There were several attempted prisoner rescues though, somewhat surprisingly, relatively few were successful.[12]

Violence was commonplace in mid-century Huddersfield and the police had a central but hazardous role in containing it. Stopping a fight between men or women, especially if inebriated, or intervening in a domestic quarrel, let alone quelling an Irish row, was a high-risk activity. At 7 p.m. one Saturday evening in early May 1864 PC Boler encountered two women fighting in Castlegate. As he stepped in he was attacked by four men who inflicted upon him 'the gross indignity of dragging him up and down the street by his beard' which was described as 'very flowing'.[13] Five years later, attempting to break up a drunken brawl outside Matthew Moran's beerhouse, also in Castlegate, he was once again 'brutally assaulted'.[14] Similarly, PC Worsnip was subject to a violent mass assault when he was called to stop a fight in Swallow Street one Sunday in June 1859. A crowd estimated to be between 200 and 300 had gathered to watch the fight and did not welcome Worsnip's intervention. Amazingly, he parted the fighters on two occasions before being driven off by members of the crowd.[15] On another occasion, attempting to stop a brawl in Manchester Road, a woman 'bit him ... seized him by the hair, scratching and mauling him' as he effected an arrest.[16] A number of assaults were so serious that men were unfit for duty for days, even weeks. PC Benjamin Crowther, an ex-soldier with a distinguished military record, suffered a broken nose, a dislocated ankle and was 'otherwise badly injured' when he went to the assistance of Mrs Flanagan, who was being beaten by her husband in Water Lane, 'a low Irish-street' off Manchester Road. Her husband barricaded himself in his house and proceeded to throw at Crowther various items, including part of a fire grate, which broke the constable's nose. Eventually forcing his way into the house, Crowther was attacked by both husband and wife![17] Thomas Graham was more fortunate, not having to go on sick leave despite the fact that part of his finger was bitten off in an Irish brawl in the *Wheatsheaf* in Upperhead Row in 1857.[18] Finally, brief mention needs to be paid to the enduring hostility between the police and soldiers. There were a number of unpleasant clashes, though none that assumed the proportions of the Leeds riot of 1844.[19]

There were other sources of physical danger, not least from the 'furious driving' of cab-men, lurry-drivers and the like. Patrolling in Westgate, as people were leaving church one Sunday in 1862, PC David Hutchinson narrowly escaped serious injury as a driver 'with a profane expression threatened to drive over him.[20] But not all injuries were sustained in physical encounters with members of the public. PC Joseph Haigh was on night duty, checking the security of property, when he had a near-fatal accident when he fell down some unguarded stairs in White Horse Yard, Beast Market. With a broken collar-bone and severe head injuries he managed to crawl into the open where, at about 11 p.m., he was found 'leaning over a railing in a state of stupefaction'.[21]

The physical dangers of policing were clear to see but the mental pressures were less obvious. Although most policemen were not attacked on most days and nights of the year, the risk was ever present. There was considerable hostility to the police, particularly in areas with a large number of Irish, such as Castlegate or Upperhead-row and their surrounding lanes and yards. Patrolling such areas required a strong nerve as well as a physical presence. In addition, there were the verbal threats and abuses that the police (and occasionally their family members) faced.[22] In hindsight, it is clear that the threats to 'poise [kick] the b★★★★y bobby' or the appeals to mount a rescue of a prisoner more often than not came to nothing, but such an outcome was far from guaranteed. Dispersing a crowd of a dozen young men, especially after a drinking session, let alone a crowd of 200 watching a fistfight or a dogfight was not to be taken lightly. There were other sources of psychological pressures that are easily overlooked. Violence was also self-inflicted and dealing with suicides and attempted suicides added to the mental pressures of the job. Between November 1860 and March 1862 PC Joseph Graham arrested three attempted suicides – one threatening to throw herself out of an upstairs window, another attempting to drown herself in the canal at Aspley and the third swallowing oxalic acid – and was called upon to cut down the body of a man, suffering from 'bodily illness and depression'.[23] Similarly, PC Boler on two occasions dragged the lifeless bodies of men from the canal at Aspley as he worked his night-time beat.[24]

Reflecting a wider societal concern, the police also devoted much time to the problem of vagrancy. For the most part this was mundane – arresting rough sleepers, 'professional' beggars and those with no visible means of support – but some of it was harrowing and occasionally it was dangerous. When PC Hamor Sedgwick arrested Benjamin Taylor at 5 a.m. in February 1857 for sleeping on a step in Threadneedle Street, it transpired that Taylor had recently been discharged from the army and did not have enough money for a night's lodging.[25] Similarly the vagrant that PC Worsnip arrested at 3 a.m. for sleeping in the open at the back of the bazaar in Lord Street had arrived in town from Guiseley 'to seek work on the new railway' but with little money and not knowing the town had 'no where else to go'.[26] Other vagrants made their way to the lime kilns at Aspley to get some warmth as they slept rough and hoped to escape arrest. Periodically, men were brought to court but few officers were as zealous as PC Boler who, ascertaining that the sleeping vagrant (one Joseph Hicks) had 'no visible means of subsistence', proceeded to kick him 'three or four times before he awoke'.[27]

And finally, there were the unusual incidents that throw light, not just upon the variety of police work, but on the wider tensions in society. Two examples must suffice. In June 1868 PC John Nutton was assaulted by a stone-throwing crowd, largely made up by angry Irish men and women, as he escorted a Mr. Flynn to the railway station. But this was not an 'ordinary' demonstration of anti-police feelings. This was the culmination of events that had been sparked off by a provocative series of five lectures on Roman Catholicism, advertised under the slogan 'Popery and Puseyism Unmasked', given at the Gymnasium Hall. The original lectures, given by James Houston, including one entitled 'The Seven Sacraments of the Church of Rome: Unscriptural and Superstitious', had aroused considerable hostility from the local Irish community, notwithstanding advice from two local priests to treat Houston with 'silent contempt'.[28] On the fifth evening Houston was replaced by the openly avowed Murphyite, Flynn, whose lecture was provocatively entitled 'Maynooth and its teachings and the confessional unmasked, showing the questions bachelor priests ask married and single women in private'.* It had its desired effect but the unfortunate PC Nutton had to run the gauntlet of irate Irish on two occasions: the first, attempting to find refuge for Flynn after the lecture and the second escorting him to the station the following day. The second incident coincidentally also took place near the railway station. In April 1867

---

* William Murphy, born an Ulster Catholic but a convert to Protestantism, was the best-known and most inflammatory of a number of Protestant lecturers who were highly critical of Catholicism. In the 1860s organisations such as the Protestant Evangelical Mission hired Murphy (and others) to deliver lecture tours on the mainland. There were anti-Murphy riots in several places. See D C Richter, *Riotous Victorians,* Athens, Ohio University Press, 1981, chapter three.

PC Boler was sent to arrest the leaders of a group of lurry-drivers who were creating a disturbance. The men, all employees of Mitchell Brothers, an important local haulage firm, were protesting against one of their fellow-workers for 'ill-using his wife'.[29] An effigy of the offending man, bedecked with placards stating 'C Beckett woman tamer' and 'Charles Beckett, woman hammerer, furniture smasher', was carried through the streets to the station warehouse, where it was exhibited all afternoon. The intention was to take the effigy and burn it outside the man's house in Albion Street. However, Boler was sent to seize the effigy and arrest the ring-leaders. He failed. Faced with 'hundreds of spectators, who hooted and yelled vociferously', he was unable to seize the effigy and was forced to look on as men took it to the *Wellington Inn* in Westgate, where another large crowd had assembled. The significance of events such as these will be discussed more fully later, but suffice it to note at this point that they reveal the limitations of police powers when faced with a large and determined group and the ease with which the police could be associated with unpopular figures or ideas when simply carrying out their normal duty of preserving the public peace.

The experience of long-serving constables has been discussed at length, partly because they constituted the largest group of 'career' policemen, and partly because the experience of beat policing was common to all, including the most successful men. No one career can encapsulate their experience but the words of one of the longest serving men, James Gledhill, captures much of the essence. Gledhill was one of the founding members of the borough force and had served as a night-watchman before 1848. He had arrested more than his fair share of petty thieves, common prostitutes and offending beerhouse keepers in a career that ultimately lasted thirty years, during which time he never rose beyond the rank of first-class constable. He had been attacked on duty several times, though his worst injuries were sustained when the stairs in the police house collapsed in 1867. A 'much respected figure, an old and trusted officer', in October 1873 he was asked, at the fourth annual police dinner, hosted by the mayor of Huddersfield, to reply to the toast 'The health of the Force'. He spoke 'from experience of the boisterous wind, rainy, snowy weather which policemen had to brave in their nightly perambulations' and concluded that 'the shattering of their [policemen's] health was out of all proportion to their remuneration, considering that in the discharge of their duty they incurred much unpopularity'.[30] It might not have been the sentiment his superiors expected, or wished to hear at such an occasion, but it provides an insight into the views of men whose voices otherwise do not appear in the historical record.

Promotion Through the Ranks

Since the creation of the Metropolitan Police in 1829 the principle of promotion from within was clearly enunciated. In theory, the prospect of a career pathway through the ranks was one of the attractions of the job. In practice life was somewhat different. In the larger city forces and the more-rapidly expanding borough forces there was a realistic chance of an able and ambitious man gaining promotion. In the smaller and more stable borough forces such as Huddersfield, promotion opportunities were limited. When the force was first established in 1848/9 the only senior officers were a superintending constable, an inspector and a sergeant of night constabulary. This changed in the early-1850s when the number of sergeants was increased to two and then three but an additional inspector's post was not created until the late-1850s. This remained the position until the mid-1860s when an additional sergeant's post was added. Only in 1868, as preparations were made for the larger force required to police the new, larger incorporated borough, did promotion opportunities open up significantly. Put another way, for most of the 1850s and 1860s there were only five or six senior posts and four men dominated these positions. Jonas Mellor was promoted to sergeant in May 1849 and remained in that post until 1868. Abraham Sedgwick was a sergeant in January 1849 before being promoted to inspector in April 1852, a post he held until his resignation in 1856. The beneficiary, on both occasions, was Ramsden White who succeeded Sedgwick as sergeant and then inspector. The fourth man was William Townend. Promoted to sergeant in 1850 and to inspector in 1858, he remained in post until the early 1880s. These men were undoubtedly able and experienced but they were also promotion-blockers to their colleagues. Nonetheless, a further ten men were promoted to sergeant and two to inspector during the period of the Improvement Commission.

For the sixteen men who made the rank of sergeant, it took on average five years from appointment to gain promotion but this figure hides significant variations. Such was the rapid success of

Mellor, Sedgwick and Townend that men such as John Kaye and Benjamin Marsden, despite having been appointed in the earliest years (1849 and 1850), had to wait almost eight and in the case of William Ramsden eleven years to achieve their first (and only) promotion. Hugh Moore, appointed in 1854, had to wait almost ten years to become a sergeant, though within five years he had become a sub-inspector and then an inspector. Similarly, Thomas Galvin, appointed in 1860, became a sergeant in 1866 but had to wait until after incorporation to reach the rank of inspector. Even the very energetic and able David Hayes had to wait five years for his first promotion, though it took him only a further four years to become an inspector. The careers of Moore, Galvin and Hayes abundantly demonstrate the importance of opportunity. Without the expansion of 1868, either their careers would have stagnated or they would have had to be pursued in another force.

The Next Rung on the Ladder: Sergeants

The role of a sergeant in any police force was crucial to its effectiveness. A sergeant was responsible for the conduct of the constables under him, ensuring they were sober, properly dressed and ready for work, and aware of any orders of the day. Their responsibilities also included ensuring that beats were properly worked and that any breaches of discipline were recorded and reported to superior officers.

In terms of day-to-day experiences, their working-lives were very similar to the men under them. They took part in raids on public houses selling outside licensing hours and beerhouses permitting gambling and prostitution; they were assaulted on the streets of the town as much as the ordinary constables; and their disciplinary records were not always perfect. Sergeant Kaye failed to report one of the constables in his section for drinking on duty and later disobeyed an order from Inspector White. Within a matter of months, he had resigned to go into an unspecified business. Two others – Sergeant Morton and Detective-sergeant Partridge – were asked to resign and one, Sergeant Marsden, was dismissed for drunkenness and neglect of duty. The numbers in this category are too small to draw meaningful conclusions but an examination of the careers of three of these men throws further light on the realities of mid-nineteenth century policing and the problems of establishing an efficient 'first generation' police force.

Jonas Mellor was undoubtedly a stalwart of the force but his career also illustrates that trade-off between experience and efficiency that characterised every force. Long years of service were undoubtedly important in building up knowledge and developing skills but the demands of the job also took their toll. Described as a man who was 'strict, punctual and steady ... stern and severe when on duty' his obituarist also noted that 'in the vigour of his manhood, he was hale, hearty and strong.'[31] Sadly, his strength had been failing for some while and he died only months after retiring on the grounds of ill-health in 1869 at the age of sixty-two. Mellor was one of a number of ex-army men recruited into the new borough force. He had already been a night-watchman before 1848 and his army experience stood him in good stead. In May 1849 he was made drill sergeant, a post he held, and for which he was praised, until 1860. His record, in terms of arrests, was one of the best in the force in the late-1850s and early-1860s. Living in Dock Street, off the notorious Castlegate, he was a well-known figure both on and off duty. Mellor met more than his fair share of violence. On a dozen or so occasions during his nineteen-year career he was assaulted by various members of the public. In September 1852, for example, he was stoned by a crowd while arresting a drunk; and a similar occurrence took place in the summer of 1859 when he tried to arrest a violent drunk, the notorious local criminal Joshua Stringer and the prostitute with whom he was consorting at midnight in Castlegate.[32] Mellor was clearly a hard man who knew how to look after himself. Earlier in 1852 he had been the victim of an attempted rescue as he arrested a drunk in Upperhead Row but found himself facing a counter-claim of violence. The charge was thrown out by the magistrates but the following month a further accusation was made relating to the same incident. The court heard how Mellor 'and seven or eight officers' beat a man they had thrown to the floor during an arrest. The assault charge, however, related to the man's twenty-year-old sister, who claimed that Mellor had beaten her with his stave. Mellor claimed he had been defending himself in the face of a mob attack but the magistrates found him guilty of using unnecessary violence. Several more routine arrests were also dangerous. On one occasion, a drunk with a mattock-shaft attacked him, while on another he found himself face-to-face with Nick Hannigan, 'a notorious prize-fighter and beerhouse keeper in Post-Office Yard.'[33] He also arrested on three occasions another violent local criminal, 'Slasher' Wilson, though on all three occasions the charge was permitting gambling and harbouring prostitutes. Indeed, much of Mellor's time was given over to preserving public decorum from the threat posed by beggars, gamblers and other undesirables on the streets. On a few occasions he was involved with more serious crimes. In October 1855 he was sent to investigate a house robbery in Quay Street at 4 a.m. The burglar had clearly jumped from an upstairs window and, having made a soft landing, made his way home. Mellor, spotting the footprints in a dung heap, followed the manure-strewn trail until he found the accused, whose shoes he seized and matched with the prints at the scene of the crime. Such was the highlight of Mellor's crime-fighting career. Mellor was a man of action; his strength lay in maintaining or restoring order, and he led from the front. There is no evidence to suggest that he wished (or was considered) for further promotion. Despite an impressive arrest record, there were signs that his health was beginning to fail. In 1861 he relinquished his position as drill sergeant to William Ramsden, though he still drilled the force at the annual inspection as late as 1865. By 1866 he was not fit for beat work. As part of the reorganization introduced by the new Superintendent Withers, and recognizing his long service, Mellor was put in charge of the police office during the day (i.e. from 9 a.m. to 6 p.m.). Such was his failing health that he was 'privileged by Mr. Withers to commence and cease duty at his own will and pleasure' until in March 1869 he was finally declared to be medically unfit for duty. His retirement was short – within three months he was dead. Two important conclusions can be drawn from this brief account of Sergeant Mellor's career. First, on the positive side, through his persistence and physical presence he made a significant contribution to the creation of an 'efficient' force – in terms of the elite values of the day – maintaining order and decorum in the streets of Huddersfield. Second, on the negative side, his recurrent conflicts with certain sections of Huddersfield's working-classes, not least but not exclusively the Irish, his career illustrates the limits of police legitimacy in the public eye, the resultant difficulties facing the individual policeman and, more generally, the limits of police power.

Edward Morton was a very different type of policeman, whose relatively short and troubled career throws light on some of the problems and tensions that beset the early force. Morton's strength was his administrative skills. Superintendent Hannan praised him for 'abilities of the highest order' while his obituarist described him as 'a most intelligent officer'.[34] It was a measure of his ability, and the relative absence of such skills among employees of the Improvement

Commission, that he was seconded to reorganise and rationalise the library of patent books held by the commissioners and was responsible for the collection of statistical information for the commissioners for their discussion of the abolition of the Moldgreen toll bar.[35] He was also largely responsible for the compilation and writing of the superintendent's annual report. His career started conventionally enough. He was initially appointed as an extra winter night constable in 1856 before becoming a permanent officer, quickly becoming a day constable. He was one of the more successful officers in terms of arrests and was involved in number of more serious cases, not least the embezzlement charge against a well-known local figure, Titus Thewlis.[36] Nonetheless, it was his administrative skills that led Superintendent Beaumont to use his talents in the police office, effectively doing those parts of his job that the superintendent was unable to do.

Ironically, the employment of Morton in the police office was to lead to Beaumont's downfall. It was clear that police book-keeping was deficient at best, corrupt at worst. For many months there were suspicions that Beaumont and his large family were living in a style well beyond his means but the Watch Committee were determined to stand by its man. However, the meticulously detailed evidence provided by Morton made this impossible as he demonstrated 'not a single or isolated offence but a series of petty but fraudulent acts' by the superintendent over several months.[37] With the removal of Beaumont, who had blocked his promotion to sergeant, Morton's career resumed its upward path under the new superintendent of police, but he clashed with Priday's successor, William Hannan, over the question of amalgamating the day and night force in 1863. The matter was resolved without any immediate dismissals and, at the next annual police dinner in March 1864, there was a symbolic reconciliation as Sergeant Morton proposed the toast: 'The health of the Superintendent'.[38] Yet within little more than six months he was asked to resign. The formal record stated that Morton, along with PC Cummings, had been drinking in the *Ramsden Arms* while on duty. For a man with an unblemished record this was strange but even more unusual was the presentation ceremony in January 1865, at which Hannan praised the former sergeant, referring in passing to a 'certain misunderstanding' that had caused Morton to resign. In his speech thanking his colleagues for their generosity, Morton spoke of 'something strange and something wrong somewhere' which had forced him to leave the force 'with some regret'. Had men been honest, saying to his face what they said behind his back, he claimed that he would still have been in the town force. It is impossible to determine what had happened. Hannan's claim that he was simply enforcing discipline in the force is not entirely convincing, but Morton had no friends on the Watch Committee to argue his case.[39] Although only moderately successful in personal terms, Morton's career highlights another set of problems related to the management of an emerging and increasingly complex organisation. Poor book-keeping had been identified on a number of occasions by the inspector of police but bureaucratic skills were not readily found among the men who applied to join the town force. This impacted on efficiency but also opened up opportunities for corruption.

The final man to be considered, Nathaniel Partridge, highlights a different set of problems as more emphasis was placed on the detection of crime. He was one of several Huddersfield policemen who had served in the army but unlike the others had been a policeman before a brief spell of service during the Crimean War. Partridge was discharged from the army as 'unfit for further service' in July 1856 and later that year he was taken on again, initially as a supernumerary constable. In August 1858 he was promoted from night- to day-constable and six months later he became a detective constable in the first class. His early career was undistinguished as he dealt with a predictable round of badly-run beerhouses and disorderly drunks. On his return it was a very different story. In the late-1850s and early-1860s he was the most successful officer in the force. At a time when the median number of arrests per officer was in the region of fifteen to nineteen a year, Partridge's tally was over seventy. In 1861 he was responsible for ninety-one cases. Predictably many of these were for low-level offences but, as the only detective in the force, he was also involved in a number of high-profile cases. In 1859 he was awarded a gratuity of £1 for his 'meritorious conduct' in identifying and arresting men responsible for a series of robberies from the Cloth Hall; while in 1862 he solved another major cloth robbery for which he was given a reward of £5. It is difficult to judge Partridge's detection skills – hiding in the Cloth Hall and spying through a hole drilled in the roof was hardly sophisticated. Rather, Partridge's success was based on good contacts with local pawnbrokers and beerhouse keepers and on his contacts with the criminal fraternity and their hangers-on. It also depended on a willingness to bend rules when necessary. As a consequence, alongside his commendations were a series of official rebukes. On more than one occasion he was cautioned by the Watch Committee for 'not strictly obeying orders' and admonished by the magistrates for the less-than-careful way in which he gave evidence. His involvement with the criminal classes also caused him trouble. In November 1862 a beerhouse case was dismissed because the magistrates 'did not like the source from which the information came … [believing] that with a well-organised, active and efficient police force, information might be obtained from other sources'.[40] This was somewhat harsh as the only direct witnesses were the two girl prostitutes who testified that their mistress had refused to pay their fines. There were more firmly based suspicions. The *Chronicle* damned Partridge for 'taking men honester than himself through the streets of Huddersfield with handcuffs on their wrists'.[41] Even more problematic was his financial involvement in 1864 with the landlord of the *Globe Inn*, from whom he borrowed £2, which was almost certainly related to his drink problem. By the mid-1860s, although he was still playing an active role, not least in the pursuit of the so-called Irish Small Gang, problems were becoming apparent. In March 1865 the Watch Committee was informed of his drink-related 'ill health' and a month later he asked to resign. He was treated generously. Commissioner Tolson conceded that 'Partridge might have gone a little beyond discretion' at times but rationalised this by arguing that 'in the obtaining of evidence it was almost impossible to avoid having a drink'. Further, he was promised 'employment until he could get something else to do' and a gratuity of £20.[42] In fact, he struggled to find work. In 1869 he was recorded as a coalman – he was accused of embezzlement from the coal dealer who employed him – and in 1871 he was a labourer in the iron works. Partridge was undoubtedly an important figure in the policing of Huddersfield in the 1850s and 1860s but his career highlights the rudimentary, and potentially counter-productive, nature of detective work.

Inspectors

Under the Improvement Commission only five men achieved the rank of inspector, two of whom were promoted in 1868 on the eve of incorporation. One, Hugh Moore, was something of a slow-burner. First appointed in 1854, it was almost exactly a decade before he was made a sergeant. For much of this time his experiences were very similar to those described above. However, from the early 1860s he worked on a number of cases with detective Partridge connected with beerhouse prostitution, and in August 1863 he was made a detective constable. The police campaign intensified with the appointment of William Hannan as superintendent. One target was Charles Shaw, a Zetland Street beerhouse-keeper. At his trial in November 1864 Moore and Partridge 'described minutely the details of their several visits, showing that the house was full of abandoned women, and that men were constantly in the habit of visiting it'.[43] Moore also gave evidence that the women of the house frequented the railway station, the *Argyle Music Hall* and other places of amusement, touting for custom. Notwithstanding 'a long "sensation" speech ... stigmatizing the conduct as the police as "incompetent, insulting and tyrannical" by the well-known defence lawyer, W P Roberts, Shaw was found guilty of brothel-keeping. Having proved himself in a number of similar cases and a major robbery at Beaumont's tobacco warehouse in 1867, it was no surprise that Moore was promoted, first to the rank of sub-inspector, then later to full inspector in 1868. In contrast, David Hayes was a rising star from his appointment in 1859. A sergeant after five years, he was promoted to inspector at the same time as Moore. Even as a constable he was involved in a number of more serious, robbery cases. In one, a burglary at the *Star Inn*, Moldgreen, Hayes arrested (among others) James Sutcliffe, a shoemaker from Castlegate. Sutcliffe, better known as 'Old Sut' was none other than the self-styled 'King of Castlegate' the notorious beerhouse-brothel keeper of the late 1840s, who had been transported for a robbery committed in the yard of his beerhouse.[44] Hayes had ability but he was fortunate to be in post at a time when new opportunities opened up. He was seen as 'a very meritorious officer ... [whose] promotion in the service was rapid and creditable'.[45] The early promise was never fully realised. He was badly injured when making an arrest and was on sick leave for much of 1869. He returned on desk duty but his injury deteriorated to the point where his hand had to be amputated and within months he died.

Of the remaining three men, the most interesting is Abraham Sedgwick. He had been appointed a parochial constable in 1845 and was one of several of the town's 'old police' who were sworn in as members of the borough force in January 1849. His rise was dramatic but doubly fortuitous. Within a month he was made sergeant, following the early dismissal of Sergeant Brown; within another few months he was made an inspector as John Thomas became police superintendent, following the unexpected incapacitation of the first superintendent, John Cheeseborough. Sedgwick was a determined and able officer, even as a parochial constable. He was highly visible on the streets of the town and was involved in a number of serious disturbances. He was also a man who was not afraid to criticise his senior officer, if he believed wrong had been done. His first clash was with a drunken Superintendent Thomas, who had verbally abused him in the street. Later the same month Sedgwick was one of two officers accusing Thomas of immoral conduct. Thomas escaped dismissal but the incident did not have a serious effect on Sedgwick's career. To the contrary, he was held in high regard by many of the Improvement Commissioners. Unfortunately, his career ended dramatically when he fell foul of the regime implemented by the new superintendent, Beaumont. The precise details of the dispute between the two men was never recorded but Sedgwick had confided to a sympathetic commissioner that he could 'neither speak right, act right, nor do anything to the satisfaction of the Superintendent'. The debate that took place among the commissioners was bitter but critics of Beaumont complained that 'there was no end of the surveillance and pettifogging interference of every kind' that drove out 'all efficient and spirited officers.'[46] Sedgwick's abrupt departure from the borough force was not the end of his police career. In moves that reflect the complexity and fluidity of policing in the mid-nineteenth century he first became the paid constable for the nearby village of Meltham before joining the newly-formed WRCC with whom he served as a sergeant until his retirement in 1872.

Sedgwick's resignation opened the way for Ramsden White, who was another founding figure and whose career mirrored that of Sedgwick. At the young age of twenty-two White became night sergeant when Sedgwick was promoted to inspector; and then inspector when Sedgwick resigned. For much of his early career he worked closely together with Sedgwick, particularly on a number of more serious robbery cases.[47] He was the obvious choice to replace Sedgwick and in the late-1850s and early-1860s he played an active part in the moral crusade against beerhouses, prostitution and gambling but he also successfully investigated a number of serious thefts. In one high-profile case in 1864 the superintendent of scavengers, John Broome, a long-time servant, absconded with £100 that belonged to the Improvement Commissioners. White finally arrested him in Liverpool as Broome was trying to buy a ticket to America where he planned to meet his daughter.[48] Scarcely less dramatically he was responsible for the identification and arrest of thieves responsible for a series of thefts from the Cloth Hall in late 1864.[49] Such was success that in October 1865 he was made detective inspector.

White continued to serve in the new borough force until in 1880, 'unable to walk' and with 'no probability of him ever being able to do so', he retired after over thirty years as a policeman. His career was unusual in that he was promoted twice and at an early age. In other respects, it was more typical. Much of his time, even as an inspector, was taken up with relatively minor offences against the licensing or vagrancy laws; and such policing brought him into contact (and conflict) with certain sections of local society. He was the victim of assault on more than a dozen occasions. In 1854 as a sergeant he was knocked senseless by a crowd of men and women, estimated to be at least 100-strong, and responding to 'the Irish cry' as he attempted to bring a drunk back to the prison house.[50] Fourteen years later, in a similar situation but as a superintendent, he was savagely attacked by several men 'each armed with a stout stick'.[51] Such were the harsh realities of mid-nineteenth century policing.

White was a stalwart of the Huddersfield force for many years. As an inspector he provided continuing leadership at a time when the position of superintendent of police in Huddersfield was precarious indeed. And yet the surprise is that his career as an inspector did not end almost as soon as it had begun. White was at the centre of a highly-publicised sex scandal which could easily have ended his career. In August 1858, rumours spread through the town about the behaviour of Inspector White and his 'improper intimacy' with Sarah Kearney, also known as 'Black Damp'![52] An incredible story unfolded. Initially, White had been a regular visitor to Kearney's cellar-dwelling in Dundas Street. Amazingly, White then proceeded to take her in as a lodger in his house in Prospect Row where, or so it was said, 'Mrs Kearney and Mrs White became very intimate, dressed exactly alike, were often out walking together and were frequently mistaken for sisters'. It might have remained a bizarre story when Kearney left to live in Halifax but it became a scandal when White visited her there and she visited him in Huddersfield. Matters came to a head on the Sunday of Almondbury rush-bearing, which White and his wife attended. Claiming 'he had to return to Huddersfield for "night duty"', the inspector went home. Neighbours noticed 'Black Damp' nearby and alerted Mrs. White who was still in Almondbury. She returned to Prospect Row at 1 a.m. (Monday) to find 'Mrs Kearney sleeping on the sofa in a position so questionable as to raise the gravest suspicions'. An angry crowd assembled but 'Black Damp' 'escaped from the house and took refuge in a cellar in John Street'. White returned – presumably from night duty – and 'gave his wife a sound thrashing'. The crowd re-assembled and remained outside the house for most of the day. Such was 'the demonstration of public feeling' that Inspector White was 'overpowered ... and unable to go out on duty that night'! The saga continued. 'Black Damp' returned to collect her clothes; only to be refused entry by Mrs. White, who demanded payment of rent arrears and 'a bonus of £5 for "extras" she had received'. Yet again a crowd assembled and forced 'Black Damp' to flee. Indeed, 'the mob ... followed and it was feared would have given her a specimen of Lynch law if the police had not intervened, put her in a cab and guarded her safely out of town'. The Watch Committee had to act. White was suspended and he secretly left town while an inquiry was held. In early September the Watch Committee announced its decision: White was to be reprimanded. They explained their decision thus:

> altho' no positive criminality has been established between the Inspector and Sarah Carney [*sic*], yet this committee considers that such Inspector has acted very indiscreetly in having a woman of such questionable character lodged in his house.'[53]

Perhaps White was helped by the fact that his misdemeanours were overshadowed by the greater scandal involving Superintendent Beaumont; perhaps his undoubted effectiveness as a police officer won him friends in influential places – whatever the reason, White was lucky to survive but the leniency of the Watch Committee was rewarded by the success of his subsequent career.

The final career to be considered is that of William Townend. It was highly unusual in that he served in all for thirty-five years, reaching the rank of Superintendent in 1875 and retiring at the age of seventy-five in February 1885; and yet it encapsulated so much of the experience of 'new policing' in Huddersfield. A whitesmith by trade, he was elected a parochial constable in 1845, along with

Abraham Sedgwick. Having proved his ability as a constable, he was sworn in as a day constable in the new borough force in January 1849. A year later he was promoted to sergeant but his career almost came to an end in 1852. As noted in chapter two, his disciplinary record was far from exemplary but his reputation as a policeman saved his career. When the Watch Committee recommended his dismissal, the commissioners were persuaded not to proceed in the face of 'numerously signed memorials [all] praying for the reappointment of Townend.'[54] Their faith in the man was rewarded. His arrest record in the late-1850s and early-1860s was second only to PC (later detective) Partridge. Furthermore, as Inspector of Common Lodging Houses and Master of the Vagrant Office he played a key role in tackling two of the most pressing problems facing the town. Despite his contribution to the policing of the town, he was overlooked for the post of inspector on the resignation of his close colleague, Sedgwick. However, in the interim, following the dismissal of Superintendent Beaumont, it was Sergeant Townend (rather than the philandering Inspector White) who became *pro-tem* superintendent. Townend was duly rewarded a month later when he was made an inspector, albeit with no increase to his wages. History repeated itself following the enforced resignation of Superintendent Priday in 1862. This time Townend was included on the list of candidates for the vacant post. After a long discussion, in which it transpired that Priday did not hold Townend in high regard, a motion to appoint Townend was defeated by nine votes to five.[55] The man appointed, William Hannan, was in post for five years and, following his resignation, Townend once again filled in. [56]

After incorporation Townend took on a more administrative and ceremonial role – he became mace-bearer to the corporation and court crier – but under the commissioners he remained an active figure, well-known in the town. In 1866 the Philosophical Hall became the scene of regular Sunday night disturbances. Revivalist meetings held by 'the Hallelujah Band' led to crowds of several hundred, mainly young men and women, gathering and 'making a burlesque of these strange proceedings'.[57] Refusing to obey the instructions of Superintendent Hannan, 'a ruffianly crowd unflinchingly stood their ground' which necessitated 'immediate corporal punishment' by the police. Within minutes 'a handful of energetic police-officers, foremost among whom was Inspector Townend, actively and promptly cleared the streets'.[58] Townend was a mere fifty-seven years old. Like other long-serving men he spent much time dealing with furious drivers, disorderly drunks, lewd prostitutes and homeless (and often helpless) vagrants. Winning popular acceptance (let alone support) was a long, difficult and never wholly successful process. Unsurprisingly in a long career, he found himself under attack from both truculent individuals and angry crowds. His 'domestic missionary' responsibilities brought him into conflict with notorious beerhouse-keepers, such as 'Big Dick' Ramsden, and local villains, such as 'Slasher' Wilson.[59] In the narrower role of crime fighter, the cases were often undramatic – thefts of tools or clothing – and, lacking the skills of fellow inspector White, only very occasionally was he involved with more serious crimes but in this respect he was more typical of the force at large than other senior figures.[60]

Conclusions

Huddersfield was not unique in experiencing a high turnover of men during the first generation of 'new policing' but it was highly unusual in having such a high rate of turnover of police superintendents. Whereas in some forces strong leadership from the very top was a key element in the creation of an efficient force, this was not the case in Huddersfield. Nonetheless, after the introduction of government inspection, the town force was always deemed to be efficient. Credit for this goes to the various long-serving men, whose careers have been considered in this chapter. They were at the core of the force, providing continuity, local knowledge and, increasingly, experience of the practicalities of policing. At almost any time from the mid-1850s onward, there were a dozen or more men with at least five years' service to their name. In 1868, on the eve of incorporation, twenty men fell into this category.

However, there are three important qualifications to be made. First, the whole question of efficiency is problematic in theoretical and practical terms. What constituted efficiency and how could it be measured? Did a high rate of crime indicate an efficient or inefficient force? Did a high arrest rate indicate an efficient or officious constable?[61] Efficiency in the minds of mid-Victorian inspectors was, more often than not, considered pragmatically and defined in purely quantitative terms – the police population ratio – and even this was not rigorously defined. Further, annual inspections were not necessarily sufficiently rigorous to pick up problems – and local police chiefs and politicians were hardly willing to point up problems with their forces. Second, there was an almost inevitable trade-off between experience and effectiveness. When the borough force was established the Improvement Commissioners appointed a number of men with proven ability but who were relatively old. While this made much sense in terms of founding a force, it created a problem that would only become apparent a decade or so later. As demonstrated by the figures compiled for the Watch Committee when it considered its annual allocation of the perquisite fund, there were a number of men who made little contribution to the force. Furthermore, the belated creation of a superannuation scheme meant that Huddersfield policemen were more likely to work on even though facing ill-health and injury. Again, the minutes of the Watch Committee bear witness to the men whose health failed them and yet remained on the books, blocking a new appointment, for months, in some cases years. Finally, the nature of crime in Huddersfield – its blatancy and persistence – must be noted. The blatancy of much petty crime can hardly be overstated. It took no great effort to find landlords selling liquor out of hours, permitting gambling on their premises, failing to maintain order or harbouring known thieves and prostitutes. For reasons that will be considered in more detail later, the art of policing was knowing when not to prosecute. As a consequence, the recorded crime figures provide, at best, a very rough guide to the actual level of crime and the effectiveness of the police in dealing with it.[62] Similarly, the sheer stupidity of many petty criminals has to be acknowledged. Year after year petty criminals effectively handed themselves in as they took their stolen goods to local pawnbrokers. The local press may well have praised gallant policemen for their skill and determination in apprehending daring or audacious thieves but little detective skill was required (or used) to effect an arrest. In a number of cases arrests followed a period of surveillance by police officers. In a smaller number of cases the ability to match up boots and footprints at the scene of crime was critical but for the most part the police relied upon identification by victims of crime or information from members of the criminal fraternity as well as the public at large. Similarly, the persistence of certain problems, notwithstanding the wishes of the Improvement Commissioners and the actions of the police, cannot be ignored. In the late-1840s the beerhouses of Castlegate, not least that of John Sutcliffe, with its barracks for prostitutes in the yard, gave rise to moral outrage, police action and a successful prosecution. Two decades later, Superintendent Hannan was battling the same problems. Likewise, violence towards the police was as much an unsolved problem in the late-1860s, as the Irish Small Gang stoned the police and terrorised the public, as it was in the late-1840s when the police were driven from Market Square on the 5th of November. There was only so much the police could (or chose to) do. To examine this further we must take to the streets of mid-Victorian Huddersfield.

Endnotes

1 All police superintendents in Huddersfield were appointed from outside the town, even though there was at least one able and experienced candidate from within. On three occasions the Watch Committee had the option of appointing a local man to the most senior position in the town's force; on three occasions it chose not to do so. There were several examples of men who had worked their way through the ranks to become the head constable of a borough force. See, for example, the success of William Ashe in Middlesbrough, discussed in detail in D Taylor, *Policing the Victorian Town: The Development of the Police in Middlesbrough c.1840–1914,* Basingstoke, Palgrave, 2002, pp.47–9.

2 The analyses are based on the careers of thirty-four men. A small number, for whom information was extremely patchy, have been excluded but this is unlikely to have any significant effect on the general findings.

3 The situation in Huddersfield (as in some other towns) was complicated by the fact that some members of the police force doubled as firemen. As explained above, the details of this responsibility fall outside the scope of the present study, though they are of significance regarding the fundamental question of police legitimacy.

4 This does not mean that the items stolen were not important to both the thief and the victim. Historians, in talking of 'petty thefts', have often given the misleading impression that the loss of a pair of boots, for example, or the theft of half-a-crown (12½p) was of little matter. For many men and women, who lived lives of poverty and economic insecurity, the items involved were important indeed. See chapter six for a fuller discussion.

5 'Long-serving' is defined, somewhat arbitrarily, as being in post for at least five years. The Improvement Commissioners were aware of the need to address the problems of men who had been in the force for several years without gaining promotion but never formally defined 'long-term'.

6 The most detailed information relating to performance (i.e. arrests) comes from the information put before the Watch Committee when the annual distribution of the perquisite fund was approved, particularly for the years 1857 to 1862. This has been supplemented by information from the local

press. However, press coverage of the local magistrates' court was not comprehensive.

7 The precise date of his retirement is not recorded in the Watch Committee minutes but there is no reference to him in the 1862 perquisite fund list.

8 The classic statement is R Storch, 'The policeman as domestic missionary', *Journal of Social History*, 9, 1976.

9 The question of prostitution is considered in detail in chapter five.

10 *HC*, 28 April and 16 June 1855.

11 *HC*, 5 & 19 December 1863, 27 April and 14 September 1867. See chapters five and eleven.

12 See for example *HC*, 30 October 1852, 16 February 1856, 13 September 1862 & 11 April 1863.

13 *HC*, 7 May 1864.

14 *HC*, 23 January 1869. In all Boler was the victim of serious assaults, including attempted rescues, in at least seven years between 1861 and 1869.

15 *HC*, 25 June 1859.

16 *HC*, 23 March 1861.

17 *HC*, 11 July 1863. Crowther had also been badly lamed in another assault in 1861. Crowther had been awarded three medals during his army career and he wore these on his police uniform as he worked his beat. Not everyone respected his heroism once he swapped the red for the blue.

18 *HC*, 23 July 1853.

19 See for example *HC*, 4 October 1856. For details of the Leeds disturbance see R D Storch, 'A plague of blue locusts: police reform and popular resistance in northern England, *1840*–1857', *International Review of Social History, 20*, 1975, pp.74–5.

20 *HC*, 22 November 1862. See also 23 June 1860 & 21 November 1863 for similar incidents with a van driver in Kirkgate and a lurry-driver in John William Street, respectively.

21 *HC*, 5 November 1853.

22 Very occasionally cases of verbal abuse came to court. See for example *HC*, 16 July 1864. It is very difficult to establish the extent to which family members were subject to verbal or physical attack but the incident in May 1867, while unusual, was probably not unique. William North was fined 5s (25p) for using 'opprobrious epithets' against Alice Sedgwick, the wife of PC Thomas Sedgwick, as the couple were walking in Kirkgate. *HC*, 18 May 1867.

23 *HC*, 3 November 1860, 20 April 1861, 13 July 1861 & 1 March 1862.

24 *HC*, 30 December 1865 and 25 April 1868. The second incident was not clear cut and the death may have been accidental but Boler still had the unpleasant job of retrieving the corpse from the canal.

25 *HC*, 21 February 1857.

26 *HC*, 29 April 1865. The magistrates discharged the case but ordered Carr to leave Huddersfield immediately! See also *HC* 10 September 1859, 16 July 1864 & 7 September 1867.

27 *HC*, 20 February 1864 but see also 20 January 1866.

28 *HC*, 27 June 1868.

29 *HC*, 27 April 1867.

30 *HC,* 17 October 1873.
31 *HC,* 19 June 1869.
32 *HC,* 9 July 1859.
33 *HC,* 22 May & 25 September 1852.
34 *HC,* 21 January 1865 & 3 February 1866.
35 *HC,* 10 January & 7 March 1863. See also his two guinea (£2-20) reward for 'extra services ... in the commissioners' office.' 8 January 1859.
36 *HC,* 30 July 1859.
37 Watch Committee Minutes, KMT 18/2/3/14/1, 11, 8 October 1859.
38 *HC,* 26 March 1864.
39 In the immediate aftermath of his resignation, Morton set himself up as an 'accountant, commission agent, rent & debt-collector etc'. He soon returned to policing, joining the Dewsbury police and becoming a sergeant before his sudden death in January 1866. *HC,* 1 April 1865 & 3 February 1866.
40 *HC,* 15 November 1862.
41 *HC,* 30 July 1864.
42 *HC,* 10 June 1865.
43 *HC,* 26 November 1864.
44 This case is discussed in more detail in chapter seven.
45 *HC,* 1 April 1871.
46 *HC,* 9 February 1856.
47 See for example *HC, 9* October 1852, 19 February 1853 and 16 June 1855. The problem of unlicensed lodging houses was a major concern. (See also chapter five) For examples of police action see *HC*, 22 April & 23 September 1854 & 26 May 1856.
48 *HC,* 23 & 30 April 1864.
49 *HC,* 31 December 1864 & 14 January 1865. For other cases in which White played a major role see 7 & 14 November 1853 for thefts from local counting houses, 6 February & 28 April 1866, 3 December 1864 & 13 July 1867 for warehouse robbery and 26 January 1867 & 25 July 1868 for housebreaking.
50 *HC,* 25 February 1854.
51 *HC,* 15 February 1868.
52 *HC,* 7 August 1858.
53 Watch Committee Minutes, KMT 18/2/3/14/1, 11 August 1858.
54 *HC,* 7 August 1852.
55 *HC,* 4 October 1862.
56 This was not the last time that Townend stepped into the breach. In 1878 he became acting-superintendent due to the illness of Superintendent Hilton.
57 *HC,* 20 January 1866.
58 *Ibid.*
59 See chapters five and six for further discussion of local crime and criminals.
60 Townend was involved with a number of embezzlement cases as well as a child-murder and a rape.
61 The Improvement Commissioners clearly put great emphasis on arrest rates. In the late-1850s/early 1860s the arrest rate per constable per annum was about fifteen. Putting this into context is difficult. Returns a decade earlier, excluding Huddersfield, showed considerable variation in Yorkshire. The

highest figure was York (twenty-two) which was significantly higher than Leeds (ten), Halifax (eight), Sheffield (seven) and Wakefield (six). The figure for both Bradford and Hull was four. City and borough police. Abstract of returns, *Parliamentary Papers,* 1854 (345).

62 It is also the case that an unknown (and unknowable) number of criminal acts never came to the attention of the police. For whatever reason – the costs (not simply financial) of prosecution or the inappropriateness of formal action – a range of crimes were either dealt with informally or simply ignored by the victims.

Beats and Streets

THE CONSTABLE 'IS responsible for the security of life and property within his Beat, and for the preservation of the peace and general good order, during the time he is on Duty'.[1] Although these words were directed to newly-appointed Metropolitan policemen, they summed up a widely held view of the purpose of the new police. Furthermore, there was a commonly-held belief that 'it was indispensably necessary that he should make himself perfectly acquainted with all the parts of his Beat ... with the streets, thoroughfares, courts, and houses ... and the inhabitants of each house'.[2] The beat constable, in theory, was the enforcer, as well as the embodiment, of order and decorum in public places: his presence a deterrent to the would-be criminal and a reassurance to law-abiding citizens or those otherwise in need of help. The reality was somewhat different.

Unfortunately, given the centrality accorded to working the beat, there is very little evidence relating to the layouts and lengths of beats in Huddersfield. The Improvement Commissioners inherited a system of night-watching based on eight beats. No formal records existed and the commissioners were forced to rely upon the memories of older watchmen. The general view was that six beats were 'so extensive and the labour so heavy' that they could not be worked 'in the ordinary execution of duty' in less than two and a half hours. The proposed augmentation of the force had the effect of reducing the time per beat to under two hours. In addition, there were three constables on day duty.[3] By late 1853 there were a total of fourteen beats, six of which required ninety minutes to work, two seventy-five minutes and the remaining six one hour. It was agreed to reorganise the beats and appoint additional men so that the time for each beat would be no more than one hour. [4] The details of the beats are not recorded and there is little in the minutes of the commissioners to suggest that this was a matter of concern. By the time of the first annual inspection under the County & Borough Constabulary Act, there were sixteen beats but Colonel Woodford recommended an extension to eighteen. A compromise appears to have been struck for in February 1858 three beats (numbers 7, 8 and 9) were made into four. There was some minor tinkering with the daytime arrangements a year later when an additional constable was appointed for day duty on Tuesday (market day) who was responsible for the Market Place, New Street, Buxton Road and Cloth Hall Street only.[5] Little seems to have changed in the next decade including Withers' reorganization in 1868. On the eve of incorporation, Huddersfield was policed by fifteen night constables and four day constables, the latter operating a two shift system.

Huddersfield policemen were expected to live, as well as work, within the boundaries specified in the Improvement Act and, with the sole exception of Abraham Chadwick, who continued to live in Paddock, all did so. They were scattered throughout the area. In 1851 Superintendent John Thomas lived at 6 Swine Market, alongside shoemakers, fishmongers, an innkeeper and two publicans. PCs Graham and Hollingrake lived in Clay's Yard, off Thomas Street. PC Beevers lived in Upperhead Row amongst weavers and cloth-dressers, an upholsterer and a French polisher, while Sergeant Mellor lived in Dock Street alongside dressmakers, mule-spinners, a tailor and a boat-builder as well as some hawkers. PC Wilson was the only officer to live in Castlegate. A decade later, the pattern was very similar. The town's policemen were to be found in mixed but largely respectable areas from Spring Street and Grove Street to Prospect Street and Outcote Bank; from Princess Street to Manchester Road. They lived in the communities they policed but whether or not they were a part of those communities is a different matter.

The absence of detail relating to specific beats creates a major problem in the analysis of the realities of police work in the first generation of new policing in the town. However, by focussing on certain areas of the town, it is possible to give some indication of the nature of police work and how it changed over time. Before this is done some general observations need to be made. First, the

Huddersfield police were in a relatively favourable position – in terms of both acreage per constable and population per constable – in comparison with the police in other urban centres and, even more so, in comparison with the county force. Second, the types of problems facing the police were to be found across the town, though they were more heavily concentrated in certain districts, notably those in and around Castlegate and Upperhead Row. However, thirdly, the policing of such areas, precisely because of their problematic nature, was seen as the true test of the local force. It is no coincidence that when Superintendent Beaumont was under attack from members of the Improvement Commission one of the most telling criticisms was that he was unfamiliar with Castlegate and the problems it posed to order in the town. Lastly, while the focus in this chapter is on problems and responses, it must be stressed that there were times when beat work was uneventful and mundane. Checking doors and windows to ensure that they were secure was tedious. Indeed, it was in no small measure the boredom factor that drove the town's night constables to snatch a nap or otherwise absent themselves from duty.

Conquering Castlegate?

In the 1820s Castlegate was 'one of the most respectable parts of the town' so much so that 'to get a house in some parts of the Old Post Office Yard [people] had to get a character from their employer or a churchman of the parish'.[6] By the late 1840s this was most certainly not the case. In October 1848 the *Leeds Mercury* painted a grim picture of a street, barely 200 yards long, that boasted thirteen beerhouses and two public houses. From ten o'clock in the morning 'drinking and gaming were indulged in all day long and far into the night … rows and riots were constant … robberies were frequent … and it was dangerous to enter … after night fall'. If that was not bad enough 'the "Stews and bagnios" on the premises' of several beerhouses ensured 'the continued assembly of lewd and disorderly characters'.[7] And over it all ruled John Sutcliffe, the self-styled 'King of Castlegate'.[8] Here indeed was a challenge for the town's new police.

Castlegate ran from the confluence of King Street and Kirkgate at Shorehead to Lowerhead Row (and thence Old Leeds Road). The area encompassed two other streets (Quay Street and Dock Street) and was joined by Denton Lane. In addition, there were numerous

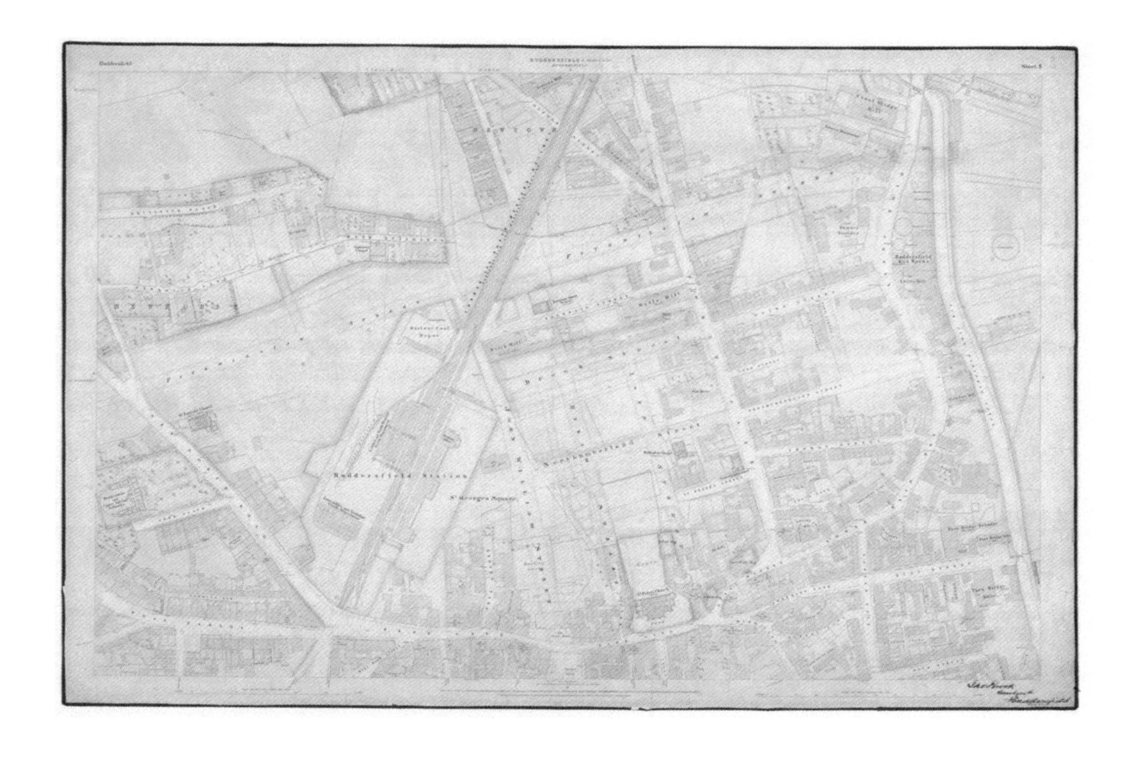

Castlegate district 1851

yards on either side of the main thoroughfare, of which Boulder's Yard and Post Office Yard (both to be found between Castlegate and Kirkgate) were perhaps the most notorious.[9] Racial and class stereotyping gave rise to crude simplification: Castlegate became a dystopia of criminality and Irishness! The reality was more complex. The Irish (including children born in Great Britain of Irish-born parents) were only a small percentage of the town's population, though there were heavy concentrations, for example in Windsor Court, and many followed poorly-paid and highly precarious occupations; but not all Irishmen and women were unskilled labourers or hawkers of pots and pans.[10] Similarly, while there were many public houses and beerhouses in the area, many were known to the authorities to be 'respectably' run. It was a relatively small number of high-profile beerhouses (and their proprietors) reported in the local and regional press that created such a negative impression. Furthermore, there was a wider mix of occupations than popular prejudice allowed. There were craftsmen and shopkeepers who clearly met contemporary criteria of 'respectability' and whose reputations were, once again, acknowledged by police and magistrates. However, there were also a large number who struggled to earn a sufficient income to provide themselves and their families with decent shelter and adequate food and clothing. Those in declining trades, such as handloom weavers, lived in pitiable conditions. Unskilled workers were similarly poorly-paid and often irregularly employed. Even the minority of skilled artisans could find themselves facing penury if there was a sustained downturn in trade. Precariousness and poverty were an enduring reality and it is not surprising to find that there was a grey economy, at best just legal, more often clearly illegal, whereby people sought to sustain themselves. And there were a few (again, well publicised) individuals who, often behind a façade of legality, made a living out of crime both petty and serious. To talk of them as a criminal class would be to exaggerate both their number and their coherence as a distinct grouping, but criminal men and women were undoubtedly part of the socio-economic mix of Castlegate. Major robberies as well as petty thefts were a perennial problem for the police. However, it is also the case that a considerable amount of police time was taken up with the enforcement of a code of behaviour that was at odds with the customs and mores of many inhabitants of Castlegate (and, indeed, other parts of town) in the mid-nineteenth century. Respectability was a complex set of values and cannot be attributed simply to one social class, but it was the working classes who most heavily felt the imposition of 'order and decorum' in public places. Restrictions on licensing hours, prohibitions on various forms of gambling and the criminalization of certain traditional sports were sources of friction and conflict.

For many contemporary observers the problems posed by Castlegate could be summed up in three words: beerhouses, brothels and brutality. These were the most spectacular manifestations of disorder and presented the police with the severest problems but there was much more to the policing of Castlegate – much that went largely unnoticed and under-reported but which constituted an important element in the complex relationship between police and policed. Furthermore, much of this activity was more facilitative, even cooperative, than coercive. Ensuring the free and safe flow of traffic is but one example. Carters taking an extended lunch-time drink in one of Castlegate's many beerhouses may well have objected to police interference but for tradesmen needing access to shops or warehouses the removal of unattended carts was to be welcomed.

Similarly, attempts to limit 'furious driving', while irksome to drivers of privately-owned omnibuses in particular, were welcomed by people who had seen, even experienced, horrific accidents as out-of-control vehicles scythed down adults and children whose misfortune it was to be in their path.[11] The police were a resource to be called upon not only in cases of street accidents. Handling sudden deaths or suicides was another important, if unspectacular, facet of day-to-day policing. These cases throw light on the often harsh circumstances in which the poor lived. When the police were called to Dock Street in March 1854 they found the dead body of five-year-old Mary Booth, who had fallen into the fire while her mother was at work as a cleaner. Although unmarried and with four illegitimate children, the 'much care worn' mother was praised for 'her untiring industry', though, cruelly, this very industry had led to the circumstances in which the child died. Later the same year, the police were called to an incident and found the body of Sarah Morris, a twenty-eight-year-old but 'who looked fully 50'. She had given birth prematurely, following a fall at home after an afternoon drinking spree, only to die the next morning.[12]

In a similar vein, working with other individuals and agencies to prosecute shopkeepers and beerhouse keepers for selling short measures offered a degree of protection to ordinary customers; likewise the periodic prosecutions for the sale of unfit meat.[13] When the butcher William Hayley was prosecuted (not for the first time) in 1860 the magistrates explicitly saw his actions as 'the more to be reprehended ... [as] it was a case essentially affecting the poor'.[14] Such prosecutions need to be put into perspective. Food adulteration cases were infrequent, penalties limited and reappearances in court suggest limited deterrent effect.[15] Nonetheless, it provided an example, however limited, of protective policing. The same could be said about prosecutions for passing counterfeit coin. Many of the victims were shopkeepers or beerhouse proprietors, not all of whom would have been, in other respects, sympathetic to the police. It is difficult to estimate the precise scale of this problem but it is clear that 'coining' was a recurrent and often well-organised and large-scale problem, whose victims included shopkeepers and publicans as well as ordinary members of the public.[16]

One final aspect of the welfare role of the police remains to be considered. Overcrowding and insanitation were major causes for concern for the Improvement Commissioners and in attempting to tackle the problems they looked to the police, not least because of the widely-made association between physical squalor, immorality and criminality. Nowhere were these problems more acute than in the unlicensed lodging houses in and around Castlegate. The *Leeds Mercury* referred to Windsor Court as 'a locality notorious for filth fever and contagion' while the *Chronicle* bemoaned the 'immense numbers … crammed into ill-ventilated and confined cellars and rooms, without any regard to sex, or other necessary requirements of civilization' and the resultant 'fever, disease, wretchedness and immorality' among the largely Irish population of Post Office Yard.[17] The largest and most notorious lodging house was that owned by Edward Dickinson in Castlegate. Following legislation passed in 1853 requiring the licensing of lodging houses, the police started a series of inspections. Inspector Sedgwick's night-time visit revealed a total of thirty-eight people sleeping in the eight rooms – including 'a lobby tenanted by nine men in eight beds' – in the house owned by Dickenson. Matters could have been worse: five beds were unoccupied.[18] He was not alone. Mary Moran was another fined under the lodging house act. In May 1855 her cellar dwelling in Castlegate, described as being 'in a state of extreme filth', was found to have two beds and a 'shakedown'. The first bed contained a man and a woman, the second two men, while the 'shakedown' was occupied by Moran herself and two prostitutes, one of whom 'danced nudely round the wretched dwelling'.[19] Despite the building of a Model Lodging House and regular attempts to enforce licensing, the problem remained. In 1866 the commissioners were still complaining of the 'filthy condition' and 'disgraceful state' of unregistered lodging houses in Castlegate.[20] Concern was not restricted to questions of public health. Lodging houses, not without reason, were seen as hotbeds of immorality and crime and subjected to close police scrutiny.

While the full range of police activities must be recognised, it remains the case that much police time was given over to a relatively small number of issues which were also more confrontational. Given contemporary beliefs that drinking, gambling and criminality were intimately linked, it is unsurprising to find that the town's magistrates and police were much exercised by breaches of the licensing laws.[21] Many of the offences were relatively minor - the sale of a jug of beer after 11 p.m. or during hours of divine service on Sunday – but not all.[22] Large numbers of men 'marrying' (that is, gambling) for ale, not maintaining an orderly house and harbouring known thieves and prostitutes were matters of greater concern. Furthermore, there were certain beerhouses – the *Talbot*, the *Butchers' Arms*, the *Blue Bell* and the *Theatre Tavern* – and certain keepers – James Cayford, John Tierney, Nick Hannigan and the Dearnleys – that crop up in the records time and again.[23]

Three problems in particular stand out – theft, prostitution and interpersonal violence. For many men a trip to Huddersfield was not complete without a visit to the drinking establishments of Castlegate. On numerous occasions, men, young and old, found themselves relieved of money and other personal possessions by the women they met there. A typical case involved a farmer from Emley Moor, who 'had come to have a little enjoyment at the fair, when his fancy led him into Castlegate' where he espied Martha Heaton, 'a nymph of the *pavé* [who] commenced "cuddling" him, and at the same time placing her hand in his pocket'. The light-fingered Heaton 'abstracted' and made off with three sovereigns, four half-sovereigns and 27s (£1-35) in silver. Only later did the police arrest her.[24] Such incidents were commonplace. The *Chronicle* reported three such cases on one day in March 1851. In the first, Martha Heaton (again) robbed a man who had 'come down to Huddersfield' to celebrate his holiday. After a lengthy session in the *Labour in Vain* beerhouse in King Street, he ended up in Dearnley's beerhouse in Castlegate where he was robbed in the backyard. Another 'young country greenhorn' went on 'a spree' on Thursday morning, fell asleep in the *Butchers' Arms* beerhouse and was duly robbed by persons unknown. Finally, while playing 'chokey' in James Shaw's beerhouse in Castlegate, Labron Longley, a local weaver, took off his coat only to have it stolen and pawned in nearby Drake's pawnshop.[25] Nor was it just the young and inexperienced who succumbed. William Kaye, a seventy-five-year-old labourer from Elland, was robbed in John Ashton's beerhouse in Castlegate in 1854 but found little sympathy from the town's magistrates. Admitting that he had visited the beerhouse on at least five occasions and had come to Huddersfield specifically for 'a spree' there, his case was dismissed and the magistrates advised him 'to keep better company in future'.[26] This was not an isolated case. The magistrates dismissed a number of theft charges, stating explicitly on one occasion that 'if persons would go into these places they must take the consequences'.[27]

Of greater concern to the commissioners was the problem of prostitution.[28] Many of the cases brought before the town magistrates involved keeping a disorderly house. In some cases, this meant permitting prostitutes to gather in a public house or beerhouse; in others it involved permitting prostitutes to work from or in the premises. In 1851 Thomas Binns, the landlord of the *Tavern Theatre* was prosecuted for keeping a disorderly house. According to Inspector Brier's evidence there were 'a number of men intoxicated and noisy and some six females, two of whom he knew to be common prostitutes, three of the females being busily engaged dancing to the enchanting strains of a 'hurdy gurdy'.[29] Some cases were truly shocking. When Jacob Senior, the keeper of the *Unicorn* public house was prosecuted for failing to keep proper order, Superintendent Heaton informed the court that he had seen 'a woman … excessively drunk, with her limbs rigid and nude and a man taking improper liberties with her' and this in the afternoon.[30] There was, however, a more serious and more persistent and unresolved problem – that of the beerhouse-brothel and what now would be termed human trafficking. In the 1840s the most notorious figure in town was John Sutcliffe, whose beerhouse in Castlegate had 'long been known as the rendezvous for thieves and prostitutes of the lowest grade'.[31] In addition, in its yard were 'barracks' in which several women lived and worked. Also known as the Jonathan Wilde of Castlegate, he appeared untouchable but changes in policing in the late-1840s, notably the appointment of a superintending constable for the Huddersfield district, led to his demise.[32] Using the powers of the 1848 Improvement Act, the commissioners ensured that 'Old Sut's' barracks were torn down in the summer of 1850.[33] Although a spectacular success, Sutcliffe's demise did not mark the end of the problem, though official concern fluctuated. In 1856, following a spate of prosecutions of beerhouse keepers, the magistrates made clear their determination 'to put down such scenes of vice and immorality' that had been made public.[34] In a long editorial the *Chronicle* asked rhetorically:

> Who is there that knows anything of the real status of the Beerhouses in and near to Castlegate but must know that the keepers of the greater portion of them harbour the vilest characters and permit practices of the deepest profligacy and vice?[35]

Of particular concern was 'the habit of decoying young girls' and taking substantial portions of the money they earned from prostitution.[36] Giving evidence in a case involving Elizabeth Lockwood, the landlady of the *Griffin*, described as 'about the best of the low class of beerhouse', Inspector Townend informed the magistrates of the sorry tale of Anne Shepherd. Engaged as a servant, she was expected to be a prostitute but with the promise of 'plenty of money'. In fact, her 'every halfpenny' was paid over to Mrs. Lockwood but worse, after a mere four months, she was dismissed and sent to the Huddersfield Workhouse in 'such a horribly diseased state'.[37] Lockwood was fined but taking effective action was far from easy. In 1861 John Smith, a Castlegate beerhouse keeper, was brought to court. Two witnesses – young women aged eighteen and twenty – 'brought from the cells to give evidence' told of the way in which Smith 'and his wife had been in the habit of hiring girls as domestic servants, and then asking them to prostitute themselves.[38] Smith's defence counsel argued that the witnesses were unreliable, not least because 'they had previously been girls of bad reputation and ... took no steps to leave the place when they discovered the true character of the situation'.[39] In the absence of corroborative evidence the case was dismissed.

Much depended upon the determination of the superintendent of police and the new man, William Hannan, proved to be a crucial figure. The successful prosecution of the 'notorious beerhouse keeper', Richard 'Big [sometimes Long] Dick' Ramsden in October 1863 was a clear indication of Hannan's determination to enforce the 1830 Beer Act (William IV c.64), which made provision for the withdrawal of a licence for a third offence under the act. The first prosecution 'for an offence against the tenour [*sic*] of his licence' was unproblematic. Not so the second. Ramsden's defence argued that this offence was not 'a second offence' in the meaning of the law, not being identical to the first. Hannan argued that this was a misreading of the act and the local magistrates accepted his argument and found Ramsden guilty. Hannan was not content with this and wrote to the editor of the *Justice of the Peace* for an opinion on the question. The reply upheld the stance taken by Hannan and the local magistrates. Duly fortified Hannan sought – and obtained – a third prosecution under the act. This time Ramsden appealed against his convictions to the magistrates sitting in quarter sessions. Hannan's groundwork stood him in good stead and the conviction was upheld.[40]

Although the success was welcome, Hannan had no illusions about the scale of the problem and the limited progress that had been made. In his annual report for the year 1863/4 he informed the Watch Committee that of eighty-four beerhouses in the town, sixty-four were effectively brothels with an average of three girls working in each. He wrote:

> No language can describe the debasing immorality of the keepers of these houses. Their victims are sought up in our and neighbouring towns and selected principally from the ranks of the poorer classes, under the pretence of hiring them as servants, when their object is to procure them for the purpose of prostitution.[41]

Complaints continued to be made to the Watch Committee regarding 'the character of many of the low beerhouses ... especially those in the neighbourhood of Castlegate' but matters did not come to a head until December 1864/January 1865.[42] Working closely with the Improvement Commissioners, Hannan put together the case against two married couples, the Hopwoods and Smiths, both Castlegate beerhouse keepers. This time the prosecution was made under the 1752 Disorderly Houses Act.[43] Subsequently the case was taken over by the poor law overseers as the costs of the case were to be met out of the poor rates.[44] The details of the case created a sensation. Although only two beerhouses were involved – the *Brown Cow* and the *Butchers' Arms* – it was claimed that there were at least eight beerhouse-brothels in the town, making Huddersfield 'the brothel of the West Riding'.[45] The details of the specific case created a sensation in court. It transpired that Hopwood had taken advantage of the distressed state of the cotton trade in Lancashire (the so-called Cotton Famine) to inveigle girls to come to Huddersfield, ostensibly as servants but in fact as prostitutes whose 'immoral earnings' paid for their board and keep. Defence attempts to delay the trial were rejected when the magistrates were informed that 'attempts had already been made to tamper with the girls upon whose evidence the prosecution were in part relying for proof'.[46] Such was the graphic evidence of the first witness, Harriet Perry, an eighteen-year-old from Ashton-under-Lyne, that William Hopwood changed his 'not guilty' plea to 'guilty' and threw himself on the mercy of the court, which sentenced him to eighteen months' hard labour. Notwithstanding evidence from the Hopwood trial that one of the young women, entrapped in Ashton and brought to Huddersfield by Hopwood, had been given to the Smiths, the recently-married couple pleaded 'not guilty'. Smith was also sentenced to eighteen months' hard labour while his wife, better known in town as 'Butter Moll', received fifteen months' hard labour – sentences that 'greatly astounded' the prisoners.[47] The magistrates were scathing in their condemnation and expressed the hope that the heavy punishments handed out in this high-profile trial would act as a deterrent to those 'systematically using and employing [their house] for the lowest purposes of immorality'.[48] So too did the Improvement Commissioners and the superintendent of police, but the decision not to follow a similar course of action for another beerhouse-brothel case in June 1865 'to save expense' was not a good omen. Even more disheartening was the fact that in the same month Mrs Hopwood, who had been too ill to stand trial in January, was charged with permitting disorderly persons, including 'women [who] were "unfortunates" [prostitutes] and one [who] was a returned convict', in the *Brown Cow* beerhouse.[49] Worse still, in February 1866, while the Smiths were still serving their 'deterrent' sentence, the stand-in keeper of the *Butchers' Arms*, Benjamin Hirst, was found guilty of harbouring prostitutes.[50] A month later when a local prostitute, Mary Garner, was arrested she informed the police of the continuing practice of bringing in girls 'from other towns … and kept in decoy houses solely for the purpose of prostitution.'[51] As Hannan's annual reports bear witness, he was all too well aware of the limited effect of successful prosecutions.

As well as having a reputation for immorality, Castlegate was also known for its violence, much of it associated with its 'low' beerhouses. Drunken brawls were commonplace and could be sparked by trivial incidents. Festival times (not simply Christmas, New Year and Easter) saw an increase in interpersonal violence as did more private celebrations at weddings or wakes. Men seeking to prove themselves came from outside town – navvies working near Skelmanthorpe, youths from Holmfirth – taking on the locals in Castlegate; but there was an underlying level of violence that shocked the more respectable members of Huddersfield society.[52] There were fights between the English and Irish, not to mention factional fights among the latter. More generally, men assaulted women, often savagely; less often women attacked men. The precise scale of interpersonal violence is impossible to establish as much went unreported. Many working-class men expected to settle their differences with their fists and not look to the courts. Similarly, they expected to discipline wives, children and servants and did so with little comment, let alone interference. To a degree (again unmeasurable) the police were happy not to interfere as long as disturbances did not threaten to escalate. Intervention was risky. Irish factionalism turned to solidarity in the face of police action, and likewise domestic discord could turn to cooperation when an interfering constable appeared. And then there was outright hostility to the police, most clearly (but not exclusively) seen among certain sections of the Irish community in places like Post Office Yard and Windsor Court. Large-scale disturbances were a recurring, though not commonplace, feature of Castlegate life. In May 1848 the unfortunate Reuben Megson, a night-watchman subsequently appointed to the new Huddersfield force, was the first man to a riotous scene in Castlegate. He was 'immediately knocked down and his skull broken with a constable's staff which had been taken from [another watchman]' and he was also kicked and bitten in the attack.[53] In April 1852, as shopkeepers shuttered their windows and closed their shops to protect their property, the police were forced to intervene in 'a violent row' between the English and Irish. With difficulty 'and after great labour', the police led by Superintendent Thomas 'quelled the disturbance and [took] the ringleaders into custody' but not before the English crowd had smashed the windows and doors of the Irish residents of Windsor Court.[54] A decade later similar problems beset the area. Superintendent Hannan was so concerned by 'the very disturbed state of Castlegate', especially on Sundays, that he drafted in extra police to maintain order.[55] Smaller-scale disturbances were more common but still carried real risks for the police. Time and again policemen found themselves faced with angry crowds as they tried to effect an arrest. It is difficult to determine whether the situation deteriorated over time or whether there was less tolerance of violence in the late 1860s compared with the early 1850s, but Hannan was in no doubt that 'the police had experienced great difficulty in doing their duty in Castlegate' so much so that he was 'obliged to send the officers there in couples'.[56] Interpreting these incidences of anti-police violence is not entirely straight forward. Men such as the Gillerlane brothers, Dan and Thomas, or Richard Ramsden, were well-known violent men who used their fists freely with ordinary men and women and had no love of the police. However, they were atypical Castlegate figures. Equally, it could be argued that assaults committed during an arrest for drunk and disorderly behaviour did not necessarily involve or imply anti-police sentiment.[57] However, not all of the evidence can be explained in this way. The large crowds that quickly gathered, throwing mud, stone and tiles at the police as they attempted to rescue prisoners, indicate a significant degree of hostility. Equally telling were the repeated incidents of members of the public refusing to come to the assistance of the police or refusing to give them information. Following an incident in which Sergeant Townend was physically and verbally abused while attempting to arrest two disorderly women, the *Chronicle* ruefully noted the 'disposition on the part of many of the low and disorderly characters in the town to annoy and abuse the police … in every conceivable manner while in the execution of their duty'.[58] Communal collections to pay fines were a further sign of hostility to the law and its enforcers. More strikingly, those suspected of assisting the police faced communal revenge. Michael Kelly, a fourteen-year-old living in Windsor Court was accused of being a 'Bobby's spy' and was duly stoned and beaten.[59] Even respectable members of the community were loath to assist (or be known to have assisted) the police. A Catholic priest, who had called the police to deal with a fight among Irish navvies, made his position very clear. He went about Castlegate 'doing a great deal of good [but] if he gave evidence it would probably have an injurious effect afterwards'.[60]

The Castlegate area posed persistent and major problems for the police. In that sense, it was never conquered, never wholly civilized, but, importantly, neither was it unpoliced. There were times when hostile mobs had to be quelled by the police force acting *en masse*; there were times when policemen patrolled the area in pairs but there was always a police presence. The fact that both Sergeant Mellor and PC Wilson lived there for several years is significant. There was a greater degree of tolerance and even cooperation between the police and the inhabitants of Castlegate than the lurid tales of large-scale attacks and prisoner rescues would suggest. In that sense, the threat of Castlegate was contained and a compromise struck between police and policed.

Upperhead Row: Something Old, Something New?

Although Castlegate remained a problem area with a reputation for immorality and criminality, its standing was challenged by those 'dens of iniquity ... the *Argyle* and *Cambridge Arms* music saloons ... [where] greater immorality is perpetrated than at any of the low houses of Castlegate' in the opinion of Superintendent Hannan in 1864.[61] This reflected a growing awareness that there were newer problem areas emerging in the town. Upperhead Row was one such hot-spot, while certain adjoining streets, most especially Manchester Street and Swallow Street, acquired a notoriety that began to match that of Castlegate. Two facts may help to explain this. The first was the growing concentration of Irish in and around Swallow Street, which gave rise to concerns about drunkenness, immorality and crime. This could be seen as a relocation of an older problem but it took a distinctive and virulent form in the shape of the 'Irish Small Gang' that came to prominence in the mid and late-1860s. The second was the emergence of new forms of popular leisure, the singing saloon and the music-hall. Again, this took a particularly distinctive form: the *Cambridge Arms* on Upperhead Row.

Upperhead Row District

Like Castlegate, Upperhead Row had once been a respectable part of town, though the presence of Lockwood's mill attracted working-class men and women to the area. Nonetheless, Schofield,

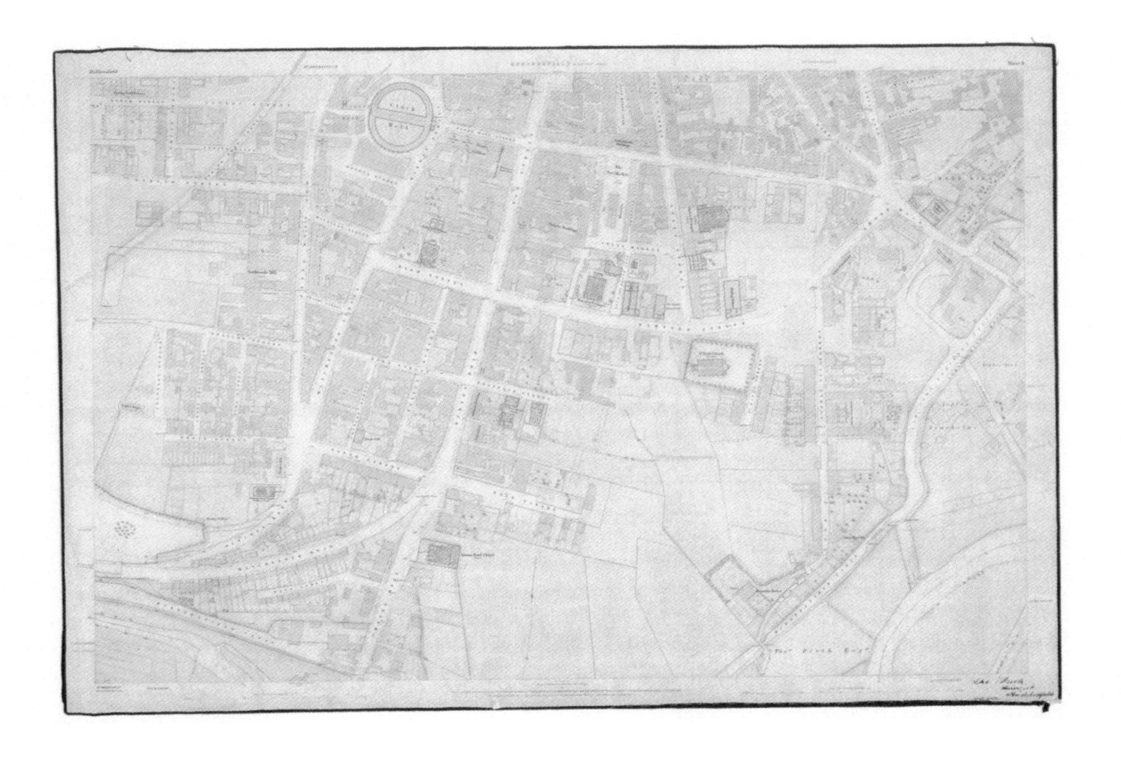

looking back from the late-nineteenth century to the 1820s, spoke of Swallow Street as 'a very good street ... inhabited by very respectable people'.[62] By the 1850s and 1860s this had changed. Although still socially mixed, there was a preponderance of working-class men and women, many of whom, not least in the Irish communities in Swallow Street and the courts, such as Connor's Yard that ran off it, were semi-skilled or unskilled. Barker's Yard and Cherry Tree Alley were 'in the most filthy state [being] chiefly inhabited by the worst description of Irish'. In the latter were thirty-two families 'in the most abject state of uncleanliness'.[63]

As in Castlegate, overcrowding and insanitation were major problems. Large families, crammed into small houses or unregistered lodging houses and with access to very basic facilities, faced a range of diseases from the commonplace, such as typhus, to the dramatic, such as cholera. Many families faced insecurity of employment and often chronic poverty. For some, small-scale crime offered a means of survival and there was the temporary escape offered by the beerhouse and the new singing saloons. Many of the policing problems experienced in and around Upperhead Row were similar to those discussed in relation to Castlegate and need not be revisited here.

The poor relations between Irish communities and the 'new' police have been well documented and Huddersfield, despite having a relatively small and dispersed Irish community, shared this problem.[64] In 1847 Sedgwick was badly kicked in a 'lawless and outrageous attack' by many Irish men and women living in Manchester Street and Granby Street.[65] The newly-formed police faced problems from the outset. In 1850, for example, the prosecution of several Irish people in Upperhead Row for lodging house offences led to a 'determination to be revenged upon the police force for having brought them before the magistrates'.[66] Within days the police on night duty were stoned by angry crowds. Sporadic assaults upon the police in the area were a feature of the 1850s but the frequency and scale of the attacks appears to have intensified in the early and mid-1860s. In January 1862 PC Sykes was 'very badly used [during] a disturbance in Swallow Street ... [he was] knocked down, struck in the face, dragged by the hair of his head by the cowardly crowd'.[67] Worse was to follow in November 1864. Joseph Carney had stripped to the waist in the street and called upon anyone to fight him. PC Nutton told him to go home but when Carney refused, abusing him with 'filthy and threatening language', Nutton arrested him.

This precipitated a major incident. Carney resisted furiously and, as Nutton and other constables dragged him towards the lock-up, a crowd, estimated to be in the hundreds, 'rushed on the constables and rescued the prisoner from them'. Eventually, Carney was arrested along with two other men who had been in the forefront of the rescue.[68] Difficult relations were exacerbated by rumours circulating in town – vigorously denied by Superintendent Hannan – that the police were operating a spy system.[69]

Such was the context from which emerged the Irish Small Gang, which terrorised parts of the town for the next decade. The precise size of 'this vicious fraternity' is unclear and almost certainly fluctuated over time. The gang probably comprised twelve to fifteen members most of the time and at its core were the Carney brothers (James, Joseph and Patrick), the Wood brothers (John and Michael) and the M'Cabe brothers (James and John).[70] This was more than a juvenile gang, though undoubtedly some members were in their teens.[71] The M'Cabes were in their late teens and at least two of the Carneys in their twenties when first they came to the attention of the police. Much of their activity appeared as nothing more than sheer vandalism. There were various incidents in which they smashed up beerhouses, 'throwing glasses and pitchers around to a dangerous extent'.[72] On other occasions they viciously robbed members of the public, usually as they left local beerhouses such as the *Wheatsheaf* on Upperhead Row or the *Cambridge Arms*.[73] Superintendent Hannan spoke of the gang 'going about the town assaulting people in the most disgraceful manner', attacking people when the police were not around and leaving town to escape arrest.[74] However, it is also evident that there was a strong sense of territorial identity. Gang members came overwhelmingly from the streets around Upperhead Row and much of their disruptive and criminal activity was directed at pubs and beerhouses at 'the bottom of town', including Castlegate. In March 1865, for example, the Small Gang wreaked considerable damage in two Castlegate beerhouses. In the second incident the unfortunate Hezekiah Taylor was assaulted (along with his wife and father-in-law) and robbed of £3-10*s* (£3.50) and a watch guard.[75] In another incident that strongly suggested territorial rivalry, John M'Cabe attacked Peter Gillerlane, a member of a family well-known to the police, in Castlegate itself.

There was a further distinctive element to the Irish Small Gang's activities that would have transcended territorial or factional rivalries

– overt hostility to the police. Reporting on the trial of some gang members in January 1865, the *Chronicle* informed its readers that 'members of this gang had bound themselves by oath to stone the police'.[76] This they most certainly did on a number of occasions and, once at least, members of the gang took to the roof of a house, smashing it with a hammer and throwing 'broken slates at the [police] officers and other persons'.[77] In other incidents members of the police force were victims of 'mob' attacks, particularly when arrests were being attempted. Perhaps the most notorious incident took place in April 1867 when PCs Ireton and Standish went to arrest John M'Cabe at his home in Upperhead Row. As soon as the police appeared M'Cabe's mother, already armed with a knife, called on eight or nine members of the gang, who then 'kicked and maltreated the officers and ultimately threw them downstairs'. The two constables, amazingly still holding on to John M'Cabe, 'were then dragged and kicked across the street and thrown into a cellar'. An estimated crowd of 100 gathered: some kicked and punched the officers and one set a dog on them. Eventually, police reinforcements ensured that the M'Cabes, mother and son, were finally brought to the cells.[78] And this was not the last incident involving John M'Cabe. In January 1870 he was brought before the local magistrates charged, for the thirteenth time, with assaulting the police. At Bradford Quarter Sessions four months later he was sentenced to seven years' penal servitude.[79] This was a major blow but their depredations continued into the early 1870s when Superintendent Withers, of the enlarged borough force, 'evinced a skill, a patience and a judgement which were beyond praise and the consequence was, in the course of time he completely destroyed the gang'.[80]

There can be no doubt as to the bitter animosity shown by members of the Irish Small Gang to the police over almost a decade. This was the most virulent outbreak of anti-police sentiment in Huddersfield. Unlike other outbursts in the town (and elsewhere) this was – at times quite literally – a running battle with the police that lasted not days, or even weeks (as was the case in well-known incidents in Leeds and Colne in the 1840s) but for months and years.[81] Clearly there was a significant portion of the town's population, predominantly but not exclusively Irish, that viewed the police as an alien and threatening force. However, there is a peculiar, personal dimension to the M'Cabes ongoing battle with the forces of law and order. In 1847, the very year in which John M'Cabe was born, his father Michael M'Cabe had been accused of being involved in a particularly gruesome triple murder in nearby Mirfield. M'Cabe and his fellow accused, Patrick Reid, was found guilty and sentenced to death. The case attracted nationwide attention when Reid confessed to being solely responsible for the murder. M'Cabe, however, was not released. In circumstances that remain unclear his death penalty was commuted to transportation for life because of 'evidence' that had come to light after the trial and that was never tested in court. In the 1851 census Mary M'Cabe (living with her sister in Upperhead Row with two small sons, James and John), was returned as 'lodger – convict's wife'. Michael M'Cabe was released - after a campaign supported by none other than Seymour Digby - and returned to his family in Huddersfield. Little is known of his subsequent life, except that he and his wife were arrested for assaulting the police in the late-1850s, shortly before his death. His wife and sons continued their battle with the police in the next decade. The penury that the wife and two boys endured in the early 1850s is likely to have had a profound effect on their view of the criminal justice system in general and the police in particular. However, while the M'Cabe experience was unusual in its intensity, it was by no means unique. Given the well-documented over-representation of the Irish in Victorian crime statistics, there would have been many others who felt that they were victims of a system that equated being Irish with criminality. It is hardly surprising that anti-police sentiments remained strong in these communities for many years.

If tensions between immigrant communities and the police were a well-established feature ofVictorian Britain, it was also the case that popular leisure activities were another source and site of conflict. Old pastimes were declining – few dogfights took place in the town in the 1860s – but the new could still be problematic. Pigeon flying and foot-racing drew large crowds that blocked thoroughfares and encouraged gambling. Beerhouses remained a source of concern, for polite society and the police alike, but the new forms of popular entertainment were often little better. Despite the harshness of life for many working-class people in the mid-nineteenth century, some had money to spend on the music saloons and music halls that began to develop. Much attention has been focused on developments in London and the larger cities, such as Manchester and Leeds, but it was not only in the cities that these new forms of entertainment were to be found. Great claims were made for the new forms of entertainment. Speaking positively of the *Cambridge Arms* in 1863, Mr. Learoyd, representing the proprietor, Mr. Allen Hoyle, was disparaging about 'the lowest beerhouses [and] the lowest class of entertainment resorted to' whereas 'nothing was so well calculated to draw people from these low and vitiated amusements, and thereby to prevent vice and immorality, as furnishing them with amusement of a higher character in the shape of good theatrical representations'.[82] The reality was somewhat different.

Under Hoyle's proprietorship, the *Cambridge* enjoyed a chequered history for just over a decade from the late 1850s to the late 1860s. He invested several thousand pounds in expanding his establishment in the late 1860s when it could boast an auditorium that held around 1,000 people. In 1858 Hoyle had taken over the *Black Swan*, renaming it the *Cambridge Arms Music Saloon* and advertising it as a 'Temple of Harmony', complete with a 'first-class pianoforte' to be played by 'the eminent pianist' Mr. Wilson, a man known for his performances in both Glasgow and Sunderland.[83] According to *Era* in August 1865 'a most agreeable hour may be spent at this [the *Cambridge*] the only place of amusement open in Huddersfield'. Throughout the 1860s the *Cambridge* offered a range of entertainments. Singers, dancers and comics (of varying descriptions but many Irish) were the mainstay while 'Negro entertainments' were a regular feature. Gymnasts and trapeze artists, such as 'The Great Pedanto! The Daring Pedanto' from America were to be found along with performing animals but 'The Sensation of 1867' was to be 'Madame Conrade and her Celebrated Troupe of Females Artistes ... in their Grand Entertainment of Poetic Groupings [and] Classical Statuary'. Despite the positive comments in *Era*, the *Cambridge* had a reputation locally as 'a den of iniquity' and Hoyle appeared in the local magistrates' court on several occasions, facing charges associated with selling alcohol outside licensing hours and permitting gambling and prostitution on his premises.[84] The presence of an onsite dram-shop added to its attractions but Superintendent Hannan was shocked by the numbers of juveniles drinking there and committing petty thefts.[85]

Matters came to a head in 1869. In March of that year Hoyle announced the forthcoming appearance of the seemingly innocuous Mr. & Mrs. White, 'Negro Comedians, Vocalists, Instrumentalists and Dancers'. Their act was to be Hoyle's downfall. Two of the local police visited the *Cambridge* and gave a detailed account of the evening's entertainment. The nub of the matter was that, in one scene, involving a 'ticket of leave man' and another person, Hoyle was effectively staging an unlicensed play. Despite a spirited claim by Hoyle's defence that it was not clear whether 'the performance or conversation could be called a drama, tragedy, comedy, opera or pantomime', the magistrates found in favour of the police case and fined Hoyle £5. *Era* was sufficiently concerned to run a short piece under the heading: How Far Does The Theatrical Licence Extend? It was clearly worried that a £5 fine had been imposed simply 'for permitting the mere conversation jargon so common with Niggers to take place on his boards without a licence'. Hoyle appealed to the magistrates at quarter sessions in the October. The police stressed the immoral nature of the 'performances' at the *Cambridge*. Detective Walter Paxman recounted how he had visited on several occasions 'and had seen, more than twice, as many as six or seven prostitutes and five or six thieves present'.[86] Furthermore, he 'had witnessed the performers making indecent signs on the stage and [had] heard indecent songs'. Worse, according to fellow officer, Inspector James Whelan, 'one of the performers was a woman in male costume [who] went amongst the audience and asked the visitors to stand treat'. The magistrates saw no reason to overturn the decision of the local magistrates in Huddersfield. The *Cambridge* was now denounced as 'the greatest curse in the town'.[87] By the time of his appeal Hoyle had suffered a second, more serious blow. After thirteen years his licence was not renewed at the annual Brewster Sessions in August 1869. The Town Clerk objected to the renewal of Hoyle's licence, citing his prosecutions for permitting gambling and prostitution and his most recent prosecution for 'permitting stage plays of an immoral character, without a licence'.[88] The magistrates upheld the Town Clerk's objection. By December 1869 the fixtures and fittings were sold.[89] Hoyle himself was soon declared bankrupt and, in an ironic final twist, the *Cambridge* itself was put up for sale and purchased by the teetotallers of Huddersfield, who renamed it the *British Workman*, but as an alternative and uplifting venue for the working men of Huddersfield it was a very short-lived venture.

Conclusion: Problems and Priorities

Although attention has been focussed on two specific areas, many of the problems to be found in Castlegate or around Upperhead Row were to be found elsewhere in the town. Back Buxton Road, with its drunken brawls between men and women and the presence of several squalid brothels, acquired a reputation for 'the disgraceful and heathenish manner in which the inhabitants are in the habit of conducting themselves'.[90] The *Gypsy Queen* beerhouse in Old Street, especially when 'Slasher' Wilson was the licensee, was one of the worst in town; little better were the nearby *Dog Inn* and the optimistically-named *El Dorado*. Equally problematic was Kirkgate.

The problems discussed in this chapter are interesting and important in their own right, particularly as they relate both to contemporary perceptions of criminals and criminality and to contemporary priorities in terms of crime control. The almost unchallenged belief that drinking and gambling led to petty crime and thence to serious crime ensured that much police time was devoted to the surveillance of public houses and, even more so, beerhouses. However, the prosecution of beerhouse-brothels owed much to the determination of individuals such as Superintendents Heaton and Hannan. This chapter has provided further insight into the day-to-day realities of policing, but necessarily from a police perspective. To gain further insight into the society which generated these problems we need to look next at the men and women who found themselves before the magistrates in the 1850s and 1860s.

Endnotes

1 *General Regulations, Instructions and Orders for the government and guidance of the Metropolitan Police Force,* London, 1851, p.49.
2 *Ibid.*
3 HIC Minutes, KMT 18/ 2/2/1, 3 November 1848.
4 HIC Minutes, KMT 18/ 2/3/13/1, 21 November 1853.
5 Watch Committee Minutes, KMT 18/2/3/13/1, 28 December 1858.
6 E J Law, *Huddersfield in the 1820s,* Huddersfield Local History Society, 2009, p.36.
7 *LM,* 14 August 1848.
8 This is discussed further in chapter six.
9 L Browning & R K Senior, *The Old Yards of Huddersfield,* Huddersfield Civic Society, 2nd edition, 2004.
10 The 1851 census returns show that 53 per cent of the inhabitants of Castlegate were born in Huddersfield or the immediate surrounding district. A further 23 per cent were born in other parts of Yorkshire. 14 per cent were born in Ireland.
11 For examples see *HC*, 24 & 31 May 1851, 2 July & 6 August 1853, *HEx*, 1 May 1852 and LM, 8 November 1858. Children were particularly vulnerable in a variety of ways. For death due to fire-burns (*HC*, 25 March 1854 & 2 November 1867), drowning (*HC*, 13 July 1867) and overdose of Godfrey's Cordial (*HC*, 10 February 1866).

12 *HC,* 25 March and 22 July 1854. Following her death, Morris's husband had to be kept in the police cells to ensure that he was sober for the inquest.
13 See for example *HC,* 7 February & 9 December 1854, 5 July 1856, 17 July 1858 & 9 July 1859.
14 *HC,* 8 December 1860. For other examples see 20 December 1851, 21 February 1857, 8 October 1859 & 11 January 1862. Hayley was not the only repeat offender. Another Castlegate butcher, Francis Senior, was prosecuted on a number of occasions.
15 J Burnett, *Plenty and Want: A Social History of Food in England from 1815 to the Present Day,* London, Routledge, 1989, esp. chapter ten.
16 See for example *LM,* 2 December 1848, *HC,* 16 October1852, 15 April 1854 & 14 July 1866.
17 *LM,* 16 June 1849 and *HC,* 10 August 1850. See also the description of 'Castlegate and the courts and alleys branching out of it' where 'masses of people were crowded indiscriminately into lodging houses and rooms which possessed neither size, light nor air'. *LM,* 1 March 1851.
18 *HC,* 22 April 1854.
19 *HC,* 26 May 1855. Moran was again fined 5s (25p) for keeping an unregistered lodging house, 13 September 1856.
20 *HC,* 8 September & 8 December 1866.
21 *HEx,* 22 April 1854. For details of changes to licensing legislation see *B Harrison, Drink & the Victorians,* Keele University Press, 1994, esp. chapter fifteen.
22 Most cases were clear-cut but some appeared petty-minded. Thomas Binns, the landlord of the *Theatre Tavern,* also owned a small shop. He was seen during the hours of divine service by Inspector Thomas and charged accordingly. The magistrates fined him 5s (and costs) for selling mint drops to a little girl. HC, 7 June 1851.
23 Examples in the *HC* court reports include the *Talbot,* 24 August 1850, 26 April & 19 July 1851, 21 May, 20 August & 22 October 1853; the *Butchers' Arms* 22 February, 15 March, 2 August & 13 December 1851 and 7 February 1852; the *Blue Bell,* 24 May 1851 & 22 May 1852; the *Theatre Tavern,* 7 June & 6 September 1851. James Cayford, 26 April & 19 July, 1851, 21 May, 20 August & 22 October 1853 and 25 November 1855; John Tierney, 21 February, 1 May & 18 September 1852, 17 September 1853, 18 August 1855, and 4 & 11 February 1865; Nick Hannigan, 14 June & 11 December 1851 and 16 October 1842; and the Dearnleys, 15 March 1851, 31 January 1852, 8 January 1853, 11 March, 17 June, 12 August & 25 November 1854; 20 June 1857, 8 May 1858, 5 October 1861 & 12 December 1863.
24 *HC,* 17 May 1852. On occasion considerable sums were stolen. A Wyke cattle dealer was robbed of £84-10s (£84-50), *HC,* 9 June 1855.
25 *HC, 15 March 1851.*
26 *HC,* 23 September 1854. He was not alone in being rebuked. Joshua Stringer, robbed in the *All Nations* beerhouse by a local prostitute, was told by the magistrates that 'he ought not to go to such disreputable places', 30 January 1858 while 'an elderly gentleman' (whom the press let remain anonymous), who had come to Huddersfield from Ossett not only had his

case dismissed but was described by the magistrates as 'a remarkably stupid old man'. 16 October 1858.

27 *HC,* 18 August 1855.

28 See chapter six for a more detailed discussion.

29 HC, 6 September 1851. See also 25 January, 19 July, 2 August & 22 November 1851, 9 October 1852.See also *LM*, 2 September & 14 October 1848.

30 *HC,* 10 February 1855.

31 *LM,* 4 November 1848.

32 Townend and Sedgwick attempted to bring him to court but with limited success. Initially Heaton fared little better, achieving a successful prosecution in July 1848 but a modest fine of 5*s* (25p). *LM,* 15 July 1848. Heaton's career as superintending constable is discussed in detail in Part 2, especially chapter seven.

33 *LM,* 8 June 1850.

34 *HC,* 19 July 1856.

35 *HC,* 21 February 1857.

36 *HC,* 24 January 1857 and 10 September 1859. *HEx,* 22 & 29 November 1862 & 10 December 1864.

37 *HC,* 29 November 1862.

38 *HC,* 26 July 1861.

39 *HC,* 26 July 1861.

40 *HC,* 24 October 1863.

41 Annual Report, 1863/4, September 1864 reported in *HC,* 4 February 1865.

42 *HEx,* 3 & 10 December 1864 & *HC,* 7 January 1865.

43 25Geo.II, c.36 An Act for the Better Preventing Thefts and Robberies and for Regulating Places of Public Entertainment, and Punishing Persons Keeping Disorderly Houses.

44 This was under legislation passed in 1818 during the reign of George III.

45 *HC,* 10 December 1864.

46 *HC,* 7 January 1865.

47 *Ibid.*

48 *Ibid.*

49 HC, 24 June 1865. See also *HEx*, 6 May 1865.

50 *HC,* 3 February 1866.

51 *HC,* 24 March 1866 and *HEx,* 24 March 1866.

52 *HEx,* 19 August 1865.

53 *LM,* 22 May 1847. Among three men sent for trial at York was John Sutcliffe, who was found not guilty.

54 *HC,* 17 April 1852.

55 *HC,* 27 August 1864.

56 *HC,* 27 April 1867 and for examples of 'routine' anti-police violence, see 26 April & 8 November 1851, 21 February & 11 December 1852, 4 November 1854, 19 February 1858, 31 January & 12 December 1863, & 23 April 1864.

57 Similarly, when Mary Curtis smashed the windows in PC Wilson's house in Castlegate, she did so to be sent to prison. The magistrates obliged and she was sent to the Wakefield House of Correction for fourteen days. *HC,* 26 March 1853.

58 *HC,* 1 January 1853.

59 *HC,* 25 April 1857.

60 *HC,* 26 August 1865.
61 *HC,* 3 September 1864.
62 Cited in Law, *Huddersfield in the 1820s,* p.10.
63 *LM,* 8 August 1846.
64 See for example, R Swift, 'Another Stafford Street Row', *Immigrants and Minorities, 3, 1984, pp.5–29*, and D Taylor, 'Policing and the community: late-twentieth century myths and late-nineteenth century realities' in K Laybourn, ed., *Social Conditions, Status and Community,* Stroud, Sutton, 1997.
65 *LM,* 13 November 1847. See also *B.Obs,* 11 November 1847.
66 *HC,* 10 August and 21 September 1850. See also *HEx,* 23 September 1854. In a large crowd 'someone spoke a few words in Irish' and an attempted rescue ensued.
67 *HC,* 4 January 1862.
68 *HC,* 19 November 1864. The three men were each fined 5*s* (25p) and costs, making totals of 14*s* (70p), 15*s* (75p) and 16*s* (80p). In default they received one month's imprisonment. For other incidents in Upperhead Row and Manchester Street see 27 March & 20 November 1851,31 July 1852, 29 July 1854, 28 July 1855, 30 March 1861, 9 April, 7 May & 11 July 1863, 1 October & 17 December 1864, 5 August 1865 & 20 July 1865.
69 *HC,* 26 November 1864.
70 21 members have been identified in the mid and late-1860s from the local press reports with a further likely 3 members, not all of whom would have been involved at the same time.
71 The local press also reported a Junior Irish Small Gang and a Girls Small Gang who emulated M'Cabe's gang, but details are very scant.
72 *HC,* 7 January 1865.
73 *HC,* 14 January & 14 October 1865 and *HEx,* 1 April 1865.
74 *HEx,* 14 October 1865.
75 *HC,* 4 & 25 March 1865, *HEx,* 24 June 1865, & LM, 3 March 1865.
76 *HC,* 14 January 1865. See also *HEx,* 16 September 1865.
77 *HC,* 31 December 1864. See also *HEx,* 14 October 1865 for another rooftop incident. For other stoning incidents see *HC,* 14 January & 16 September 1865.
78 *HC,* 6 April 1867.
79 *HC,* 15 January and 28 May 1870. The assault took place in Spread Eagle Yard where detective inspector White had confronted five men and three women.
80 *HC,* 14 November 1874. The words are those of Alderman Mellor at a Town Council meeting debating (and agreeing to) an increase in Withers' salary. The details cannot be explored here but it is worthy of note that Superintendent Hannan had struggled to bring gang members to justice because of the unwillingness of members of the public to provide information or give evidence in court, particularly while the M'Cabe brothers were on the scene.
81 The most spectacular outburst was in Honley in 1862. See chapter nine.
82 *HC,* 10 October 1863.
83 *HC,* 25 July 1858.

84 *HC,* 3 & 10 September and 26 November 1864.
85 *HC,* 9 December 1865 and 4 August, 22 & 29 September 1866. The problem was not unique to Huddersfield. Similar comments were made by the chief constables of Bradford and Leeds.
86 *LM,* 23 October 1869, though the Huddersfield detective is wrongly named as 'Pazman'.
87 Letter to *HC,* 4 September 1869.
88 *HC*, 28 August 1869.
89 *HC*, 11 & 18 December 1869.
90 *HC,* 26 July 1862. See also 25 July 1864, 18 March, 5 August & 4 November 1865 and 26 May & 2 June 1866.

Criminals or Victims?

MANY MIDDLE-CLASS Victorians were worried by the squalor, immorality and criminality to be found in the midst of growth and prosperity. There were deep fears that the (ill-defined) 'dangerous classes' might sweep away the prosperity and civilization that marked out mid-Victorian society. The denizens of this 'other' world were described in demonic, almost apocalyptic terms, but who were the criminals of Huddersfield? What lives did they live? And what light do their lives throw on the nature of the economy and society of this expanding, prosperous mid-Victorian town? Contemporary fears of a criminal class threatening the fabric of society were misplaced. Many crimes were mundane – non-violent thefts – and most criminals were ordinary working-class men and women. In so far as they were habitual criminals, this was a product of economic insecurity and social marginalisation. They tended to be the 'losers' in society – the men and women, who for a variety of reasons, often beyond their control, were unable to make a living in a prosperous town that was at the forefront of industrialisation and urbanisation.

Crimes of violence exercise a particular fascination. There are many studies of Victorian murderers but the pre-occupation with such criminals, especially when their crime was particularly gruesome, gives as reliable a guide to criminality as an episode of *Midsomer Murders* or *Inspector Morse*. Non-violent crimes against property dominated the statistics of serious (indictable) offences tried at assize or quarter sessions and, even among petty offences, assaults were a minority of the cases that were heard by local magistrates. In 1863, for example, exactly 5 per cent of all persons charged with crime in Huddersfield were accused of an indictable offence. There were no cases of murder or manslaughter in the town; no robbery with violence and in the one case of burglary the thief had made off with a few bottles of porter.[1] Superintendent Hannan, having served for several years in Middlesbrough, repeatedly stressed the absence of serious crime in the town. This is not to say there was none – there were beerhouse brawls that led to fatalities and manslaughter charges on more than one occasion – but these were the exception rather than the rule.[2] The emphasis in this chapter will be upon the less dramatic offences and those who perpetrated them. The men and women who became before the town's magistrates and who, (on being found guilty) became criminals, defy easy categorization. Even if it were possible to establish accurate crime-specific gender, age and occupational profiles, such generalizations obscure important variations. As other studies have shown, there was no such thing as a criminal class – though there were people who relied heavily upon criminal activities – and there is little evidence of criminality running in families from generation to generation. Persistent offenders were a minority but even among this group heterogeneity is the striking feature. As Godfrey *et al.*, have argued there was 'a continually varying cohort of individuals ... rather than an easily categorized group of like-minded people capable of undermining the cohesion of society'.[3]

John Sutcliffe, 'The King of Castlegate', Henry 'The Burton Slasher' Wilson and Other Notorious Local Criminals

Although the evidence does not indicate the existence of a criminal class in Huddersfield there were a number of individuals, and their coterie of associates, who, while retaining a 'legitimate' exterior, were clearly involved in a variety of criminal activities. In the 1840s the most notorious figure in Huddersfield was John Sutcliffe, a Castlegate beerhouse keeper, the self-styled 'King of Castlegate'. The 1841 census lists him simply as a beer retailer but he had a hand in a variety of illegal activities. His beerhouse achieved notoriety as 'the rendezvous for thieves and prostitutes of the lowest grade'.[4] It was a centre for coiners, targeting nearby villages, while robberies were planned and some even carried out there, but despite a number of brushes with the parochial constables no charge was brought successfully against him. Such was his success that he was able to purchase the beerhouse and build in its yard 'a barracks', rooms in which he rented out to certain 'members of the frail sisterhood'.[5] His relationship with the constables is undocumented but his sobriquet – the Castlegate's Jonathan Wilde – is suggestive.* Whatever the reasons, his good fortune held until late 1848. His downfall is interesting for a number of reasons, though the actual crime – robbery and assault – was not uncommon, especially in Castlegate. James Speight 'an old man from Askern Spa near Doncaster' visited Huddersfield and after 'he got fresh [drunk] somewhere in the town and rambled down into Castlegate … he went into a public house, but he did not know which one … he went into the yard shortly after and was there seized by three or four men, who lifted him off his feet and placed him across the channel. One of them placed his hand over his mouth … and another took the remaining sovereign from him'.[6]

The initial outcome was equally predictable. Sutcliffe and an accomplice were arrested and identified by several witnesses. Speight did not help his cause by admitting that he was so drunk at the time that he was unable to identify the beerhouse in which he was robbed. However, the defence were able to call an array of witnesses who claimed that Speight had been robbed in the street while Sutcliffe had been quietly minding his business in his beerhouse. The fact that one of these witnesses was the 'protector' of one of Sutcliffe's female tenants did not prevent the magistrates from dismissing the case. At this point events took a different course. The determination of the new superintending constable, Thomas Heaton, and of one of the town's parochial constables, Abraham Sedgwick, led to the discovery of further evidence, including a stolen handkerchief, which greatly strengthened the case against Sutcliffe. Equally determined was James Speight, who walked some thirty miles from Askern to pursue his case in court. This time Sutcliffe (and his younger accomplice Joshua Armitage) were committed for trial at the York Assizes, where, in a session dominated by the trial of the Chartist leaders, they were both found guilty and sentenced to ten years' transportation.[7] 'Old Sut's' barracks were demolished a year later and there is no further record of him in Huddersfield for almost twenty years.[8]

---

* Jonathan Wilde, or Wild, the notorious eighteenth-century thief-taker, escaped the law for many years because of his ruthlessness in prosecuting some (but not all) thieves for whom he had acted as receiver of stolen goods.

Sutcliffe's departure was not an end; rather, it opened the way for others to take over the mantle of most notorious criminal in town. The man who made the strongest claim in the early 1850s was Henry Wilson, also known as 'the Burton Slasher' or simply 'Slasher'. A pugilist with a reputation for violence, who turned beerhouse keeper, he was involved in a variety of criminal activities. His career appeared to be living proof of the validity of local magistrates' analysis of crime. During his mid-twenties, in a six-year period (1852–57), he appeared in court on some forty occasions. He was fined for being drunk and disorderly on five occasions, for fighting on seven occasions (including a vicious assault on a woman) and for gambling a further four. He was found guilty of seven licensing offences (including permitting gambling (twice) and harbouring prostitutes (three times). He was also found guilty of theft on six occasions, the sums involved varying from 8*s* (40p) to £91 and four further offences involving dogfighting, while he was also charged with passing bad coin and attempting to bribe or intimidate a jury. To make matters worse he was married to a well-known prostitute, who herself was involved in a number of robberies, and the beerhouse they ran, the *Gypsy Queen* in Kirkgate, was notorious as a meeting place for known criminals. Not all of his offences were petty. In the winter of 1855/6 he and his wife and associates faced two charges of highway robbery. The first took place in Moldgreen. The victim, Christopher Smith, of Jockey Hall, had been drinking in a number of beerhouses in 'the bottom of town' and was followed before being knocked down and robbed of nineteen sovereigns and sixteen shillings (£19-80) by 'Slasher' and two other men at the gateway to his house.[9] The second 'garotte robbery'** took place in similar fashion but this time on Kilner Bank. A local butcher, Richard Poppleton, who had been drinking in 'Slasher's' beerhouse, was followed home and robbed of £91 in gold, notes and bills. Wilson and three others were arrested and brought before the town's magistrates. Identification proved difficult and ultimately only one man, William Pitchforth, stood trial at the York Assizes, where he

** The sensationally-named garotte robberies generally took the form of an attack from behind in which the victim was held round the neck. There were 'moral panics' surrounding such attacks – particularly in London in the early 1860s. See G Pearson, *Hooligan: A History of Respectable Fears*, Basingstoke, Macmillan, 1983, chapter six and Rob Sindall, *Street Violence in the Nineteenth Century*, Leicester University Press, 1990.

was found guilty and sentenced to eight years' penal servitude.[10] Wilson was able to prove his *alibi*, though not for the first time there was a suspicion that 'hard-swearing' [perjury] was involved.

'Slasher's' lifestyle revolved around drinking, gambling and fighting and, while he made some money from the legitimate beer trade, his income was clearly supplemented by earnings from prostitution and theft. He moved within a relatively small circle of like-minded individuals.[11] The same names crop up either as fellow spectators, attending (and gambling on) dogfights and footraces, or as partners in crime. The inter-relationship between these activities is well illustrated by a case from 1855 when Wilson and two others were charged with stealing £15 from Arthur Warburton in the *Dolphin* beerhouse, Castlegate.[12] Entertained by 'Butter Moll', the keeper's wife, Warburton revealed to her the contents of his purse as he went to purchase cigars. Within minutes Wilson and two colleagues appeared and after some 'milling practice' by Wilson, Warburton was knocked into a corner and relieved of two £5 notes and five sovereigns (£5). The three made their way immediately to 'Malley Pashley' at Dogley Lane, where they spent the afternoon gambling away the money on a dogfight.

Wilson led something of a charmed life in court, managing 'to elude the penalties of the law'.[13] Nonetheless, he was successfully prosecuted on a number of occasions and it is striking that, more often than not, his fines (which could run to as much as £20 when costs were included) were paid immediately. Furthermore, Wilson had the money to ensure that he (or his wife) was properly represented when the need arose. Nowhere was this more clearly seen than when his 'paramour', Sarah Sutcliffe, was charged with stealing a gold watch from James Brook in Hull. Brook, a preacher amongst the New Connexion Wesleyan Methodists, had meet Mrs. 'Slasher', as the papers reported it, on a steamboat from Goole to Hull and was aware that she was married and her husband at home in Huddersfield. Nonetheless, he bought her a drink and a meal at a cook shop in Hull before retiring with her to an upstairs room in the *Victoria Hotel*. Meanwhile, 'Slasher' took an adjoining room. Brook, claiming no immoral intentions but merely wanting a rest, was duly robbed. Brook later identified Sarah Sutcliffe, who was eventually tried at the quarter sessions, where she was defended by the well-known legal figure of Digby Seymour.[14] 'Slasher's' reign collapsed rapidly and mysteriously soon after. By 1858 he was charged with being a vagrant and found himself facing trial for passing counterfeit coin while purchasing muffins. He was sentenced to three months' imprisonment at Wakefield, 'a decision which appeared to afford great satisfaction to a crowded court'.[15]

Sutcliffe and Wilson were exceptional but there were other men, and a few women whose lifestyles were not that dissimilar. Many were keepers of various beerhouses and they inhabited that borderland between legality and outright criminality. Men like John Conroy, James Cayford, John Ashton and another 'low beerhouse keeper', Richard 'Big Dick' Ramsden, regularly appeared in court and their careers bring out the harsh realities of life for certain sections of the working classes.[16] Infringements of the licensing laws and permitting (or taking part in) fighting on the premises were the most common offences, but there were others, not least receiving stolen goods and buying pawn tickets for stolen goods, that hint at an informal/illegal economy whereby they and their customers could offset their poverty.[17]

By the time he fell foul of Superintendent Hannan in 1863, Ramsden had been charged twenty-five times and convicted thirteen times since first being granted a licence for the *Forge* beerhouse in Castlegate in 1861. He was part of the beerhouse-brothel trade and, no doubt shockingly for respectable readers, he had 'the most lascivious prints of the French school' on his walls and 'everything ... which pander to vice and lust'.[18] In fact, his criminal career extended back at least until 1855. He was well-known for his violence against both men, women and the police and was arrested for criminal damage in several town drinking establishments.[19] Like 'Slasher' Wilson, 'Big Dick' also had the money to hire the best defence. In another assault case, brought by Mary Waddington, he was defended by the distinguished 'miners' counsel', or 'Mr Roberts of Manchester' as he was widely known.[20] Equally violent was John Conroy, who at various times in the late-1850s and 1860s was the keeper of beerhouses in Castlegate, Kirkgate and Old Street. When one of his assault victims appeared in court his 'face was covered with bandages and plasters and he presented a very sorry spectacle'.[21] In another incident it was alleged that he had 'danced on the head' of a labourer as he shouted 'I'll poise [kick] the eye out of ye'.[22] But not all violent beerhouse keepers were men. One of the most formidable figures in town was Hannah Armitage, 'a woman of gigantic breadth' who weighed more than twenty stone and was more than capable of holding her own in a fight. When William France's taunts provoked her, she gave him such a beating that he appeared in court some days later with a 'shockingly disfigured' face.[23]

Not all violent men were beerhouse keepers. Daniel Gillerlane lived off Castlegate in Post Office Yard, and from his late-teens onwards, was involved in a number of vicious assaults. His violence might have been channelled differently had he made a success as a soldier but he absconded from the West Yorkshire Rifles, soon after joining as a twenty-year old in 1855. He resumed his assaults in Huddersfield and increasingly focused his anger on the police.[24] After one particularly vicious attack on Sergeant Kaye, the *Leeds Mercury* described him as 'a truculent vagabond' and the *Chronicle* as 'a brutish-looking fellow' responsible for several 'savage attacks both on the police and other people'.[25] Also involved in petty theft he was imprisoned in Wakefield for periods ranging from one to eight months, but the theft of a purse in Tierney's beerhouse brought him a sentence of seven years' penal servitude.[26] Similarly Andrew Dearnley spent time in and out of Wakefield prison for a variety of assaults, but he was also involved in several incidents of theft.[27] Violence was not confined to the semi-criminal fraternities that men like Gillerlane and Dearnley frequented. George Dyson, on the surface at least, was a moderately successful man, a butcher, living and working in the Shambles; but he was a violent man. On at least eleven occasions between 1859 and 1867 he was found guilty of fighting or committing an assault. On four occasions the fight was with fellow butchers and another involved a lawyer's clerk, who was bringing Dyson his expenses for a court appearance. His cohabitee was knocked down and kicked insensible in Kirkgate and he also threatened the landlady of the *Bull and Mouth Inn* with violence, though the threat was never carried out.[28] Dyson did not win every fight. Indeed, so badly was he beaten in 1865 that Superintendent Hannan withdrew the case against him on the grounds that he had been punished enough.[29]

Acts of violence were very much a part of mid-century Huddersfield life. Some were unequivocally criminal but others less so. It was commonplace for working-class men (young but also old) to settle disputes with their fists. Although this could lead to a court appearance the 'offence' was viewed with ambivalence, unless it was a blatantly unfair fight. Another problematic area was domestic violence. It was commonly held that men had the right to physically chastise their wives, children and (if they had them) servants or apprentices. As Victorian masculinity was re-defined in the mid-nineteenth century, such actions were increasingly condemned and prosecuted, though the provisions of the law were often woefully weak in terms of punishment. The town magistrates were increasingly vocal in condemning 'the disgusting prevalence of the cowardly offence of wife-beating' though the police were often reluctant to intervene, not least for fear that the fighting couple (and even neighbours) might turn on them.[30] Many cases were brought by the victims themselves, 'praying for sureties of the peace', and reveal the often wretched lives led by these women. Many assaults took place after lengthy drinking sessions and over many years, involving beatings and kickings, even strangulation. Furniture was broken, windows smashed and clothes torn, often before the eyes of children and neighbours. The economic insecurity of the women was also very apparent. Elizabeth Haigh, 'like most wives was unwilling that [her husband Thomas] should go to prison' but sought an escape from violence via separation and support for her and her children.[31] There was a clear class dimension to the condemnation of domestic violence both nationally and locally, but it was not simply middle-class magistrates and reformers who condemned 'wife-beating'. When the co-workers of William Horsfall became aware of 'his habit of severely beating his wife … they burnt him in effigy to show how deeply they execrated his inhuman conduct'.[32] There were other acts – large-scale and planned thefts, for example – which were clearly criminal, but it is to a different range of offences and offenders that we now turn.

Drunks, Whores and Beggars

There was a growing demand for 'order and decorum' in public spaces but while the emphasis on civilizing the streets says much for largely-elite Victorian values, the cases that came into court also tell much about the lives of overwhelmingly poor, working-class 'criminals'.[33]

Working-class drunkenness was a problem that exercised the minds of many respectable Victorians (working-class as much as middle-class) and Huddersfield, with a strong temperance presence, was no exception. Letter-writers to the local press regularly condemned the extent of inebriety in the town and, in 1867, there was an unpleasant row among the Improvement Commissioners and the superintendent of police over the 'supposed extraordinary prevalence of drunkenness in Huddersfield'.[34] Huddersfield, or so it seemed, was the fifth worst town in England in terms of drunkenness per head of population and little better than such notorious places as Liverpool and Middlesbrough. In fact, the analysis was fundamentally flawed as recording practices varied considerably from town to town, as Superintendent Hannan forcefully pointed out to his critics.[35] Unlike in many other towns every case of drunkenness brought to the attention of the police was recorded. Although the problem of under-recording was not entirely eradicated – not all drunks came to the attention of the police – the local figures give a reasonable approximation to the scale of the problem. Hannan defended Huddersfield's position but his figure for the number of residents charged with drunkenness (203) in 1866 was equivalent to one person in every hundred of the town's population.[36] Further, he claimed that two-thirds of the cases were associated with the 'low beer-houses' in town.

Drunkenness presented a range of problems to the police. At the most basic level incapable men and women had to be removed from the streets or alleys. This was not always easy. James Beaumont was 'in such an incapable condition that a wheelbarrow had to be got to convey him to the lock-up'.[37] Likewise, Susannah Gibson.[38] People put themselves in danger. Sarah Beasley was found in Horseshoe Yard able 'neither to stand nor walk … in an exposed state with a large number … around her'.[39] In some cases drunks fell into the canal and drowned. John Wagstaff was one of many who, the worse for drink, fell into the canal basin at Aspley and drowned, though some, like James Duffy, were fortunate enough to be rescued.[40] In other cases they collapsed in the streets or nearby fields. Elizabeth Shaw, 'compelled to obtain a living by plain sewing', even though she was seventy-one-year-old, spent an afternoon and early evening drinking in Castlegate before setting off home in the dark. Between 7 a.m. and 8 a.m. the next morning she was found in a field 'running down from the New George into Northumberland Street … in a state of utter exhaustion'.[41] She died less than three hours later. Others deliberately attempted (and in some cases succeeded) in ending their lives. Thomas Driver, a seventy-year-old shoemaker 'well known for his intemperate habits' returned to his home in Manchester Street where he attempted to slit his throat while Mary Padley, also inebriated, threatened to slit her throat or jump out of her bedroom window – drink and desperation were a powerful combination.[42] What drove people to excessive drinking is not always clear. There was a culture of heavy-drinking among many working-class men and women for whom it provided an escape, however brief or costly, from the harshness and apparent hopelessness of their lives. However, in some cases there was a more immediate and tangible cause. John Lunn was arrested for being drunk and disorderly in King Street (a second such offence in a matter of days) but it transpired that his son had recently been run-down and killed in Quay Street.[43] Mary Cryan was found drunk and smashing windows in Swan Yard. When she appeared before the magistrates the following day she explained that she had been deserted by her husband and that the windows were in to the house of a local prostitute, Mary Rowe, with whom he was now living. The magistrates thought the 'circumstances sufficiently mitigatory' to dismiss the charge.[44]

As can be seen from the Cryan case, drunkenness was often associated with disorderly behaviour. Verbal and physical abuse in the streets was a recurrent feature. The involvement of men in acts of violence has been commented on and analysed extensively but less attention has been paid to disruptive women.[45] Irish rows were a regular feature of working-class life in Huddersfield and many involved women rather than men.[46] Many of the women involved were described as prostitutes (though in a number of cases this probably meant that they were cohabiting and not married) and it is clear that there was a significant number of women whose life experiences and lifestyles led them into various forms of criminal behaviour. Reconstructing the lives of these women is difficult given the limited and often biased evidence that survives. However, an analysis of local press coverage combined with the use of census material enables a picture, albeit partial, to be drawn of these women.

Prostitution, the great 'social evil', was a major concern in the mid-nineteenth century, not least because of the frightening revelations about the prevalence of venereal disease among soldiers and sailors fighting in the Crimean War. Huddersfield was not a designated area under the Contagious Diseases (CD) Acts but there was considerable local concern about the moral and health threats posed by prostitution in the town. Technically, prostitution itself was not an offence but women could be arrested for being 'lewd and disorderly', 'drunk and disorderly' and for importuning. However, it is clear that the term 'prostitute' was used in a subjective manner, labelling women who did not conform to mid-Victorian standards of female behaviour. However, matters are confused by the plethora of terms used – 'fallen woman', 'unfortunate', 'soiled dove', 'member of the frail sisterhood', 'nymph of the *pavé*' and so forth – sometimes for the same individual. It is not clear if such terms were interchangeable or reflected some form of hierarchy based on the permanence, or otherwise, of the individual's involvement in prostitution. Describing a woman as an 'unfortunate' or a 'soiled dove' suggested a degree of sympathy; calling her a 'fallen woman' carried a more explicit moral judgement while using the term 'nymph of the *pavé*' and even 'frail sisterhood' implied both a lifestyle choice and an 'otherness', apart from respectable society. Our knowledge of Victorian prostitution and prostitutes owes much to Walkowitz's classic study, which exposes the inadequacies of contemporary explanations of prostitution.[47] Prostitutes, she argues, tended to be heavily drawn from the daughters of the poor; for many, particularly before the CD Acts, it was a temporary phase into and from which young women moved; and the motivation for becoming a prostitute was to be found in lack of skill/education and poverty. More recently, Lee's work on prostitution in Kent argues for a more complex pattern of behaviour and has stressed the degree of agency exercised by the women involved.[48] To what extent was this the case in Huddersfield?[49]

Press accounts were profoundly influenced by contemporary attitudes. Men were portrayed as the innocent victims of immoral temptresses.

> Many decent men might go into one of these [beer]houses with the best intentions, only to get a glass of beer as numbers of respectable working-men did, without knowing the temptation therein, but the moment they were sat down one of the girls was placed besides him; he was led to ruin and his family to destitution.[50]

Accounts of arrests combined titillation and moral shock. Sergeant Townend proved remarkably adept at arresting women 'in an improper position behind the Cloth Hall', Detective Partridge caught a couple 'in an act of prostitution' while strange sounds led PC Worsnip to the shooting-gallery booth in Lord Street where he found Mary Ann Preston 'with two men in a shamefully disorderly position'.[51] Even when the women are accorded their names they are either dehumanized or distanced, as an unnatural 'other'. Mary Ann Pearson was a 'social evil' while Ann Ashton became 'a notorious "social evil"'; Catherine Hopkins, likewise, 'a well-known social evil'.[52] There was something voyeuristic in the description of Mary O'Neil as a one-armed drunk and something unnatural in the description of Mary Kaye as 'a masculine looking Irish woman'.[53] Other descriptions, emphasizing famished and cadaverous looks, dishevelled appearance and diseased condition, reinforced the image of 'the prostitute' as a 'threatening other'. And the importance of appearance was also highlighted in the rare (or rarely reported) case of a wrongful arrest. When Susannah Dent appeared in court, accused of an act of indecency, she was described as 'respectably-attired and rather ladylike' and suffering 'great mental anguish'. The case was dismissed after her father, a respectable old man, gave evidence of her good character.[54]

Looking beyond these comforting fictions one can see a more complex reality. Men, rather than being innocent victims, knew full well what was on offer in a large number of the town's beerhouses. They may have acted foolishly – as the magistrates reminded them on occasions – but they actively sought out the delights of Castlegate or the *Cambridge*, be they farmers coming to market, youths coming from outlying villages or residents of the town. There were victims, most notably the young girls, brought in from other towns and villages on the promise of a job as a servant, only to find that they had to pay for their board and keep through prostitution. Others may well have made a conscious choice but were still victims of poverty and lack of opportunity, particularly for unskilled women. It is no coincidence that many of these women were either domestic servants, hawkers, or the wives of hawkers and labourers, or widows. It is also striking that several had either been abandoned by their husbands or ill-used; unsurprisingly many of them were repeat offenders, preferring to be in the Wakefield House of Correction – for security and medical reasons; and a significant minority attempted suicide. It is not possible from the surviving evidence to determine how many women moved out of prostitution to become 'respectable'. 'Slowit Hannah' (Hannah Armitage) had by her own confession led a dissolute life as a young woman when first in Huddersfield in the mid-1840s but by the late 1850s she was the wife of James Armitage, who kept the *Dog Inn*, on the corner of Kirkgate and Old Street. Unfortunately, the *Dog Inn* was a well-known centre of prostitution but she was very much the exception in Huddersfield.[55] Many of the repeat offenders clearly never escaped a life of prostitution, though there were a number of reported one-time offenders for whom prostitution may have been a short-term expedient.

These broad socio-economic characteristics confirm the view that those women for whom prostitution was a longer-term option, were drawn from the poorest strata of society and lived lives of considerable hardship and danger. The complexities of their lives can only be fully appreciated by looking at specific case studies. In February 1861, under the sub-heading, 'Shocking Death' the *Chronicle* carried an account of the coroner's inquest into the death of Isabella Taylor, aged thirty-nine, and 'for a long time one of the frail sisterhood'. Her body had been found at the foot of the cellar-kitchen steps of the *Croppers' Arms* beershop at 7.30 a.m. one Tuesday. In tracing her last steps, it was ascertained that at 1 a.m. that day, she was seen struggling with a farm labourer, James Cotton, who was trying to drag her into the *Rose and Crown* dram-shop. That was the last time she was seen alive. The coroner's conclusion was that

> having no place of abode, and knowing the beerhouse well had wandered there with the intention of going to the water-closet at the bottom of the steps and that she either accidentally fell down, or was pushed down by the iron gate which hangs only on one hinge and falls too heavily.[56]

The jury, it should be said, also recommended that 'the iron gate ... should be put in a proper state of repair'. Nothing more was said about the woman but what little is known about her life is instructive. Born in Kendal in 1823, she had come to Huddersfield as a young woman, probably in the late 1840s. In 1851 she was recorded as being single, a lodging house keeper, living in Rosemary Lane. Soon after she was known to be living as man and wife with John Stock, who was fined 5*s* (25p) for assaulting her. By 1852 she was described as being 'of notorious bad character' and was variously charged and imprisoned for importuning and theft from the person. She was assaulted on at least two occasions by punters as she eked out a livelihood from prostitution and petty theft. In April 1860 she appeared once again at the Wakefield Quarter Sessions charged with the theft of a handkerchief. Unfortunately, the grand jury threw out the bill and, instead of being sent to the relative safety of prison, she was free to return to Huddersfield where she met her tragic death.[57]

Equally instructive is the case of Elizabeth Long. She had come to Huddersfield from Cumberland (precisely when is unclear) and by 1851 was thirty-four years old, married to a man almost twenty years her senior, with a young child, and living in Spring Street. Three years later, and still married, she was found guilty of 'being lewd and importuning passers-by on Sunday evening' but she was discharged early from Wakefield 'for behaving well in gaol and her extreme destitution'.[58] Later that year she appeared in court, labelled one of the 'fair and free nymphs of Castlegate', though the theft charge against her was dismissed. The following year, now described as 'an impudent looking wretch' she was sentenced to two months at Wakefield for 'wandering abroad in Kirkgate … for the purpose of prostitution'.[59] By now 'a character well-known to the police', in July 1856 she became the 'keeper of a house of ill-fame in Castlegate' and later that year she was sentenced to eight months imprisonment at the Leeds Quarter Sessions for the theft of a sovereign (£1) from a solicitor, Thomas Leadbetter, in a beerhouse in Old Street.[60] In the next two years she appeared in court at least five times on charges of theft from the person. Now in her mid-forties, she was described as 'a miserable looking dirty woman ... [and] a miserable specimen of depravity'.[61] Apparently still a prostitute (her 'bully' rescued her on one occasion) she was trapped in a life of criminality. In October 1861 she was sentenced to four years' penal servitude for the theft of clothes and, almost immediately on release, stole a shawl from off a washing line. This time her sentence, at the Bradford sessions, was seven years' penal servitude.[62] She was released on a ticket-of-leave and returned to Huddersfield, living in Duke Street. Her reputation went before her and she was arrested 'for prowling about at four o'clock in the morning', though the case was dismissed. Later that year the 'unfortunate and returned convict' was found guilty of the theft of 18*s* 6*d* (92½p) and, at the age of fifty-four, was sentenced to a further ten years' penal servitude at the Wakefield intermediate sessions.[63]

Other lives are even less well documented but the fragments point to very similar conclusions. Mary Ann Hilton was married to an ex-soldier, who was unable to find employment. Their relationship was troubled and she was assaulted by other men as well. 'So frequently [had she been] committed to Wakefield that she could not tell the number of times.'[64] Like Elizabeth Long, her sentences lengthened as her criminal career continued. After a number of short sentences in Wakefield, Hilton was sentenced to five years' penal servitude in 1865 and, having been released early, to ten years' penal servitude in 1868.[65] Mary Kelly (of Castlegate), 'a somewhat massive member of the "fair and free" circles inhabiting Rosemary Lane', as an old woman, after a lifetime of often violent petty crime, attempted to commit suicide by throwing herself into the canal.[66] It was not just the old who tried to end their lives. Emma Edwards, a prostitute aged twenty-five, tried three times to commit suicide by drowning, only to be rescued by PC Partridge.[67] Others sought a short-term break. When Julia Carney was committed to the Wakefield House of Correction for the thirty-fourth time, the *Chronicle* flippantly called it 'a singular instance of prison infatuation', failing to grasp that prison was a place of refuge for these women.[68] Mary Curtis knew well what she was doing when she smashed the windows in the house of PC Wilson in Castlegate. It was not because she hated the police but, as she told the magistrates, 'in order that she might be sent to prison'.[69] The oft-convicted Bridget Killarney was even more explicit: 'I would rather be in Wakefield [House of Correction] than out'.[70] It was a simple but eloquent statement, born of an awareness of the limited opportunities for poor, unskilled women and of long knowledge of the harsh realities of the prostitute's life.

In his annual report for 1857 Superintendent Beaumont told 'the inexperienced ... [but] innocent sympathisers ... that the greatest portion of crime is committed directly or indirectly by [vagrants]'.[71] He was wrong, but many contemporaries shared his beliefs and, as a consequence, much police time was devoted to dealing with beggars and other vagabonds. This was another ongoing problem. In 1847 the *Leeds Mercury* noted that 'the number of beggars has lately increased in Huddersfield to an alarming extent, many of whom are destitute Irish'.[72] It was not, however, a problem confined to recently-arrived Irish migrants. Eighteen-year-old Elizabeth Scott was arrested for begging in John William Street, having come from Leeds to look for work but was 'sadly in want of the common necessaries of life'. She was discharged on condition she left town at once. Such was her plight that a woman in court came forward to pay her fare back to Leeds.[73] A decade later, Sarah Thompson found herself before the magistrates for begging but it transpired that, having recently arrived from Carlisle, she had been deserted by her husband and to support herself and her five month-old child she tried 'earning her living by selling a few needles on the road', while Mary Ann Reynolds, 'a miserable looking creature with a child in her arms' was found guilty of begging from door to door.[74] In hindsight many of these cases appear to be nothing more than the criminalization of poverty but the magistrates could be more sympathetic. Mary Walker, a tramp, arrested at 2 a.m. in the company of two men, having 'tearfully pleaded her utter desolation and destitution' was freed on promising to leave town immediately.[75] Similarly, Thomas Kilroy, when charged with begging, received a caution but was allowed 2*s* 6*d* (12½p) from the charity box once he explained that illness had 'reduced [him] to absolute want'.[76] Others were less fortunate. Jane Grey and George Berry were sentenced to seven days in Wakefield House of Correction for sleeping in a cart in Brierley's Yard, King Street; Sarah Jones, a sixty-three-year-old seamstress, to fourteen days for sleeping in the open air, and David Beardsall and Robert Burns, to a month for sleeping in a tenter store in Armitage & Kaye's Yard in Quay Street.[77] One of the most attractive places for rough sleeping, and therefore the most likely place to be arrested, was the lime kilns at Aspley. In 1861 James Green was given an hour to leave town (the alternative being a month in prison) for sleeping there.[78] It was a risky matter, especially as many rough-sleepers fortified themselves with several drinks. When PC Marsden went to arrest a drunk, 'sleeping close to the mouth of the Aspley lime kilns', he was unable to do so immediately because the man's 'clothes were too hot to handle', but less fortunate was David North, a forty-year-old coal-heaver, who died as a result of sleeping too close to the fire.[79] These were men and women who, for a variety of reasons, did not have a permanent place to sleep, nor have the money to find accommodation for the night. As such they were victims of laws that penalised those who were the economic losers in a seemingly prosperous town such as Huddersfield.

One final group of 'criminals' remains to be considered: suicides and attempted suicides. Again, it is difficult to categorise the people who fall into this group but a number of common themes emerge. Older men were vulnerable. James Dearnley, a weaver living in Northgate, hanged himself, three weeks after the death of his wife, to whom he had been married for thirty-eight years.[80] But Michael Boyle was only twenty-nine when he tried to kill himself in Old Post Office Yard, being 'very despondent ... owing to the faithless conduct of his wife who [had] abandoned him and left

Castlegate

Old Cottages,
Denton Lane

The Old Shears Inn, Beast Market

Upperhead Row

Spring Street

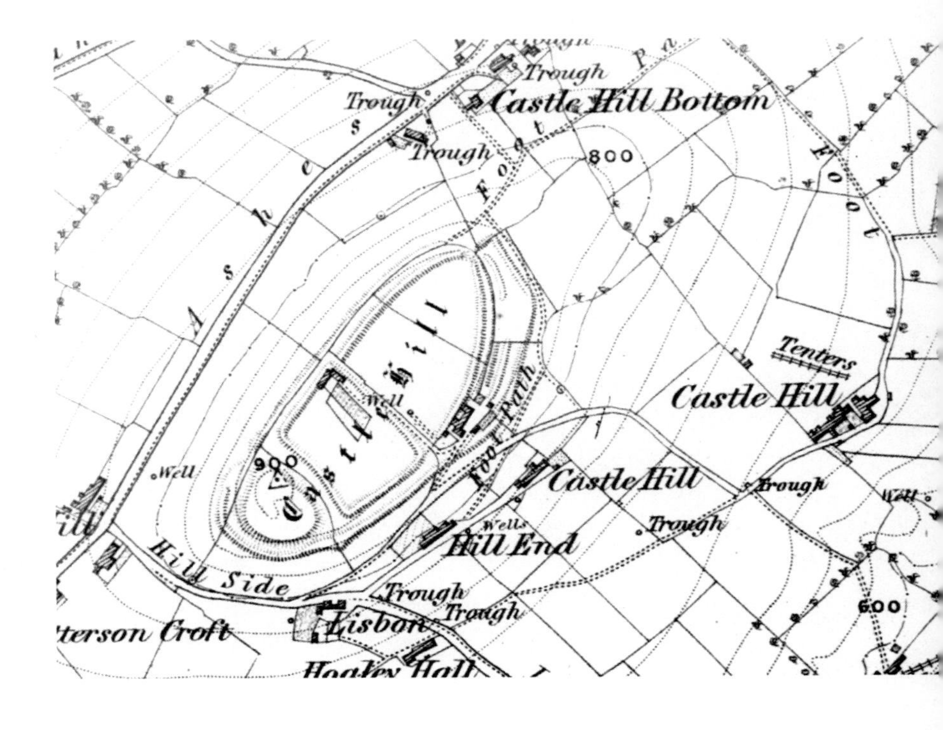

Castle Hill (map)

Honley, Town Gate

Marsden

him disconsolate'.[81] A second cause for men was physical frailty, which undermined their sense of masculinity. Seventy-one-year old John Schofield, a veteran of the battle of Waterloo, also living in Northgate, suffering from depression brought on by concern with increasing bodily frailty, hanged himself when left alone by his wife.[82] Similarly, Henry Lindsay, although only fifty, was depressed by the fact that he was 'too old to work' and strangled himself in the Model Lodging House.[83] But there were also younger men who took their lives. Joseph Sewell, an out-of-work plasterer, first took to heavy drinking before killing himself at the age of thirty-six.[84] Of the women who committed (or tried to commit) suicide, personal problems predominated. Mary Manning drowned herself in the canal after Christmas Eve Mass, when she discovered that her husband, to whom she had been married for thirty-three years, had been having an affair with a neighbour in Back Buxton Road for over two years.[85] Emma Walker, pregnant at eighteen, was abandoned by the father. She too ended her life in the canal.[86] Sarah Sutcliffe (not related to the woman of the same name mentioned previously), also eighteen, drowned herself after 'some unpleasantness ... between her and her mother with reference to love affairs'. The coroner returned an open verdict, noting simply that she had been 'found drowned'.[87] All suicides/attempted suicides were tragic but in some cases the tragedy was compounded by macabre black-humour of the incident. The stableman Joseph Hirst, known as 'Deaf Joe', tried to commit suicide by jumping into the canal but he became stuck in the mud, the water was insufficiently deep to cover him and he was found exhausted by his efforts to force his head under water.[88]

Conclusion

This chapter has not attempted to provide a comprehensive (let alone statistical) analysis of crime in mid-Victorian Huddersfield. Rather it has sought to bring out the diversity of criminal behaviour and to set these actions into a broader social and economic context, thereby throwing light on the society in which these crimes took place. A number of broad themes stand out. Although Huddersfield did not experience a high level of crime – particularly indictable offences but also petty crimes – there were a substantial number of offences involving violence, drunkenness and prostitution. These need to be considered in a wider context. First, there was a growing demand for 'order and decorum' especially in public spaces. There was less tolerance of certain types of behaviour than a generation earlier. The casual poor, in general, were subject to greater scrutiny and control; street prostitutes, in particular, more so. Terms such as 'prostitute' or 'beggar' were not neutral but were labels that carried strong (and negative) moral overtones and had the effect of creating a distant 'other', perceived to be a threat to 'normal' and 'respectable' society. The introduction of the new police both reflected and strengthened these new expectations. Second, and in many ways cutting across these wishes for greater respectability, was the existence of an economy characterised by considerable inequalities – reflecting occupational, gender and racial differences – and a society with relatively few institutions to alleviate poverty. There was a grey economy, which was criminal in formal, legalistic terms, but was less obviously so from the perspective of those who benefitted, for example, from the sale and purchase of stolen foods and goods. It was also, particularly for single or abandoned women, a makeshift economy in which people struggled to devise survival strategies, cobbled together from ill-paid, casual work, begging, charity and petty crime. Thus, there were many 'criminals' who were as much victims as criminals. This was particularly true of unskilled, working-class women, especially those from an Irish background. Prostitution, on a part- or full-time basis, was for many of these women the best of a bad set of options: high-risk in a variety of ways – short-term, violence and disease; longer-term an inescapable life of crime – but bringing in more money than being a hawker, a servant or even a factory hand. And then there were those who occupied an ambivalent middle ground. Hannah Armitage and Sarah Sutcliffe were both victim and perpetrator.

There are problems with the use of the term 'victim', not least the danger of perceiving certain people as powerless, having no choice and unable to influence their lives. To deny any sense of agency to the people discussed in this chapter would be wrong. There were choices to be made. Lee has argued that, because some poor women chose to resort to prostitution and others not, there was a degree of agency that is denied by labelling such women as victims.[89] There is force in such an argument, albeit more so for a Hannah Armitage than an Isabella Taylor, and it could be extended to include those who committed (or attempted) suicide but there is a danger of overstating the degree of freedom (real or perceived) and minimizing the desperation that many such people felt and the dilemmas that such a course of action (be it prostitution or suicide) created. Further, it overlooks similar problems for those who, for whatever reason, chose not to adopt such a course of action but were still faced with the threat to life of self and family of, in Acton's phrase, 'cruel, biting poverty'.[90]

Third, there remained a 'rough' working-class male culture in which physical prowess, including heavy drinking, was paramount. There was also a sub-culture that tolerated more, but not all, violence than many in the 'respectable' classes would do and, finally, and this is a theme that will be explored more fully in the conclusion, there was a complex relationship between these criminals and the agents and agencies of the criminal justice system. Beerhouse keepers were prosecuted as were bullies and beggars but there was no simple 'hunter/hunted' distinction. Beerhouse keepers called the police to clear their houses of unwanted and truculent customers; women went to court to prosecute troublesome neighbours, even violent partners. Further, though more exceptional, some of Huddersfield's most notorious criminals called upon distinguished legal figures to defend them in court. Conversely, the police often turned a blind eye to crimes – discretion literally being the better part of valour in certain cases – and the magistrates threw out cases or inflicted nominal fines to mitigate the harshness of laws, if strictly applied. Such was the complex and at times contradictory world of law and order in mid-nineteenth century Huddersfield.

Endnotes

1 Superintendent Hannan, Annual Report, 1863 *HC,* 14 November 1863.

2 In 1861 Thomas Norton was charged with the manslaughter of Joseph Smith, following a fight in the *Black Lion* beerhouse in Upperhead Row. The Grand Jury at York returned a verdict of 'Ignoramus' and Norton was set free. *HC,* 9 February 1861 and *LM,* 9 February & 12 March 1861. Similarly, in 1865 Michael Hayley was charged with manslaughter, after a fight led to the death of John Mylett. This was a classic case of manslaughter, starting in a dispute in the Marble Masons beerhouse again in Upperhead Row after a lengthy drinking session and resolved by a fight in nearby Marsh Delph. Mylett died when he fell back from a punch by Hayley and struck his head on a stone. Hayley was tried at Leeds and (again) the case was dismissed. *HC,* 22 April 1865.

3 B S Godfrey, D J Cox and S D Farrall, *Criminal Lives: Family Life, Employment and Offending, Oxford, Clarendon*, 2007, p.166.

4 *LM,* 4 November 1848.

5 *Ibid.*

6 *Ibid.*For a similar case see the arrest and subsequent transportation of 'Lindley Lyd' Clay for robbery from the person (two £5 notes) in the Green Dragon, Castlegate. *LM*, 16 August 1845. See also 31 July 1848 for another violent robbery from the person in Castlegate.

7 *York Herald* 23 December 1848. In February 1849 Sutcliffe was taken from York Castle to Millbank prison London to await transportation. *Ibid* 24 February 1849.

8 In 1864 James Sutcliffe of Castlegate, referred to as 'Old Sut' was tried, along with five other men, for robbery, though this may have been John Sutcliffe's son. *HC,* 13 February 1864.

9 They stood trial at York and were acquitted, a verdict which 'created some surprise' given the strength of the evidence. *HC,* 1 & 17 November & 15 December 1855.

10 *HC,* 26 January & 22 March 1856.

11 Certain names, for example George Broadbent, William Stancliffe, Daniel Byram and Charles Kendal, crop up regularly in the court reports.

12 *HC,* 26 May 1855.

13 *LM,* 30 January 1858.

14 *HC,* 9 August 7 25 October 1856 and *Hull Packet*, 24 October 1856. Sarah Sutcliffe was eventually found guilty (the jury was evenly divided and the decision depended on the foreman's casting vote) and she was sentenced to twelve months' hard labour. It was not uncommon for people from Huddersfield to take a train and boat day out to Hull. The train was taken to Goole and a steamboat from Goole.

15 *HC,* 30 January 1858.

16 Ramsden, also known as 'Long Dick' on account of his height, should not be confused with 'King Dick' who was a chimney-sweep, living in Old Street!

17 See for example *HC,* 25 November 1854, 21 April 1855 and 14 November 1863. Almost all were fined at one time or another for having faulty measures and several were also prosecuted for using their houses as lodging houses without a licence.

18 *HC,* editorial, 24 October 1863 and *HEx,* 6 & 27 December, 1862.

19 See for example *HC,* 24 November 1855, 19 April 1856, 7 March & 13 June & 21 November 1863.

20 Roberts played a prominent part in the trial of the Honley rioters. For details see chapter nine.

21 *HC,* 20 February 1864, Conroy was fined 10*s* (50p) and ordered to pay £1-10*s* (£1.50) to his victim whose face he had slashed with a broken glass.

22 *HC,* 28 July 1866. Another fine of 10*s* (50p) was imposed, though the total costs took the figure to £2-4*s* (£2.20).

23 *HC,* 10 October 1857.

24 See for example *HC,* 27 August 1853, 30 May 1857, 29 December 1860, 13 July 1861, 8 August & 12 December 1863 & 10 August 1867.

25 *LM,* 12 November 1859 & HC, 12 November 1859.

26 *HC,* 11 February 1865.

27 See for example *HC,* 27 May 1854, 26 June 1856, 4 July 1857, 5 October 1861, 21 November 1863, 30 January & 10 September 1864. *HEx*, 27 May 1854.

28 For fighting with butchers see *HC,* 15 March 1862, 16 April 1864, 28 April 1866 & 15 August 1868. The assault on his partner was reported 21 November 1863 and the threat of violence 27 July 1867.
29 *HC,* 9 September 1865. Among other injuries Dyson suffered a broken arm but this did not end his fighting career.
30 *HC,* 11 July 1863. See also 1 June 1861.
31 *HC,* 29 June 1861.
32 *HC,* 25 January 1856.
33 This highlights a problem of evidence. The people who appeared in court are not necessarily a random sample of, say, beggars, drunks or prostitutes. To that extent it is impossible to say for how many begging or prostitution was a temporary expedient.
34 *HC,* 7 September 1867.
35 *Ibid.*
36 *Ibid.* Hannan also drew attention to the larger number (326) non-residents of the town who were charged with drunkenness in the local courts.
37 *HC,* 1 October 1853.
38 *HC,* 28 April 1855.
39 *HC,* 17 November 1855.
40 *HC,* 17 March and 10 November 1866. Some deaths were more suspicious. George Clayton was found drowned in the same spot but there was a suspicion that he had committed suicide. *HC,* 2 June 1866
41 *HC,* 30 November 1850.
42 *HC,* 14 October 1854 & 3 November 1860.
43 *HC,* 7 October 1854.
44 *HC,* 3 March 1855. This was not the end of the case as Rowe brought a case for damages to which the magistrates acceded. *The Chronicle* was unimpressed, claiming that they 'fined innocence and threw the mantle of justice over vice'.
45 S D'Cruze, *Everyday Violence in Britain, 1850–1950,* London, Longman, 2000, C Emsley, *Hard Men: Violence in England since 1750,* London, Hambledon, 2005, M Weiner, *Men of Blood: Violence, Manliness and Criminal Justice in Victorian England,* Cambridge University Press, 2004 and J Carter Wood, *Violence and Crime in Nineteenth-Century England,* London, Routledge, 2004.
46 For examples of such disturbances in Castlegate see *HC* 14 September 1850, 15 November 1851, 7 June 1856, 4 June 1862 and 5 November 1865; for Manchester Street see *HC,* 23 October 1851, 5 February & 21 May1853 & 23 March 1861; for Upperhead Row see *HC,* 5 February 1853, 16 June 1855, I May 1858 & 11 June 59; and for Windsor Court see *LM,* 22 May 1849, 8 November 1859, *HC,* 25 April 1857 & 22 March 1858.
47 J R Walkowitz, *Prostitution and Victorian Society: Women, class and the state, Cambridge,* Cambridge University Press, 1989. See also C Lee, *Policing Prostitution, 1856–1886: Deviance, Surveillance and Morality,* London, Pickering & Chatto, 2013.
48 Lee, *Policing Prostitution,* esp. chapter one.
49 The following analysis is based on evidence relating to approximately 150 women who appeared in court in the 1850s and 1860s. While this cannot be

considered, in strict terms, as a representative sample, the characteristics that emerge provide an indication of the underlying realities.

50 *HC,* 11 March 1865.

51 *HC,* 4 October & 27 December 1856 and 29 November 1860 and *HEx,* 17 January 1863.

52 *HC,* 28 February 1860 and 24 January & 23 May 1863.

53 *HC,* 3 September 1859 and 27 October 1860.

54 *HC,* 25 July 1863. In fact, the case appears less straightforward. Several witnesses spoke of Dent's improper behaviour but the case was not well handled by the police. PC Marshall wanted to give further evidence after the verdict had been delivered but the magistrates refused to hear him. Later that year a Susannah Dent, 'an alleged prostitute,' was arrested for a beer-house theft case. It is not clear whether this is the same woman.

55 *HC,* 19 July 1862. A crowd of some 1,500 turned out to watch the funeral cortege for what the paper, in a masterpiece of understatement, called 'a most remarkable woman not only in character and conduct but also in size'. The only other woman to have explicitly stated that she had abandoned her dissolute ways since becoming a married woman, Margaret Kelly, was also charged with running a brothel. *HC,* 1 July 1865 & 6 October 1866.

56 *HC,* 16 February 1861.

57 *HC,* 7 June 1851, 5 June & 9 October 1852, 15 January 1853, 25 March 1854, 18 July 1857, 3 December 1857 & 7 April 1860.

58 *HC,* 11 February 1854.

59 *HC,* 6 January 1855.

60 *HC,* 18 October 1856.

61 *HC,* 19 November 1859 & 1 December 1860.

62 *HC,* 19 October 1861 & 28 October 1865.

63 *HC,* 27 May 1871, 22 July & 26 August 1871.

64 *HC,* 26 July 1856.

65 *HC,* 21 & 28 January & 25 February 1865 and *B.Obs, 11* December 1868.

66 *HC,* 21 October 1854, 20 October 1866 & 13 March 1869.

67 *HC,* 18 June 1853.

68 *HC,* 27 July 1850. See also 10 May 1851 for a similar comment. Julia Carney was born c.1815. In 1841 she lived in Windsor Court with the family of John Gannon, labourer. No occupation is recorded for her. In 1851 she was serving time in the Wakefield House of Correction on the census date. This time under occupation is the clear entry 'none'. Her criminal record goes back at least to 1846, probably before, and lasted until 1853, when (not for the first time), she was sent back to Wicklow. This time she appears not to have returned. See *LM* 10 January & 12 September 1846, B.Obs, 10 September 1846 and *HC,* 9 November 1850, 10 May 1851, and 30 April 1853.

69 *HC,* 26 March 1853. The magistrates obliged with a fourteen-day sentence.

70 *HC,* 14 April 1864.

71 *HC,* 5 December 1857.

72 *LM,* 30 January 1847. See also 6 March 1847 for references to beggars being 'chiefly Irish and Scotch mendicants'.

73 *HEx*, 27 May 1854.
74 *HC*, 12 February 1859 & 24 September 1864.
75 *HC*, 14 April 1855.
76 *HC*, 15 January 1853. It helped that he was 'respectable and apparently well-educated'.
77 *HC*, 3 & 17 April 1858 & 6 June 1867, John Delaney was fined for sleeping in a pigsty in Boulder's Yard but he was also drunk at the time. *HC*, 16 June 1855.
78 *HC*, 9 February 1861. See also 30 May & 4 July 1863.
79 *HC*, 20 January 1855 & 3 May 1856. An unnamed man was more fortunate, being rescued with his trousers ablaze. *HC*, 24 January 1863. See also the death of John Flood, *LM*, 2 January 1847.
80 *HC*, 3 April 1857.
81 *HC*, 25 April 1863.
82 *HC*, 22 February 1862.
83 *HC*, 6 October 1861. See also James Chapman, who killed himself at the second attempt, following a prolonged illness, which resulted in his heavy drinking. HC, 31 May 1862.
84 *HC*, 1 January 1859.
85 *HC*, 5 January 1867.
86 *HC*, 9 April 1859.
87 *HC*, 20 December 1862. See also Margaret Bell, twenty-eight, who drowned herself, having fallen out with her parents over her 'late hours and questionable conduct'. *HC*, 7 June 1862.
88 *HC*, 30 June 1861.
89 Lee, *Policing Prostitution*, esp. chapter two.
90 William Acton, *Prostitution Considered in Its Moral, Social and Sanitary Aspects*, 2nd ed., London, Churchill & Son, 1870, p.180.

PART TWO

THE HUDDERSFIELD DISTRICT (UPPER AGBRIGG)

Upper Agbrigg, 1844.
Courtesy of Cassini Maps.

Thomas Heaton and the Superintending Constable System

THE RESPONSIBILITIES OF the Huddersfield borough force extended to the limits specified in the Improvement Act; for policing the rest of the Huddersfield (or Upper Agbrigg) district, responsibility rested with the magistrates of the West Riding. Their decisions led to a distinctive, but neglected, form of policing, and one that casts new light on a neglected aspect of the mid-nineteenth century experimentation in police reform. Marginalized in most police histories have been the 'Tory initiatives' embodied in the Parish Constable Acts of 1842 and 1850, which provided for the appointment of a paid superintending constable responsible for coordinating the activities of parochial constables - and other paid constables - in any petty sessional division.[1] Although this model of policing was 'decisively rejected in 1856', these acts were used in the West Riding of Yorkshire, particularly in the Huddersfield district, to create a system of policing that satisfied many of the needs and expectations of local magistrates and manufacturers, who voted consistently not to establish a county force under the 1839 Rural Police Act. Furthermore, despite difficulties that were perceived at the time, the superintending constable system was an important transitional phase in the policing of the West Riding, providing significant elements of continuity, in terms of personnel and policing practice, which linked the 'old' police with the more 'closely supervised' 'new' police.[2]

The Parish Constable Acts of 1842 and 1850 were an important element in the mid-nineteenth century debate on policing. A number of counties, notably Kent and Cheshire – both at the forefront of thinking on police reform – adopted the superintending constable system in an attempt to introduce 'some measure of professional policing' into the old parish constable system.[3] The 1842 Act provided for the appointment of superintending constables, paid for by the county and responsible to quarter sessions, but linked these appointments to the establishment of lock-ups. The 1850 Act dropped this requirement and enabled the appointment of superintending constables with oversight of all unpaid and paid parochial constables in any petty sessional division. This system has been criticised by several police historians as little more than a dead-end, being unable to deal with anything other than relatively minor offences.[4] While many superintending constables were professional, it has been argued that the men under their command, the parish constables, 'were not, and had no intention of becoming such'.[5] Even more sympathetic historians have argued that 'their great defect was particularly felt in cases where they had to deal with serious violence, robberies and burglaries'.[6] Even in counties heavily committed to the superintending constable system, by the mid-1850s magistrates were convinced that a system heavily reliant upon parochial constables could not deliver the protection deemed necessary at the time.[7]

Much of the evidence on which these judgments rest is drawn from proponents of county-based police forces, many of whom had direct experience of the much vaunted Essex county force.[8] Witnesses from county forces, in addition to extolling the virtues of their own forces, condemned failures in neighbouring counties. Captain John Woodford of the Lancashire County Constabulary lamented the 'want of a proper police establishment in Yorkshire' and complained of the 'great disorder and rioting in Yorkshire, immediately over the borders of Lancashire'.[9] Given the volume of contemporary criticism, the decision of the Yorkshire magistrates to implement the superintending constable system requires some explanation and this can be found in their debates in the 1840s.[10] Financial considerations undoubtedly played an important part, not least the fear that relatively quiet rural areas would be unfairly burdened by the cost of a county police, but many of the magistrates were confident that traditional parish-based policing could be modernised. Within months of the passing of the 1842 Act, the county magistrates received applications for the appointment of superintending constables from eighteen towns, including Bradford, Huddersfield and Halifax, even though in only four were lock-ups already in existence.[11] In view of the set-up costs involved, the magistrates proceeded with caution. In June 1843 they voted that lock-ups be provided and superintending constables appointed for Bradford, Knaresborough, Dewsbury, Halifax and Huddersfield.[12] More superintending constables were subsequently approved and by the time of the 1852/3 Select Committee twenty-two had been appointed, covering almost all of the county.[13] Among the first was Thomas Heaton who assumed responsibility for the Upper Agbrigg district in June 1848 and held the post until December 1856, at which point he became superintendent of the Upper Agbrigg division of the newly-founded WRCC.[14] Little is known about Heaton when he first took up office, despite being presented to the county magistrates as 'the unanimous choice of the Huddersfield bench from a number of candidates' by proposers who paid 'a high compliment to his character and qualifications'.[15] He had had a seventeen-year career in local government, first as clerk to the Board of Highways and later as poor-law relieving officer for Huddersfield.[16] There is no record of his views on policing at the time but, from later comments he made to newly sworn-in parochial constables, he believed in a causal link between gambling, drinking and criminality. In his mind the contamination that followed from the intermixing of petty and serious criminals added urgency to his task of controlling beerhouses and brothels. As superintending constable, Heaton had responsibility for the local lock-up and for the oversight of annually-appointed parochial constables and any paid constables in the district.[17] Although appointed by the county magistrates, he was expected to work closely with their local counterparts.[18] The magistrates (both county and local) saw the dissemination of information and the regulation of parochial constables as central aspects of his work but also expected him to play an active role, including cooperating with existing local law-enforcement agencies, particularly the Woollen Inspectorate that dated from the late-eighteenth century.[19] Taken together, though never formally defined, these elements constituted the superintending constable system as it operated in Upper Agbrigg.

The central role of superintending constable was challenging and Heaton, though relatively old and inexperienced on appointment, proved to be a highly active police-officer. To dismiss him simply as a 'neighbourhood pest' does not do justice to the scope of his activities, nor to his beliefs about the causes of crime.[20] He was undoubtedly greatly exercised by illegal, out-of-hours drinking and 'unacceptable' working-class leisure activities. In particular, he set his sights on those 'vile places, [the] sinks of iniquity and vice', the beershops in Castlegate, but his net was cast wider.[21] Success was hard to come by. An early attempt to tame Guy Fawkes celebrations in the town's market square was an ignominious short-term defeat. The sight of a mud-sodden police superintendent, his uniform torn, struggling to his feet, as young men kicked out at him, did little for dignity or reputation.[22] Heaton was undeterred and continued his energetic attack on local crime.[23] His pre-occupation with breaches of the licensing laws, especially at Easter, Christmas and during local feasts; his determination to stop young men taking part in 'nude' races or playing pitch and toss* in the highway; and his willingness to use arcane and ancient pieces of legislation to prosecute make him appear a driven and somewhat ridiculous figure.[24] Above all he kept a close eye on publicans and beer-house keepers who sold liquor outside licensing hours (and particularly during the hours of divine service), and on their customers, and brought many of them to court. His methods could be dramatic. Suspecting malpractice at the *Horse and Groom*, Linthwaite, one Sunday in the summer of 1852, he drove there from Huddersfield, 'ran round the front door and met two men coming out'. Suspicions roused by the fact that 'the passage was wet here and there, as if some liquor had recently been spilled' he entered the bar to find 'a can containing about a quart of ale of fresh-drawn ale, having the froth upon it.'[25] In another case his detective skills came to the fore when he raided a Lindley beer-house, run by a Mr. Walker. As the press reported the case, 'the superintendent spied some wet marks upon the [beer-house] table which Mrs Walker said were caused by her child's breakfast cup; but the cup would not fit the impression. Looking under the settle [Heaton] saw a beer glass and on the carpet alongside its recent contents'.[26] Individual cases do not do full justice to Heaton's commitment. Take for example a day's work in the winter of 1852. In the morning, while out in his gig, he found the landlords of both the *Sovereign Inn* and the *Star Inn* in Fenay Bridge serving drinks illegally between 10 and

---

* Pitch and toss was one of the most common forms of gambling. Players would pitch coins at a mark (or a wall) and the person closest to the mark had the right to toss all the coins into the air, winning all those landing heads up. Variations were to be found in different parts of the country. Rudyard Kipling, in his much-loved poem *If*, seen by some as a guide to manliness, extols the virtue of being able to shrug off the loss of 'all your winnings' on a game of pitch and toss!

11 a.m. Continuing on his way, just before midday he came across some young men, playing pitch and toss and causing an obstruction in the road, near Shepley, whom he apprehended and summonsed, before arriving at the *Sovereign Inn*, Shepley, where he found the landlord selling alcohol out of hours. Not content with that haul, between 3 and 4 p.m. he found time to catch the landlord of the *Star Inn*, Shelley, and a beer-house keeper in Netherton similarly breaking the law. In total he had travelled over 20 miles that day in his pursuit of lawbreakers. All were subsequently prosecuted; and the precise date – the 25th of December, Christmas Day![27] Much of his time was concerned with petty crime, particularly non-violent theft. Heaton arrested servants who had stolen linen and clothing from their masters and mistresses; workmen who had stolen from their employers; and workmates who had stolen from each other. In most cases little in the way of detective skills was required as the stolen goods were quickly pawned and there was a good working relationship between local pawnbrokers and the police, which regularly resulted in the latter reporting suspicious characters to the authorities.[28] Heaton was nothing if not tenacious and patient. James Aspinall stole and subsequently hid money from his employer. He confessed and Heaton arrested him and took him to the county lock-up, where 'he was placed in an upstairs room … [Heaton] alone remaining with him' through the night. The wait was worthwhile as 'at four o'clock in the morning in the ordinary course of nature a sovereign and two half-sovereigns (£2) passed from his body and were identified as the property of the prosecutor'.[29]

Heaton's police methods made him unpopular. Using men in plain clothes led to accusations of introducing a despotic 'Austrian' spy system while, more mundanely, checking public houses and beerhouses as soon as the church bells stopped ringing gave rise to charges of unreasonable zealotry. Undoubtedly Heaton was at odds with late-night drinkers, cockfighters and players of pitch and toss, but he was not acting simply on his own beliefs and initiatives. The local magistrates repeatedly stressed the importance of containing and restricting gambling and illegal drinking at the annual swearing-in of parochial constables; and many local organisations and individuals were similarly concerned with the threat posed by working-class leisure activities and particularly by the 'wild, rough youths of the neighbourhood'.[30] The scale of police activities and their success in marginalising pastimes such as cockfighting and prize fighting in the early and mid-1850s was considerable, not least at a time when the advent of the railway made it easier for people to travel to such 'sports' from miles around. When Heaton first took office, well-organised and well-attended fights took place not just close by the town, notably on Castle Hill, but even in Castlegate itself. Acting in line with the local magistrates' condemnation of the 'disgraceful pastime' of dogfighting in particular, Heaton, sometimes alone, at other times accompanied by two or three constables, first succeeded in disrupting such events and dispersing the crowds and then gradually drove them into remoter locations further into the Pennines.[31] By the mid-1850s, to escape 'the vigilance of Superintendent Heaton, battles [cock fights] are generally fought among the moors and thinly populated districts on the confines of Yorkshire, Lancashire and Cheshire'.[32] Even then Heaton continued his campaign despite the more difficult terrain on which the fights took place. For instance, forewarned of a cockfight that was to take place on an isolated farm, close to the *Victoria Inn*, Upper Maythorn, over ten miles from Huddersfield, Heaton and two police officers were able to arrest and bring to trial the major protagonists.[33] This success (and it was not unique) was the product of Heaton's personal determination and his ability to coordinate the activities of parochial officers.

Although Heaton's campaign against petty crime had its limits, there was a greater degree of effectiveness than is often suggested by police historians with their eye to a model of policing that was to triumph in 1856. However, the question remains: could the superintending constable system cope with public disturbances and serious crime? The evidence from the Huddersfield district suggests that it could. Despite the turbulent history of the town and the surrounding district in the late-1840s, Heaton, as superintending constable, had to deal with only one major incident of public disorder. Early in his career, in April 1849, there was an 'alarming riot' at Milnsbridge, just under two miles outside the town, involving the navvies building the Manchester to Huddersfield railway. Tensions fuelled by the non-payment of wages were exacerbated by hostility between English and Irish labourers. Acting on a tip-off that the Irish were planning to drive out the English workers, Heaton arrived while the men were being paid out and managed to arrest and handcuff seven suspected ringleaders. This sparked the riot. An eighth man 'set up one of those dismal yells peculiar to the Irish' which led to a full-scale assault by a crowd estimated to be 500 or 600 strong. Heaton, unable to prevent the rescue of the prisoners, managed to send word to Huddersfield requesting reinforcements. Abraham Milnes and twelve men, constituting 'the whole of the night watch' duly arrived. The rioters were eventually put to flight and twenty-nine men (including but two of the original arrestees) were brought to the town's two lock-ups. Eventually fourteen men were found guilty at York Assizes of conspiracy, riot and assault.[34] It would be foolish to generalise from one incident but the Milnsbridge riot revealed both the immense self-confidence of Heaton and, more importantly, the ability of the local police to come together and successfully contain a major disturbance.

Heaton, who often worked closely with the town constables, Sedgwick and Townend, was also determined to bring to justice high-profile local criminals, such as John Sutcliffe and Henry 'Slasher' Wilson. Almost from the day he took up post Heaton determined to bring to book John Sutcliffe, the notorious 'King of Castlegate' and a few years later Heaton showed equal commitment in prosecuting 'Slasher' Wilson. His involvement with serious crime was not restricted to local 'celebrity' criminals. His skills of detection enabled him to arrest three weavers guilty of a particularly bloody assault in nearby Kirkheaton; one of several such cases with which he dealt in the winter of 1849/50.[35] Most serious crime was more mundane. Thefts of cloth were not uncommon. In 1851, for example, his investigation of the theft of thirty-two yards of cloth from William Ashton, a cloth-dresser of Folly Hall, brought him to a beershop in Sheffield where the stolen material was being sold.[36] Heaton was also successful in a safe-breaking case at Meltham Mills, 'a robbery of somewhat extraordinary character both as to boldness in design and dexterity in execution', which brought nationwide coverage.[37] Horse thefts, similarly, were relatively common occurrences and offered him opportunities to demonstrate his skill and determination in apprehending law-breakers. On more than one occasion, Heaton came into conflict with the Seniors, father and three sons, a well-known family of horse thieves who also carried on 'a wholesome trade in horse flesh'.[38] Heaton's 'persevering and unceasing activity', involving a trip to London to arrest one of the sons, finally led to the arrest of three of the four men. Not for the last time there was a touch of the melodramatic. Having traced them to their dwelling in Lowerhouses, Heaton had the house surrounded. Two men were arrested but it was feared that George Senior had escaped. Heaton led the search of the house and

> on examining the bedroom chimney ... found the extremities of the unfortunate culprit dangling down the chimney within reach. Mr Heaton seized hold of the legs but found Senior had squeezed himself so unmercifully into the small aperture as to require the utmost exertion to release him.[39]

Heaton gave evidence at Senior's trial at York Assizes and was praised by the magistrates for his perseverance.[40]

Heaton's undoubted enthusiasm and success in pursuing petty and serious criminals could, nonetheless, be seen to confirm the judgement of the 1852/3 Select Committee, namely that individual superintending constables could be 'useful as police officers'. However, there was more than individual commitment. This can be seen, firstly, in the way in which he cooperated with other formal and informal law-enforcement agencies and, secondly, in the way in which he worked with both unpaid and paid constables.

The most important of the local law-enforcement agencies was the Huddersfield and Holmfirth Manufacturers' Association, whose chief inspector was R. H. Kaye, who regularly prosecuted under the Worsted Act. On numerous occasions Kaye and Heaton took action on behalf of the Manufacturers' Association, bringing men and women before the local magistrates.[41] Often there was a suspicion that stolen material was being sold in local public houses and beerhouses and on several occasions Kaye was involved in police raids on licensed premises.[42] A similar pattern of cooperation can be seen with the prosecution of local 'whisky spinners'; that is, men and women operating illicit stills.[43] This was a matter for the local Inland Revenue Officer, Mr. Wallis, who needed to work with the police who had the power of arrest. Intriguingly, in at least one raid Wallis was accompanied by Kaye (the Woollen Inspector) as well as Heaton.[44] Significantly, local manufacturers and magistrates expressed themselves satisfied with the effectiveness of such policing arrangements.

The relationship between Heaton and the various local prosecution societies is less easy to establish. Such societies were to be found in the 1850s in Holmfirth, Kirkburton, Lindley, Longwood, Marsh, Meltham and Saddleworth. All claimed to be 'prosperous' and 'efficient' but much of their time was devoted to giving salutary lessons to young boys guilty of trespass and the like. There were, however, more serious concerns. Following a successful arrest for robbery with violence, the Meltham society gave a reward of £10 to their local parish constable; likewise the Saddleworth society gave rewards of £2 and £4 to local constables for their 'active exertions in detecting offenders' and the Longwood society bestowed praise (and a small memento) on Superintendent Heaton for 'the tact and energy that he displayed' in capturing a gang of burglars.[45] The importance of such societies and their actions must not be overstated but the fact remains that they did have links with parochial constables and the superintending constable, which could lead to successful prosecutions.

The greatest weakness of the superintending constable system, in the eyes of nineteenth-century police reformers and later historians, was its dependence upon parochial constables (unpaid and paid) who were simply not willing or able to be effective officers. Locally, the *Leeds Mercury*, ever-ready to criticize and deride Heaton, thought little more of the men under him. It observed sarcastically that 'it is amusing to read the recorded exploits of the parochial constables in the Huddersfield district, many of whom are wretchedly deficient in that tact and resolution in the discharge of their duties'.[46] There were also some concerns expressed in the local Huddersfield press about the lack of cooperation, though the local magistracy continued to view the parochial constables as 'indispensable officials'.[47] It is clear that Heaton made a conscious attempt to create a more coordinated and effective system. He advised parish constables of their duties and on occasion disciplined those who neglected them.[48] He tried assiduously to 'communicate frequently' with the constables in his district, which was no easy task in a district that had some 181 parochial constables in thirty-one locations.[49] In addition, the local magistrates, on swearing in the parochial constables, regularly recommended 'a small book of instruction for them' that had been compiled by Heaton as early as 1848.[50] Predictably it put emphasis on the need to keep public houses and beerhouses under close scrutiny and to guard against gambling, 'the greatest evil in the district'.[51]

It would be naïve to suggest that there were not shortcomings in this parish-based system. On a number of occasions, the meetings called to nominate parish constables were poorly attended; on other occasions, questions were raised about the number and quality of men being put forward. However, it would be misleading to suggest – as many police reformers did at the time – that parish constables were uniformly decrepit and incompetent. Ultimately, it is impossible to offer a precise evaluation of the quality of parochial constables in Upper Agbrigg in the 1850s. Undoubtedly a small minority were totally incompetent, if not verging on the corrupt. John Halliday, one of the Kirkheaton constables, was described as 'a fatherly Dogberry', while constables in Longwood and Lindley were dismissed in similar 'worthy Dogberry' terms.[52] Ephraim Kaye, a Dalton constable from 1851 to 1854 appears to have had more success at the Kirkheaton horticultural show than in the courts.[53] Many more were well-intentioned but hampered by the fact that they were unpaid constables and had to look elsewhere for their income. John Cooper, elected parochial officer for Fartown in 1855 was a carpenter and wheelwright who spent more time earning a living than enforcing the law.[54] However, there were also some – again a minority but too easily overlooked – who were competent and aspired to be 'professional' in terms of their conduct, their commitment to enforcing the law and their ability to establish a degree of order and decorum even in localities such as Kirkheaton, Kirkburton and Scammonden, all known for their hostility to the police.[55] Francis Goodall, first appointed as parish constable for Marsden-in-Almondbury in 1851 was praised for 'doing all that one man could do to preserve order' and his 'vigilance and successful efforts to preserve the peace' at Marsden Feast in 1852 brought praise, especially as he was one of the unpaid [constables] to boot'.[56] William Taylor, a long-serving constable in Honley, was a well-respected local figure. Much of his work involved drunks and itinerant hawkers but he played an important part, along with Inspector Kaye and John Earnshaw, the Holmfirth constable, in a serious embezzlement case that saw five men brought to trial.[57] Similarly, Matthew Riley, a Berry Brow constable, effected a number of arrests for theft (and one case of highway robbery) as well as prosecuting dogfighters and offending local landlords.[58] Riley's enthusiasm brought him a rebuke from the magistrates who dismissed a case against the keeper of the *Morning Star* beerhouse and told him 'You've been too hasty, Matthew'.[59] The laughter in court was a blow to pride but Riley also suffered blows to the body on several occasions. In April 1850 two men were charged with assaulting Riley during an attempted prisoner rescue. The case was dismissed, 'an announcement which seemed to give great satisfaction to a crowd of spectators from Berry Brow' and the *Chronicle* noted that Riley was 'not very popular among the working classes'.[60] Other parochial constables stand out for their assiduousness, none more so than the long-serving Holmfirth constable, John Earnshaw, who dealt with a wide variety of crimes, both petty and serious. Like Heaton he brought charges against landlords who served alcohol outside hours and prosecuted lads who played pitch and toss on the roads; and also, like Heaton, he could be 'indefatigable in his endeavours'.[61] More importantly, on several occasions Earnshaw worked with, or on the instructions of, Heaton. In September 1851 offending publicans in Honley were brought before the magistrates after a joint action between Heaton, Earnshaw and the local parish constables. Three months later the two were in action against beerhouse owners in Holmfirth, who were permitting gambling on their property.[62] The recognition by local magistrates of the 'efficient services of Constable Earnshaw' reflected local satisfaction with parochial policing. Earnshaw was the most active parochial constable in the Huddersfield district but he was not alone. John Shaw, the Marsden-in-Huddersfield constable, was another man who worked with Heaton on a number of occasions; nor was Earnshaw the most controversial.[63] That dubious accolade fell to the parochial constables for Birkby and Fartown, Nathaniel Hinchcliffe and Miles Netherwood, who were first appointed in 1852. Netherwood, described by a local magistrate as 'an efficient constable', often worked with Hinchcliffe, bringing several offending landlords and gamblers to court. This made them unpopular in certain quarters and liable to physical attack. In 1855 Hinchcliffe was assaulted by a group of men as he tried to make an arrest at a local public house, the *New Inn*, Cowcliffe. Netherwood came to his aid but the prisoner was rescued and the two constables 'abused and assaulted … in the public road'.[64] There were also legal challenges to their nomination as constables. In February 1854 Netherwood's nomination was almost overturned by a group of rate-payers led by the landlord of another local public house, the *Lamb Inn*, at Hillhouse, against whom Netherwood had given evidence in court.[65] The following year the two men were not appointed as parochial constables, following accusations of illegal drinking, exacting 'a kind of blackmail' and assault. Two of the three incidents brought to the attention of the magistrates involved the *Lamb Inn*, Hillhouse.

Matters did not end there as both men were nominated as parochial constables, albeit at a poorly attended meeting the following year.[66] At the swearing-in meeting before the magistrates in April 1856, the solicitor, who had spoken against the two men the previous year, again raised objections. This time Heaton gave evidence on their behalf, claiming 'no two constables had taken such pain ... to discharge their duty efficiently' and singled out Hinchcliffe for particular praise, being, in Heaton's opinion, the 'most efficient man in the township'. The magistrates agreed and appointed both Hinchcliffe and Netherwood: a decision that 'appeared to give great satisfaction to a crowded court'.[67] The *Chronicle* made no editorial comment but the *Examiner* was scathing of the two men, allegedly known for their 'officious intermeddling'. Heaton was criticised for supporting them, the *Examiner* claiming that he 'knew his men ... and used them as his pliant tools'. Netherwood and Hinchcliffe were condemned for doing 'the dirty work at the bidding of the superintendent' and the bench of magistrates was condemned for forcing 'two obnoxious, meddling constables on the ratepayers'.[68] In fact, the situation was less clear cut. The memorial opposing Netherwood had been signed by over one hundred people but an equal number had supported his nomination. Indeed, supporters of Netherwood and Hinchcliffe argued that attempts were being made to discredit the men 'simply because they had done so much to put down gambling'. The chairman of the bench, George Armitage, agreed, referring to a 'conspiracy' against two men for doing their duty. In a telling observation one supporter of Netherwood and Hinchcliffe argued that 'it was necessary for Mr. Heaton to have men with whom he could work as constables'.[69] Whatever the merits of the case, and much remains obscure, it is clear that Heaton was trying to build up a group of men with whom he could work in his fight against both petty and serious crime; but it was equally clear that this gave rise to very real tensions in certain quarters.

In terms of foreshadowing later reform, the emergence of a small group of paid constables was of greater significance. The Parish Constable Acts had provided for the appointment of a paid constable by any township that wished to do so; and the West Riding magistrates exhorted local ratepayers to take advantage of this provision more than once. One local J.P. argued specifically that the various townships in the Huddersfield district could raise £400 through contributions of £10 to £15 each, which would make possible the appointment of five or six constables under Superintendent Heaton.[70] The suggestion was not acted upon but paid constables were appointed in several townships, including

Kirkburton, Marsden, Marsh and Meltham. The appointment in Marsh was uncontroversial – indeed the absence of trouble at the local feast that year (1854) was seen as evidence of his good influence on the community – while the appointment in Marsden was welcomed and the constable praised for the 'untiring zeal' with which he discharged his duties.[71] From Heaton's perspective this boded well as here were yet more local constables with whom he could work.

Elsewhere matters were more problematic, most particularly in Kirkburton. A paid constable was first appointed as early as 1850 but had met with 'a very warm but unsuccessful opposition'. The 'poorer classes' determined to 'nurse their wrath' and Constable Glover was assaulted in 'the most cowardly and clandestinely manner' on a number of occasions.[72] Matters escalated and in February 1851 local feelings 'assumed a more excited tone, and burst out in all its pent-up vehemence at a town's meeting'.[73] The meeting voted to dispense with the paid constable at the end of his period of service but it soon became apparent that 'the manufacturers seem determined to retain the present paid constable, while the working classes seem determined to dispense with his services'.[74] There followed an acrimonious legal dispute in which 'Mr Roberts of Manchester, the high-profile radical lawyer W. P. Roberts, represented those working men seeking to dispense with the paid constable. Ultimately the challenge failed and the paid constable remained in post for another year.[75] The extent of his continuing unpopularity soon became evident. In the following months the windows of his house were broken by stones and he was physically assaulted on at least two occasions. One assault led to a trial for cutting and wounding with intent to inflict grievous bodily harm, for which sentences of seven years' transportation and twelve months' hard labour were handed down.[76] It is all but impossible to establish the specific causes of the friction between Glover and certain sections of the Kirkburton community but his close association with certain local employers did not help; nor did his zealousness in 'moving on' people and enforcing the licensing laws. Whatever the precise reasons for his unpopularity, no paid constable was subsequently appointed in Kirkburton.

A similar set of difficulties emerged in Meltham, where the question of the appointment of a paid constable was debated for several years. For some local ratepayers the 'drinking, swearing, gambling, racing and all sorts of *immoralities*' demonstrated the need for reform but others felt the concerns were overstated and the parochial constable more than adequate.[77]

Reports of the debate in 1855 are more detailed and indicate a polarisation of views and considerable animosity. The situation was not helped by the misplaced zeal of the unpaid parochial constable, whose 'considerable desire to put down all immorality' led to 'sweeping charges without proof', in the view of the magistrates at the annual Brewster Sessions.[78] The *Chronicle* reported 'a great deal of prejudice against a paid constable' and, along with the *Examiner*, referred somewhat enigmatically to 'party spirit' running high on the subject.[79] In a poll only sixteen people voted for a paid constable while 129 voted against but this was not the end of the matter. In February 1856 an officer was appointed, paid for by 'a few [unspecified] gentlemen'.[80] Despite a claim that this was 'very generally approved' the new constable (former Inspector Sedgwick, recently of the Huddersfield town police) was assaulted soon after taking up post and a few weeks later had the windows of his house broken by stones.[81] As in Kirkburton, the intrusion of the police into working-class leisure activities appears to have been crucial.

Although there were a number of energetic parochial and paid constables in various parts of the Huddersfield district under Heaton's authority, the question remains: could they be brought together, when needed, to act more as a force rather than as individuals? As noted above, Heaton worked with various constables on several occasions.[82] There were also times when he worked in conjunction with several constables in a pre-planned operation. The most spectacular example was the apprehension of the Wibsey gang in which Heaton worked with another superintending constable, three parochial constables, a paid constable and two other men with previous police experience.[83] The theft of ten pieces of cloth, valued at over £100, from a warehouse just outside Huddersfield caused a stir in August 1856.[84] The subsequent conviction of the so-called Wibsey gang was a triumph for Heaton and the men who had worked with him over several weeks in bringing the gang to trial. The first problem was to locate the stolen goods. Having been tipped off that the stolen cloth had not been 'sprung' [disposed of] but was still in the locality, Heaton called upon the experienced Sedgwick. Together they spent a whole day searching various possible hiding places before coming across eight of the ten stolen pieces of cloth concealed in a false roof in a dis-used church (now used as a school) in Quarmby, two miles from the centre of Huddersfield. There followed a period of surveillance. For a week Heaton and six constables maintained a nightly vigil, secreted in a mistal [a cowshed or byre] opposite the school, awaiting the return of the gang. The final act saw the spectacular arrest of six men during some dramatic events on the night of the 3rd of September 1856. At about 11 p.m. the gang came to collect the stolen cloth. The police were now hidden behind bushes, not far from the look-out set by the gang. The trap almost failed because 'one of the officers was troubled with a cough and Mr Heaton, to prevent him coughing and thus alarming the thieves gave him a lozenge'. It was to no avail: 'at this very moment ... the man left on watch ... called out "all away"' and a meleé ensued as the police sought to retrieve the situation. After a lengthy struggle two men were captured, one having been laid low by 'a terrific blow on the back of the head with his [Heaton's] stick'. The four other men fled the scene but, not to be thwarted, Heaton, who had recognised some of the gang members, ordered 'a coach with a pair of the best horses in Huddersfield' at 3 a.m. and set off with his men the fifteen miles to a beerhouse in Wyke Common (near Bradford) at which lived one of the gang whom Heaton had seen fleeing the school. The first arrests were made at 5 a.m. after Heaton 'hit one of the men, whose nose bled profusely'. The other gang members, including an accomplice who had not been at Huddersfield, were quickly apprehended, with the stolen goods, skeleton keys and other house-breaking tools found in their possession. The final arrest was made at 9 a.m., almost twelve hours after the police operation had begun, when Heaton personally seized the last gang member as he lay in bed in his house at nearby Wibsey Slack, outside Bradford.

Eventually five men were tried at Leeds Quarter Sessions in October 1856 and, in a widely-reported trial, found guilty and each sentenced to eight years' penal servitude. The chairman of the magistrates singled out Heaton for a £10 gratuity because 'very great credit was due to him' but also added that 'the activity, vigilance, zeal and patience of the Superintendent and the police are creditable to them in the highest degree'.[85] This was not a unique case. There had been a similar collaborative effort in the summer of the previous year. In August 1855 a major dogfight, reported as a clash between Lancashire and Yorkshire, was arranged to take place in a field behind the *Shepherd's Boy Inn* in Marsden. A crowd of between 400 and 500 assembled but Heaton mustered 'several parochial constables' of whom four were initially sent into action by Heaton, who had 'given them previous instructions what to do'.[86] The fight was broken up and forty-three men, including beerhouse keepers, labourers, miners and weavers were brought to trial.[87]

Conclusion

From these and other examples a picture emerges of a small core of men, maybe no more than ten or twelve in number, upon whom Heaton relied in enforcing the law in the Huddersfield district. However, while there was an important degree of coordination and cooperation in policing within this petty sessional district, there is little evidence to suggest similar action between the superintending constables and parochial constables of different districts, who for the most part focussed upon the problems within their localities and only infrequently helped out elsewhere.[88]

The superintending constable system was less inefficient than commonly claimed. There were a number of long-serving and capable men, though none matched Thomas Heaton in terms of his energy and resourcefulness in dealing with both petty and serious crime. Heaton's career demonstrates that it was possible to mobilise a combination of parochial and paid constables as well as working with other local law-enforcement agencies in a campaign against crime. That said, it is important to recognise the limitations of this system. In February 1857 Heaton was presented with a silver snuff box by the Longwood Prosecution Society in recognition of his astuteness and perseverance in bringing the Wibsey gang to trial and of the general 'high estimation' in which he was held. In his response Heaton made predictable reference to his commitment to make property and person safe but added that 'this had been a very difficult task, until the new system of police [the WRCC] had been brought into operation'.[89] Nonetheless, the superintending constable system paved the way for the introduction of the WRCC in terms of personnel, policy priorities and policing practice.[90] There was, therefore, a less dramatic discontinuity in 1856/7 than commonly suggested. Prior to the advent of the WRCC, Heaton, along with the paid constables and more active parochial constables in the Huddersfield district, had found through experience the limitations of proactive policing. They developed a *modus vivendi* with the communities they policed. They learnt that there were very real limits to police powers and that winning consent required discretion, knowing as much how far or when *not* to act. The enforcement of the licensing laws provides a good example of Heaton's approach. Prosecutions were brought to show that the law could not be flouted but, on several occasions, he only sought costs if there were extenuating circumstances. Similarly, at the annual Brewster's Sessions, he only objected to the licences of the most frequent and blatant transgressors. He was not wholly successful, nor did lessons learnt guarantee success after 1857. Nonetheless, the experience gained under the superintending constable system proved useful in the early years of the new county-wide force. Ultimately the superintending constable system failed to provide a robust alternative to county-wide forces. However, it was not a dead-end but rather an intermediate stage on another route to 'new' policing in England and Wales. Superintending constables like Thomas Heaton and parochial officers, like John Earnshaw, who strove to make a reformed parish-constable system work, were part of a broader tradition of local policing initiatives, which can be traced back to the late-eighteenth and early-nineteenth centuries, and which contributed to the complexity and dynamism of policing before the 'new' police.

Endnotes

1 Similar approaches to reformed rural policing can be seen in the proposals of the semi-professional, entrepreneurial Bedfordshire constable, J.H. Warden and the Hampshire magistrate, Sir Thomas Baring in the 1820s and 1830s respectively discussed in R D Storch, 'Policing Rural Southern England before the Police', in D Hay & F Snyder, eds., *Policing and Prosecution in Britain, 1750–1850,* Oxford University Press, 1989, esp. pp.217–9.

2 C A Williams, *Police Control Systems in Britain, 1775–1975,* Manchester University Press, 2014, p.52. Williams also stresses the proletarianised nature of the 'new' police.

3 R D Storch & D Philips, *Policing Provincial England, 1829–1856: The Politics of Reform, London,* Leicester University Press, 1999, p.215. See also C Emsley, *The English Police: A Social and Political History,* 2nd ed., Hemel Hempstead, Longman, 1996, pp.47-9. Buckinghamshire, Herefordshire and Lincolnshire also adopted this system.

4 T A Critchley, *A History of Police in England and Wales, London,* Constable, 1978, p.93, Emsley, *English Police, pp.*47–9 and 249, and S H Palmer, *Police and Protest in England and Ireland, 1780–1850,* Cambridge University Press, 1990, p.449.

5 Emsley, *English Police*, p.39.

6 D Philips, *Crime and Authority in Victorian England,* London, Croom Helm, 1977, p.62.

7 Philips and Storch, *Policing Provincial England,* p.231 but see also p.216-8. This conclusion is based on the direct evidence from Buckinghamshire and the assumption that 'similar cautiously negative conclusions were being drawn elsewhere' (p.218) but this was not the case in the West Riding of Yorkshire.

8 For a more detailed discussion see D Taylor, '" No remedy for the inefficiencies of Parochial Constables": Superintending constables and the transition to 'new' policing in the West Riding of Yorkshire in the third quarter of the nineteenth century', *Crime History & Societies,* 2015, 19(1), pp.67–88, esp. pp.68–70. Much of the evidence is drawn from the partisan First Report of the Select Committee on Police, *Parliamentary Papers,* 1852 (603). See especially the evidence of William Hamilton, esp. QQ *1014*–5; and of David Smith Second Report, 1852–3, (715) esp. QQ 3672 and 3691–2.

9 First report of the Select Committee on Police, 1852 (603). Evidence of Capt. J Woodford, First Report, esp. QQ 1693 and 1699.

10 *LM,* 18 April, 12 & 26 September 1840 and 17 April 1841; *Sheff.I,* 1 July 1843 HC, 10 April 1852. See also Philips & Storch, *Policing Provincial England*, p.202–6.

11 *B.Obs,* 29 June 1843 and *Sheff.I,* 1 July 1843.

12 West Riding Quarter Sessions Committees: Minutes and Reports, Lock-up Committee Minutes, 1843–59. 3 April 1843 meeting, p.1; 5 May 1843 meeting, p.5 and 9 June meeting, p.8. *West Yorkshire Archive:* Wakefield QC/4. *B.Obs,* 29 June 1843 and *Sheff.I,* 1 July 1843.

13 Seven were superintendents of lock-ups and parish constables and fifteen for parish constables only. *Parliamentary Papers, 1852*–3 (675) Returns of Superintendent Constables.

14 The Huddersfield district comprised the parishes of Almondbury, Kirkburton and Kirkheaton and also that part of the parish of Rochdale (roughly speaking the Saddleworth district) that fell in the West Riding of Yorkshire. In addition, it included the parish of Huddersfield but not the area covered by the town's improvement act of 1848. Part of Heaton's salary was paid by Huddersfield ratepayers within the limits of the act and, as a consequence, Heaton was expected to render assistance when asked by the superintendent of Huddersfield police.

15 *B.Obs,* 29 June 1848.

16 The relieving officers were essentially the front-line forces of the New Poor Law, determining the fate of those applying for relief. Hostility to the New Poor Law was particularly strong in Huddersfield.

17 *Sheff.I,* 1 July 1843.

18 For the relationship between magistrates and chief constables in the late nineteenth century see J Leigh, Early County Chief Constables in the north of England, 1880–1905, unpublished Ph.D. thesis, Open University, 2013, esp. chap. three.

19 The Worsted Acts and the committees responsible for prosecution were the most important weapons used against workplace embezzlement. B Godfrey, 'Judicial impartiality and the use of the criminal law against labour', *Crime, History & Societies,* 1999, 3(2), pp.47–72 describes 'the worsted committee and their inspectors' as 'a private, state-funded detection and prosecution agency', p.58 fn.5. See also B Godfrey and D J Cox, *Policing the Factory: Theft, Private*

Policing and the Law in Modern England, London, Bloomsbury, 2013, and for prosecution societies see D Philips, 'Good Men to Associate and Bad Men to Conspire: Associations for the Prosecution of Felons in England, 1760–1860' in Hay & Snyder, *Policing and Prosecution.*

20 R D Storch, 'The Policeman as Domestic Missionary' *Journal of Social History,* 1976, 9, pp.481–509 at p.484.

21 *LM, 24* September 1848. The attack on Beerhouse Brothels is discussed above in chapter five.

22 Interestingly, this was the last time that 'traditional' November 5th celebrations took place in the centre of Huddersfield. For a general discussion of the 'problem' of working-class leisure see H Cunningham, *Leisure in the Industrial Revolution*, London, Croom Helm, 1980. Many of the 'rioters' were otherwise respectable young middle-class men who resented Heaton's interference.

23 The extent to which Heaton's concern with Sabbath-breaking was driven by religious beliefs is unclear. He makes no explicit reference to his personal beliefs when bringing prosecutions but, in a town with strong non-conformist traditions he may well have had a strong religious belief but one that he did not feel it appropriate to articulate. It is clear that other enthusiastic figures, such as William Payne, acted on strong religious beliefs.

24 See *HC,* 3 June & 29 July 1854. Among his more bizarre but successful prosecutions was that of a seventy-year old man for shaving (another man) on a Sunday. On another occasion he prosecuted three men for watching a cricket-match, also on a Sunday, but the case was thrown out.

25 *HC,* 7 Aug. 1852. See also similar cases in Almondbury (*HEx*, 14 August 1852), Milnsbridge (*HEx*, 7 August 1852) and the Isle of Skye (*HEx*, 5 February 1853).

26 *HC,* 10 Jun. 1854.

27 *HC,* 8 Jan. 1853. Nor was this a one-off event. See *HC,* 9 Jan. 1858 for details of another of Heaton's Christmas Day peregrinations. The earliest reference to Heaton's Christmas visiting comes from 1850 when a beer-house keeper in the village of Berry Brow fell foul of him but the Superintendent must have been somewhat provoked by the name of the beer-house – *Exchange Evil for Good!*

28 See for example *HEx,* 23 February 1854 and *HC,* 3 January, 26 June & 18 December 1852; 29 January, 11 June, 2 & 9 July 1853, 20 January 1855 & 16 February 1856. See D Taylor, *Policing the Victorian Town: The Development of the Police in Middlesbrough, c.1840–1914,* Basingstoke, Macmillan, 2002, chapter four for an analysis of crime in Middlesbrough in the North Riding of Yorkshire.

29 *HC,* 29 January 1853. See also 14 December 1850, 11 January, 22 February & 28 June 1851, 7 August 1852, & 15 October 1853 and *HEx*, 3 June 1854.

30 *HC,* 16 June 1855. For a more general discussion of anxiety over working-class juvenile leisure see J Springhall, *Youth Popular Culture and Moral Panics: Penny Gaffs to Gangsta-Rap, 1830–1996,* Basingstoke, Macmillan, 1998 (esp. chapter one) and ofVictorian explanations of criminal behaviour M J Weiner, *Reconstructing the Criminal: Culture, Law and Policy in England, 1830–1914,* Cambridge, Cambridge University Press, 1990, and D Taylor, *Hooligans,*

Harlots and Hangmen: Crime and Punishment in Victorian Britain, Santa Barbara, ABC-Clio, 2010, chapter five.

31 *HC,* 5 & 12 May 1855. This is discussed further in chapter ten.

32 *HC,* 19 April 1856.

33 *HC,* 19 April, 10 & 24 May 1856.

34 *Hull Packet,* 27 April 1849, LM, 21 & 28 July 1849.

35 *LM,* 19 Jan. & 16 March, 1850, *HC,* 21 January & 14 December 1850.

36 *HC,* 22 February 1851. For similar successes in arresting thieves see the *LM,* 13 July 1850 and the HC, 15 March 1851.

37 *HC,* 29 April 1854. The wider coverage emphasised the audacity of the crime rather than the skills of the police.

38 *HC,* 5 April 1851. For other cases of horse theft see *HC,* 16 August 1851, 30 October & 27 November 1852, 10 & 17 November 1855 & 23 & 30 August 1856.

39 *HC,* 19 April 1851.

40 *HC,* 26 April & 19 July 1851.

41 See for example *HC,* 8 February, 1 March, 14 & 21 June 1851, 29 April & 27 May 1854; and *HEx,* 13 December 1851 & 13 March 1852. See also examples of Kaye working with parochial constable Earnshaw, *HC,* 4 January 1851, 13 September 1851, 14 May 1853 & 14 July 1855 but see *HC,* 2 November 1850 for magisterial complaint that Heaton was misusing the Worsted Act. Embezzlement in Upper Agbrigg is discussed more fully in chapter ten.

42 For example, the arrest for gambling in Scammonden, *HC,* 21 September 1850.

43 Illicit distillation was probably on the decline in the 1850s in the country as a whole. See B Harrison, *Drink and the Victorians: The Temperance Question in England, 1815–1872,* Keele University Press, 1994, pp.305, 327 & 359.

44 *HC,* 24 May 1851. It is not clear from the report whether there was a suspicion that there was also a case of embezzlement. Kaye appears to have taken his civic responsibilities seriously, on one occasion coming to the aid of a town constable who was being assaulted by the brothers Hulke and on another occasion trapping a mad dog and restraining it until it could be shot! *HC,* 20 March 1852.

45 *HC,* 20 August 1853, 12 August 1854, 19 January & 14 June 1856, 10 January & 7 February 1857.

46 *LM,* 25 May 1850. Such evidence, nonetheless, suggests a greater degree of activity among parochial constables than previously thought.

47 *HC,* 13 April 1850 and 3 & 10 November 1855.

48 See for example *HC,* 7 June 1856 when parochial constable Hoyle was charged with wilful neglect of duty, having been the only parochial constable not to attend during the peace rejoicings. It is difficult to establish how often Heaton took out disciplinary proceedings.

49 *HC,* 26 April 1851.

50 The handbook appears not to have survived but see *HEx,* 22 April 1854 for reference to first publication date.

51 *HC,* 19 April 1856.

52 *HC*, 10 August and 2 November 1850 and 3 April 1852. See also 11 January 1851 when two Lockwood constables were dismissed as 'two officious Dogberrys' as they summonsed various landlords for infringing licensing laws.
53 *HC*, 7 September 1850, 26 April 1851, 19 August 54 and 18 August 1855. Kaye won first prizes for his baking pears and yellow savoys but there is no evidence of him bringing any cases to court.
54 *HC*, 10 February 1855.
55 *HC*, 19 May & 16 June 1855.
56 *HC*, 18 September 1852. See also 3 January, 27 November & 4 December 1852.
57 *HC*, 14 September, 16 November and 28 December 1850, 31 March, 6 September & 4 October 1851. See also 4 June & 5 November 1853 for prosecutions for false weights and dealing with a suicide.
58 *HC*, 18 January, 1 February, 19 April 1851, 8 October 1853, 9 December 1854 & 3 March 1855.
59 *HC*, 8 October 1853.
60 *HC*, 27 April 1850, See also 12 October 1850 and 19 April 1851 for other examples of assaults on Riley.
61 *HC*, 16 November 1850. For examples of his involvement with petty crime see *HC*, 11 May 1850, 3 & 31 May, 13 September & 27 December 1851, 14 February, 29 May, 4 September, 13 November 1852, 8 January, 16 April, 25 June, 17 September, 12 & 26 November and 10 December 1853, 18 February, 15 April & 2 September 1854, 12 & 26 May 1855, 30 August & 20 December 1856.
62 *HC*, 13 September & 27 December 1851. See also 28 May 1853 & 20 December 1856 for similar joint action.
63 *HC*, 9 April 1853.
64 *HC*, 10 February 1855.
65 *HC*, 18 February 1854. Netherwood had given evidence against the same man in December 1852 and there was an ongoing feud between the two men.
66 *HC*, 10 February 1855.
67 *HC*, 19 April 1856. In contrast, Heaton claimed other parochial constables could not always be relied upon to respond to orders and discharge their duty.
68 *HEx*, 19 April 1856.
69 *HC*, 19 April 1856.
70 *HEx*, 22 January 1853.
71 *HC*, 18 February 1854 for a brief reference to the constable of Marsh and *HC*, 17 September 1853 for a longer piece on Goodall.
72 *HC*, 8 March 1851. Assaults on Glover are reported on 11 May & 17 August 1850 and 18 January 51 (the assault took place on Christmas Day, 1850). Glover was subjected to 'opprobrious epithets' including 'Duck Stealer' and 'Highway Robber'.
73 *HC*, 12 April 1851.
74 *HC*, 8 March 1851.
75 *HC*, 12 April 1851.

76 *HC*, 26 July 1851. Both men had previously been fined for assaulting Glover, though it was claimed on behalf of one of the defendants that he had been the victim of three or four summonses from Glover. See also *HC* 26 April, 12 July 51 & 25 October 1851.
77 *HC*, 11, 18 & 25 September 1852. Two years later but 'there appeared an overwhelming majority against a paid constable' because it was widely (but erroneously) believed that it would mean 'a policeman in uniform with a salary of some £50 or £60 per annum'. *HC*, 24 February 1854.
78 *HC*, 25 August 1855.
79 *HC* and *HEx*, 17 February 1855.
80 *HC* and *HEx*, 8 March & 5 April 1856.
81 *HC* and *HEx*, 17 February 1855.
82 See also *HC*, 17 August 1850, 1 February & 16 August 1851 for examples of Heaton working with men of the Huddersfield force to deal with dogfighting, prize fighting and cockfighting respectively and 17 June 1854 for a joint venture with the Kirkburton constable to prevent a cockfight. In November 1854 Heaton broke up a gambling den in Golcar in conjunction with Superintendent Thomas and two other senior men from the Huddersfield force. These cases are discussed in more detail in chapter ten.
83 *HC*, 25 August & 3 September 1856.
84 The following account is drawn from the reports in the *HC* 25 August & 3 September 1856.
85 Italics added. For details of the trial see *LM*, 18 October 1856.
86 *HC*, 14 & 28 April 1855.
87 *HC*, 15 September 1855.
88 Too much should not be made of the fact that George Shepley of Scisset was involved in the Wibsey venture. This appears to be the only serious crime in which he was involved and the location of Scisset, less than ten miles to the south of Huddersfield and within the Upper Agbrigg petty sessional district, was hardly a barrier to cooperation.
89 *HC*, 14 February 1857.
90 Active parochial constables such as John Earnshaw (Holmfirth) and William Taylor (Honley) became members of the WRCC but others, notably Riley (Berry Brow) did not. Riley remained an active parochial officer throughout the 1860s.

The Early Years of the West Riding County Constabulary

NOTWITHSTANDING ANY SUCCESS achieved by Heaton and his trusted parochial and paid constables, the national debate about policing had moved on in the mid-1850s and the superintending constable system had been found wanting.[1] Locally there remained doubts about the desirability of a county force. The *Chronicle* was concerned with the cost implications but a more principled opposition was mounted by the *Examiner*. In late 1855 it argued that 'there is still no reason for the introduction of the rural [county] police ... [as] every township has the remedy in its own hand', namely to appoint a paid constable.[2] In language echoing the fears expressed in the debates about the Metropolitan police in the 1820s, it saw a rural police as a step towards 'espionage' and 'an approximation to the hateful interference of foreign despotisms'.[3] Three months later, the language became more forceful. Opposition to the first police bill was part of 'a continual struggle on the part of the people against the unjust, arbitrary and tyrannical proceedings of government'.[4] If passed the bill would lead to 'a vast spy system under the cloak of the defence of property ... [and] confidence ... would be destroyed and results similar to those consequent upon the police systems of the continent would be experienced in this country'.[5] The *Examiner* maintained a critical stance to the new police after the passing of the (second) bill but in many respects its fears were ill-founded. The new force that took responsibility for the policing of Upper Agbrigg was too small and too inefficient to create and enforce 'a vast spy system'. Its approach was largely pragmatic and, though there were significant outbreaks of anti-police sentiment in

Honley and Holmfirth in 1862, these were exceptional. But first it is necessary to consider the basic characteristics of the local division of the WRCC.[6]

The passing of the County and Borough Police Act meant that from January 1857 the West Riding would have a county-wide police force. Parochial constables were not abolished immediately but the balance of responsibility for policing shifted decisively to the paid officers of the WRCC under its new chief constable, Lieutenant-Colonel Cobbe. Cobbe had an engineering and military background, which led (initially at least) to a dependence upon the experienced former Chief Constable of Lancashire, now Inspector of Constabulary, Colonel Woodford.[7] In his first report, Woodford praised Cobbe for selecting men 'with care and discrimination' and was confident that they showed 'promise of early efficiency … many having served with credit in other police forces'.[8] Sadly for Cobbe, Woodford's judgment was not wholly sound and, in the short-term at least, his confidence somewhat misplaced.

The WRCC was a large force, numbering just under 500 officers and men at inception and rising to over 650 by the late 1860s. The area for which it was responsible was considerable (over 1,600,000 acres) and the population (over 800,000) relatively large. As a consequence, both the police/population and police/acreage ratios were considerably higher than in Huddersfield. At the end of the period under consideration there was one policeman for every 2,235 acres and one for every 1,334 people; but these figures mask some important variations between the well-populated villages, such as Honley, Holmfirth, Kirkburton, Kirkheaton, Marsden and Meltham, and their outlying districts in which the population was well scattered. As a consequence, the police were more heavily outnumbered in the villages than the average figure might suggest and, therefore, had limited resources for the more remote areas. Furthermore, the police were also more scattered. Unlike the Huddersfield force, concentrated in a relatively small geographical area, the men of the WRCC were far more isolated from one another: a fact, easily overlooked, that had a major impact on the policing of a largely rural area. As Superintendent Heaton noted 'in the case of a disturbance, they [county policemen] could not rap the lamp-post and have a man come to their assistance immediately … officers in these isolated districts had a difficult and dangerous duty to perform'.[9]

Twenty-one police districts, based on the county's petty sessional districts, were established, each with its own superintendent. In 1857, of the twenty-one divisions in the WRCC, eighteen were headed by men who had been superintending constables in previous years.[10] Cobbe relied heavily upon these men in setting up the new force. Heaton, for example, was specifically charged with the initial training of the recently-appointed constables, several of whom came from other forces, before they went out to their various stations in the Upper Agbrigg division. His extensive experience and local knowledge and his continuing active role ensured that there was no significant departure in terms of the priorities and practices of policing.

At the next level in the police hierarchy, inspectors, Cobbe looked outside the county. Of fifty-nine inspectors appointed in the first three years of the force, fifty-three (almost 90 per cent) already had police experience in other forces. The tactic was far from successful as almost half of these men either resigned, were dismissed or demoted.[11] In Upper Agbrigg the experience was of short tenures and some unsatisfactory appointments. With Heaton residing in Huddersfield at the County Court, the first inspector, thirty-five-year-old Thomas Parkin, was stationed at Holmfirth. Born in Sheffield, Parkin had served in the Blackburn borough force for over five years and a further five years in the Lancashire County Constabulary. He was one of the more promising appointments, so much so that in June 1858 he was recalled to headquarters in Wakefield and subsequently became a superintendent. His replacement was Joseph Haworth. A Lancastrian, aged forty, Howarth had served for fifteen years including just over one year in the Manchester City Police when he was appointed as a sergeant in the WRCC in April 1857. He was promoted inspector in October 1857 and moved to Upper Agbrigg in June 1858, becoming a first-class inspector in November 1859 when he was transferred to the Ainstie division. During his brief time at Holmfirth he did much to foster good relations between the new police and the people of Holmfirth. His successor, Seth Parker, was another ex-Lancashire County Constabulary man and altogether a flintier character. His aggressive action against local beerhouses was an important factor in precipitating the mass protests of 1862 (discussed in chapter nine) which led to his transfer out of the district.[12] His successor, William Airton, born in Skipton but having served briefly in the Met, did much to restore relations in the mid- and late-1860s and it is no coincidence that his work as inspector of nuisances and particularly his actions during the cattle plague won him local support. Of the two other inspectors who served in Upper Agbrigg there is little to say. Airton's successor, the successful career policeman, Walter Nunn, who had worked his way up from constable to inspector, moved to Upper Agbrigg in January 1868 but died shortly afterwards. Samuel Hockaday was promoted to inspector and transferred to Upper Agbrigg in July 1868 but was forced to resign six months later. In view of the importance of the position in the police hierarchy, and the need for good leadership at a time when many of the rank and file officers were inexperienced, the combination of brief tenure of office and poor performance (by some though not all inspectors) meant that this level of management was weak and added to the problem of creating an efficient and effective force.

In the lower ranks were several men from outside the county, including some from the longer-established Lancashire County Constabulary, but 69 per cent were born in Yorkshire. Almost half of the men recruited to the force as a whole had some previous policing experience. Recruits were drawn from a broad socio-economic spectrum but, unsurprisingly, almost a quarter of the men were from the textile trades. Labourers, however, were the largest occupational category in the police records. It is not clear whether overall the men of the WRCC conformed to 'the image of rural class relationships' that Steedman claims was commonplace across the country in the early years of the new county forces.[13] Like most forces, the WRCC experienced a high turnover rate. Around 40 per cent of early recruits left within a year (rising to over 50 per cent after two years). In the nearby and earlier-founded Lancashire County Constabulary, the percentages were almost identical. In the Buckinghamshire force the figures were 47 per cent and 62 per cent respectively for the year 1857, falling to 38 per cent and 61 per cent a decade later, and in Staffordshire 46 per cent and 72 per cent in 1856, falling to 43 per cent and 66 per cent a decade later.[14] Half of the early recruits to the WRCC resigned and another quarter were dismissed. Nonetheless, about a fifth served for sufficient time to retire on a pension, of whom some 40 were promoted to the rank of inspector. The percentage of resignations was higher in Lancashire (59 per cent for the period 1845–70), though the figure for dismissals was the same.[15]

The main concern in this chapter is the Upper Agbrigg division from its establishment in 1857 to 1868 when its numbers were reduced as a consequence of the creation of the enlarged borough of Huddersfield. During this period 259 men served in Upper Agbrigg (two on two occasions, having left and then been re-appointed). 32 per cent gave their occupation as labourer (or farm labourer) and comprised the largest group in the force. Some 22 per cent of men were from a variety of textile trades (clothiers, spinners, weavers and wool-combers) and 26 per cent from a variety of trades (literally butchers, bakers and tallow chandlers but also cabinet makers and shoemakers). The remainder were drawn from various backgrounds, including gamekeepers and grooms, clerks and one teacher. There were also four men for whom 'no trade' was entered into the record. Almost two-third of recruits were in their twenties on appointment and one-third in their thirties. Eight experienced men were in their forties and one in his fifties; surprisingly there is one nineteen-year old recruit. Married men outnumbered single by a ratio of three to two and of these married men only a quarter had no family.[16] Cobbe placed particular value on married men, seeing them as more stable figures at a time when turnover rates were high. In addition, to prevent officers 'going native', he believed in recruiting (or deploying) men from outside the division in which they would be operating. Few men were recruited from the Huddersfield area, although almost half of the recruits were born in the West Riding and a further 20 per cent elsewhere in Yorkshire. Of the remainder, 10 per cent were from Lancashire, 10 per cent from other northern English counties, 7 per cent from the rest of England and 6 per cent from other parts of the United Kingdom; the bulk from Ireland, but one man had been born in Bombay.

Given Cobbe's preference for men of experience, especially in the earliest years of the WRCC, it is not surprising to find that 137 men (52 per cent of the total) had previous police or military experience. Surprisingly, only ten of these had served in the Lancashire County Constabulary – almost exactly the same number who had been paid or parochial officers under the previous superintending regime. Previous police experience had been gained most commonly in the northern city forces – Manchester, Bradford, Leeds and Liverpool. There were a few men (five in all) with experience of the Met – the same number as had served in Halifax – but there is little evidence to suggest that there was a flood of men from the Huddersfield force, attracted (as Cobbe claimed) by higher wages: only two men who had served in Huddersfield were appointed to the Upper Agbrigg division.[17] On closer examination, this previous police experience was less than impressive, some men having served only weeks, even days, before leaving. In total, 30 per cent of men with previous experience had served less than one year. However, more than half had been in a force for between one and four years and only 16 per cent had served for more than five years.

The lengths of service and career outcomes for the policemen of Upper Agbrigg are summarised in tables 8.1 and 8.2 below. Table 8.1 distinguishes between the time policemen served in Upper Agbrigg and their overall length of service in the WRCC, thereby taking into account transfers within the force. There was clearly a high turnover of men – half served less than one year in the WRCC and only 14 per cent for more than five years. However, this obscures the divisional experience. In Upper Agbrigg almost three in five men served for less than a year and a mere one in twenty recruits went on to serve in the district for more than five years.

Table 8.1: Upper Agbrigg: length of service, 1857-68

	CAREERS IN UPPER AGBRIGG	CAREERS IN WRCC
Less than 1 year	*59%*	*50%*
One year but less than 5	*36%*	*36%*
5 years and above	*5%*	*14%*
	100%	*100%*

Source: West Riding Police Records, Examination Books

The figures, as they stand, do not take into account prior experience with the WRCC before transfer to Upper Agbrigg. Making this adjustment increases the percentage of men serving over five years by 3-4 percentage points, and reduces the percentage of men serving less than one year by 4-5 percentage points. (The figure for those serving more than one but less than five years increases by one percentage point.) Nonetheless, the figures remain stark: over a half of recruits left within the first year and only a small percentage became long-serving men.

Table 8.2: Upper Agbrigg: career outcomes, 1857-68

	COMPLETED CAREERS	ALL MEN
Resigned	*37%*	*30%*
Dismissed	*29%*	*24%*
Transferred	*32%*	*26%*
Dies or killed	*2%*	*2%*
In service 1868	*n.a.*	*18%*
	100%	*100%*

Source: As for Table 8.1

The inclusion of the 'In service' category in table 8.2 explains the differences between the two columns of figures. The high percentage of resignations and dismissals is not significantly out of line with experiences in other county forces in their early years, if anything it is marginally better than many. However, the importance of transfers should be stressed. A significant number of men ended their police careers in Upper Agbrigg because they were transferred elsewhere. The reasons for such transfers were varied. In some cases it was due to a promotion, in others to a demotion. Whatever the reason, transfers added to the high rates of turnover and to the problem of acquiring knowledge of a particular area. There were unresolved tensions in the recruitment and deployment strategies adopted in the WRCC. There was a trade-off between the desire to have men independent of the district they policed and the need for local knowledge; similarly, there was a tension between the stability brought by married officers and the disruption they and their families faced through repeated transfers.

In view of the emphasis on the introduction of the new police in the district, the experience of the first cohort of recruits (the men appointed in December 1856 and January 1857) has been analysed separately and is summarised in Tables 8.3 and 8.4.

Of the twelve men with previous police experience, four came from the superintending constable system, including Thomas Heaton. The rest had served with local police forces (Halifax, Oldham and Leeds). By far the most experienced man was Abraham Sedgwick, who had served eleven years in the Huddersfield force. Only one other man came close to this, John Ward, a Leeds-born man who had served seven years in the Met. In total there were only seven men (excluding Heaton) who had more than three years' police experience when they were sent to Upper Agbrigg. Three-quarters of the new men had no previous police experience. In addition, the overwhelming majority came from outside the division and would have had little or no local knowledge. This presented a daunting task for Heaton, whose responsibility it was to train these men. In view of their inexperience, it is unsurprising to find that almost two-thirds had left by the end of 1857. Not all of these were inexperienced men. Earnshaw, the long-serving Holmfirth constable, was dismissed after five months and Ward retired after nine months.[18]

Table 8.3: Upper Agbrigg 1st Police Cohort: previous police experience and place of birth

	PREVIOUS	EXPERIENCE		
Army		*Police*		*% Police experience*
	Less than 1 year	*1 year but less than 5*	*5 years and over*	
2	*2*	*5*	*5*	*25*
	PLACE	OF BIRTH	*(as %)*	
Upper Agbrigg	*Other West Riding*	*Other Yorkshire*	*North-west England*	*All others*
10	*44*	*25*	*15*	*6*

Source: As for Table 8.1

Table 8.4: Upper Agbrigg 1st Police Cohort: length of service and career outcomes

LENGTH OF SERVICE	NUMBER		CAREER OUTCOME	NUMBER	
Less than 1 year	*30*	*61%*	*Resigned*	*18*	*37%*
1 year but less than 5	*12*	*24%*	*Dismissed*	*13*	*27%*
5 years but less than 10	*4*	*8%*	*Died*	*2*	*4%*
10 and above	*3*	*6%*	*Transferred*	*12*	*24%*
			In service	*4*	*8%*

Source: As for Table 8.1

It is worth noting that six of the thirty men who served for less than a year were transferred out of Upper Agbrigg. Overall, the figures for the first cohort, while not significantly out of line with those for all men serving in Upper Agbrigg, bring out clearly the scale of the problems facing Heaton. Few men had meaningful previous police experience, large numbers left within a short period of time and, consequently, few acquired experience and became long-serving officers in the district. There was a further logistical difference, which was both a blessing and a curse for Heaton. As superintending constable, he had about a dozen reliable men with whom he could work; as newly-appointed superintendent of the Upper Agbrigg division of the WRCC, he had (at any one time) over forty men under his command, many of whom were not efficient constables, and the core of reliable men at his disposal was probably little higher than it had been before 1856. The problem of recruiting and retaining good men remained unsolved a decade later. Even the Inspector of Constabulary, prone to putting a favourable gloss on matters where possible, noted in 1866 'the difficulty of procuring properly-qualified men for service in the police [which had been] so recently aggravated by the high rates of wages now paid for labour'. Indeed, he felt there was 'a danger of the service [in the county] becoming seriously impaired'.[19] Thus, one of the most striking similarities between the 'old' policing of the early 1850s and the new policing of the late-1850s and early-1860s in the West Riding of Yorkshire was the number of relatively ill-educated, ill-disciplined and often incompetent men charged with the responsibility of policing

Table 8.5: Upper Agbrigg: length of service 1868

LENGTH OF SERVICE	UPPER ONLY	AGBRIGG	UPPER & PREVIOUS	AGBRIGG WRCC EXPERIENCE
	Number	%	*Number*	%
Less than 1 year	*5*	*10*	*3*	*6*
1 year but less than 5	*16*	*33*	*14*	*29*
5 years but less than 10	*18*	*38*	*16*	*33*
10 or more	*9*	*19*	*15*	*31*
Totals	*48*	*100%*	*48*	*99%*

Source: As for Table 8.1

their local community. Only gradually did matters improve but by the late-1860s there had been some significant developments, as Table 8.5 shows. The percentage of inexperienced men (serving less than a year) was appreciably lower while the numbers with five or more years' experience had increased significantly. Even though experience did not automatically ensure efficiency, this was a stronger force than a decade previous.

The arrival of county constables aroused considerable local interest. The regional press, notably the *Leeds Examiner* and the *Leeds Time*, both unsympathetic towards the newly-formed WRCC, seized upon examples of popular hostility in various parts of the county, including the Huddersfield district. Notwithstanding the experience of more intrusive policing before 1857, the arrival of the 'raw recruits' of the WRCC gave rise to a 'popular feeling of dislike [of] the county police' in certain quarters.[20] Concerns were expressed at 'paltry' and 'trumpery' charges and 'intermeddling cruelty', particularly the excessive use of handcuffs.[21] Robert Storch concluded from evidence such as this and drawn from various parts of the West Riding, that 'the imposition of a modern, uniformed police [in 1857] called forth a bitter and often violent response ... [but] ... once the police were successfully entrenched the open warfare of initial contact was replaced by a state that one may characterize as armed truce', albeit one that could be broken and 'more or less open warfare' resumed.[22] In fact, a detailed examination of the local (Huddersfield) press reveals a more complex picture in Upper Agbrigg which points to somewhat different conclusions both in the short- and longer-term.

The first detachment of the new force had arrived in Huddersfield in January 1857 to meet Heaton for training before being sent out to various nearby villages. From the strengthening of the police presence it was hoped that 'the numerous depredations in the out-townships will thereby be held in salutary check'.[23] Such optimism overlooked the inexperienced nature of the new force. Furthermore, the simple fact of a significant increase in police personnel threatened the *modus vivendi* between police and policed that had developed in the previous decade. Initially, there was no dramatic increase in the volume of anti-police activity in 1857, particularly taking into account the sharp increase in police numbers. Further, and more importantly, much of the reported anti-police behaviour was of a highly localised nature and the *overall* popular response was less hostile than previously suggested. The local response was mixed and there is little evidence that there was any attempt to drive out the 'new' police. There was magisterial concern that 'in Longwood and other places a number of lawless characters had determined in every possible way to interfere with the police, with the view of driving them out'.[24] However, there is little direct evidence of such intent. In an isolated incident in Longwood, James Maud attacked Sergeant Caygill, declaring 'he would drive the police out of Longwood as they were determined to have no policemen there' but no support materialised.[25] There were clashes with the new police on a number of occasions in the old trouble-spot of Lindley, where in 1859 according to Heaton, 'the police [were] shockingly treated', though there were also positive comments about the behaviour of the new police in the village. There was continuing hostility in Deighton, another problematic area for the old parish constables.[26] There was open hostility here to the newly-arrived county police officers, PCs Firth and Ward, who were the victims of a savage attack in March 1857 by two men they had previously arrested for drunkenness. The claim by the defendants that they were now more determined 'to oppose the authority of "the gentleman in blue" who have been recently stationed in the village' led the Huddersfield bench to make 'a marked example' and imposed a fine and costs that amounted to the considerable sum of £13-8*s*-6*d* (£13-42½). The *Chronicle,* in an editorial, praised the magistrates for their 'signal example of severity ... imperatively called for against such brutality and lawlessness' but overlooked the significance of the fact that the fine was paid shortly after a collection had been made.[27] Heaton conceded that 'there were a number of lads and men in the villages who took it upon themselves to do all they could to annoy the police.[28] The 'annoyance' took various forms. In Golcar the newly-installed policeman was assaulted, while in Upper Mill a crowd rescued a prisoner from the police; at the Honley Feast there was a serious assault on one of the local policeman while in Crosland Moor, during a stang-riding* protest, the 'mob made a dead set at

* Stang riding was a form of 'rough music' that is, a cacophonous and mocking ritual directed at individuals who transgressed community norms of morality. A representation of the offending individual(s), astride a long pole, or stang, was carried on men's shoulders, while a crowd beat pots and pans, cheered and even threw mud and other unpleasant substances. For more detail see E P Thompson, *Custom in Common*, London, Penguin, 1993, chapter eight.

the police', but in Slaithwaite the police were criticized merely for doing 'nothing but walk the streets in their smart dresses and clean, spotless shoes'. In Kirkheaton sporadic trouble continued but in Kirkburton, somewhat surprisingly, it was claimed that 'few have proved more favourable to the new county force than the inhabitants of Kirkburton and neighbourhood' while in Meltham they were welcomed for their success in 'quelling the disorderly rows that have so long been the disgrace of that village'.[29] In other parts of the district no popular response – positive or negative – can be found in the pages of the local press.[30] The *Examiner* was (unsurprisingly) more critical of the new county police. There had been no love lost between the paper and Heaton as superintending constable and less as the new superintendent of the Upper Agbrigg division.[31] More generally, it focused on the inferiority of the county police and their preoccupation with trivial cases – the latter charge also made by the *Chronicle*.[32]

Nor did attitudes change significantly in the following years. The police continued to be unpopular particularly in Lindley, in 'the semi-civilized neighbourhood of Kirkheaton' and 'among the ruthless-looking desperadoes … [from] the wild region around Scammonden'. Their attempts to curb out-of-hours drinking and suppress cockfighting in and around Kirkburton and Holmfirth also provoked a number of violent responses. Around Jackson Bridge in the summer of 1858 the police were subjected to Saturday-night attacks by 'parties secreted on the way side, in readiness with stones, bludgeons etc'. As a consequence 'officers have resigned their duties, not daring to risk their lives in so perilous a district' but this was an exceptional and short-lived occurrence.[33] Violent incidents are scattered through the district throughout the 1860s. Four men were charged with assaulting PC Stansfield in Golcar; in Paddock ten men were arrested for stoning the police; PC Redman was attacked by three men at Lockwood Feast; and PC Long was attacked outside the *Cavalry Arms* in Birchincliffe, where one of his assailants called out: 'Come up here you ------, and I'll kill you.'[34] Undoubtedly there were those who held personal grudges against individual policemen. When Henry Sanderson, better known as 'Red Harry' was arrested in Holmfirth for assaulting two constables who had served him with a warrant for non-payment of rates, he told PC Rhodes ''Ov Ow'd thee a grudge an ol pay thee off afore theea goas 'yoat o' this heease'.[35] Certain places remained hostile to the police but in many of the out-townships there was a general if begrudging acceptance of the new county police; while in some villages, such as Honley, the demands were for more, rather than less, police action.[36]

Assaults on the police made good copy but to focus solely on manifestations of anti-police sentiment would be to paint a misleading picture. Police work – in Upper Agbrigg as much as in Huddersfield itself – covered a wide range of activities, many of which minimised and marginalised outright opposition, even winning more positive support. The crime-fighting activities of the county force rarely encompassed major crimes. Indictable offences were infrequent in Upper Agbrigg. In the late 1860s just under ten percent of all the recorded crime fell into this category and over fifty per cent of these were simple larcenies. The most frequent summary offences were begging and vagrancy (about a quarter of the total), assaults (about a fifth of the total) and then drunkenness. In the late 1860s there were as many arrests for 'family' offences (disobeying bastardy orders and neglect of family) as for common assaults. Many of these offences were largely uncontentious, the police themselves acting in response to and on behalf of victims, but were less commonly reported than more spectacular incidents. Further, certain police actions appeared positive to many Victorians, irrespective of class. In hindsight the vagrants of Victorian Britain appear more as pathetic figures, often undeserving losers in a socio-economic order that offered little protection for the unskilled and misfortunate but, at the time, such footloose, wandering people were seen as a major threat to settled society. In this sense, the police were working very much with the grain of contemporary beliefs (or prejudices) and thus their role as protectors against a threatening 'other' was seen as necessary for the wider good of society. The police also took on responsibilities as inspectors of nuisances – though this could bring them into conflict with certain propertied individuals – and, in the mid-1860s agricultural crisis, enforced regulations under the Contagious Diseases Acts that were designed to protect the wider economy of rural Britain from the threat of rinderpest, pleuro-pneumonia and foot-and-mouth disease. Police work also extended to 'welfare' activities, such as the easily-caricatured concern for lost or abandoned children.

Nonetheless, not all routine policing was uncontentious. Concerns with order and decorum, not confined to the urban middle classes, gave rise to conflict as traditional activities and events were subject to greater scrutiny. As the police became increasingly involved in curbing drinking, gambling and cockfighting, and in ensuring order at customary celebrations, such as local feasts, the scope for conflict between police and many working-class men and women (and some middle-class people as well) increased. And it was not simply a matter of inculcating new notions of order and decorum. There was an unchallenged consensus among local senior police officers and magistrates that beerhouses were a major and ongoing source of criminality and that annual village feasts provided a site for immorality and an opportunity for criminality. The police, it was argued, had a central role to play in curbing such licentious and illegal behaviour that threatened respectable, civilized society. Heaton, whose personal enthusiasm in the early 1850s has already been noted, continued to set the tone as superintendent and many of his men responded energetically. Beerhouse keepers and publicans were prosecuted for selling liquor out of hours in every village in the district though, as in Huddersfield certain men were regular attenders at the local courts. Increasingly the emphasis was on the 'crusade' against gambling, which was seen to be particularly pernicious.[37] But, in rural districts, bringing to justice landlords who permitted gambling on their premises was not easy. William Corden, an energetic sergeant, was able to prosecute successfully John Whiteley, an innkeeper from Scammonden, but only with some difficulty. With two other men, he hid himself near the inn, and 'having placed a ladder against an upstairs window … heard one of the men say "we'll play for another quart"'. On another occasion, also in Scammonden, 'the constables [Corden and two PCs] lifted each other up to get a glimpse into the room through a crevice in the blind'.[38] They then quietly entered the house and arrested the miscreants who were 'tossing' and 'marrying' each other, that is gambling together. In similar style PCs Lucas and Wardle arrested gamblers who had been 'throwing the dart' for beer' at the *Stafford Arms* beerhouse in Kirkheaton, after looking through an ill-fitting blind.[39] More problematic, but common in the more outlying districts, was 'lakin' for brass' [playing for money] in fields and bye-ways. Such events were well organised. In Lockwood between thirty and forty young men would meet regularly in a field to play pitch and toss, paying a young boy to stand watch for 3*d*. (1p) an hour. After numerous complaints and several unsuccessful attempts, the police finally managed to arrest thirteen men. The police had gone in 'disguise' (that is, in plain clothes) and had hidden behind the 'Standing stones' above Lockwood reservoir, waiting for an opportunity to catch the gamblers unawares. Eventually the watch left his position and the arrests were made.[40] Even more dramatic was the arrest of gamblers near Nettleton Hill, Longwood, coordinated by Sergeant Corden. On three previous Sundays the police had tried and failed but eventually their perseverance paid off. The police 'were dressed in blue slop, so as to imitate weavers as much as possible' but seeing a look-out, Corden advised his men to 'back off the moor'. The first attempt to capture the gamblers involved 'one of the officers mounting a donkey'. Quite what he was meant to do is unclear but he 'succeeded in coming within sixty yards of the spot where the men were playing 'shake cap'**, but the watch whistled a warning and the police retreated. The gamblers brazenly continued, which provoked Corden to order direct action. Several of the 'boys in blue slops' advanced along the footpath and asked the watch 'if the hounds were out'. Failing to recognise that the would-be gamblers were in fact officers of the law, the unsuspecting watch allowed the disguised police to proceed, having generously told them that the dogs were lower down the hill. Seven men were arrested and fined but they 'treated the matter with much levity, and said they could easily club up the money'.[41] Others were less successful. PC Wardle, of whom more later, tried and failed on several occasions to catch Sunday gamblers in Kirkheaton.

While undoubtedly police (and magisterial) priorities brought the police into conflict with men and women who felt that their legitimate pastimes were being criminalized, much depended upon the actions of the individual constable. A constable was very fortunate not to be assaulted at least once in the course of his normal duties but some men were more (often much more) unpopular than others. The experienced Abraham Sedgwick was one such man. When in the Huddersfield force he had been attacked on at least six occasions. As a sergeant in the WRCC he was subject to a number of serious attacks. Such was the beating he received at the Bath Hotel, Lockwood, during Honley Feast that he had to take time off work; a year later, this time at Meltham Feast, he was the victim of another

** A variant of pitch and toss in which half-pennies were put in a cap and the participants took it in turn to shake them out and won any coins that came down 'heads'.

brutal assault. Then a few days later he, and two other officers, were attacked by a crowd of 200 people. There were cries of 'Go into him' and 'Punch him well' as Sedgwick was 'thrown down, kicked and ill-used'. Again, he was rendered unfit for duty and confined to bed for several days.[42] It is difficult to get to the bottom of these events but a later incident is more illuminating. In late November 1863 Sergeant Sedgwick was moving on a crowd of men at 12.30 a.m. when they turned on him. Arrests were made and the case heard before the town magistrates but this time there was a counter claim of police violence. This in itself was not unprecedented but the magistrates made it clear that 'they deprecated on the part of policemen anything like officiousness such as was likely to promote a demonstration against them'.[43] This was not the only time that the magistrates criticised police behaviour. Indeed, on a number of occasions they made clear that in their opinion the police had used excessive force. Equally telling was the response in the courtroom. The magistrates' words were warmly received and those charged made it clear their hostility towards Sedgwick.

Sedgwick, a close friend of Heaton was, as far as one can judge, zealous, albeit to the point of officiousness, but other members of the force were guilty of dishonesty as well as of using excessive force. The local magistrates were outspoken on a number of occasions. Four men were charged with attacking the police in a brawl outside the *Junction Inn,* Golcar, but when the evidence had been heard the magistrates were scathing. The police 'case had miserably failed and ... the officers and the defendants ought to change places'. PC Stansfield, they continued, was responsible for 'one of the grossest assaults, in the unwarrantable use of the staff' heard in court.[44] In Stansfield's case this appears to have been a one-off incident but there were other officers who were reprimanded on more than one occasion. One such was PC Thomas Manuel, who came to the WRCC after serving three years in the army and four-and-a-half years in the Lancashire County Constabulary. He served in Upper Agbrigg from 1857 to 1862 before he was transferred to another division. Soon after his arrival he arrested James Garside, accusing him of being drunk and disorderly at midnight in Lindley. Garside had an alibi and openly accused Manuel of lying. The case was dismissed but the magistrate, in a somewhat tongue in cheek manner, observed that 'the officer might have been mistaken as to the time he had seen the defendant'. [45] Manuel soon became an unpopular figure in Lindley – 'the d----d Irish b-----' in the words of (the unrelated) Benjamin Garside, whom Manuel had arrested on a previous occasion.[46] In the summer of 1859 he was assaulted on three separate occasions and again in 1860. Manuel's unpopularity was borne out by the severity of the beatings he received. The *Chronicle*, aware of his reputation for unreliable evidence, noted 'the most convincing part of the evidence was the exhibition of a plastered nose which [Manuel] stated had been severely injured by the defendant throwing a stone at him'.[47] This time the magistrates believed him but in at least one previous case they so doubted Manuel's evidence that the case was dismissed.[48] Matters came to a head in the following year. The *Chronicle,* under the heading 'Cruel Treatment Of A Prisoner By A Policeman: Important Case', reported on the charge of cruelty brought against PC Manuel, who had kept Joseph Bottomley prisoner 'in a damp and loathsome cellar' and in handcuffs for eight hours. Bottomley's case was made by none other than 'Mr. Roberts of Manchester', the well-known scourge of the new police. The case had aroused considerable attention locally and 'it was unmistakably evident that the sympathies of the majority of those present were on the side of the plaintiff'.[49] Manuel denied that he had been removed from Lindley because of his violence but the magistrates were unconvinced and awarded £10 to Bottomley. More significantly, one told the open court that it was not for the first time he had had occasion to say in Court … that the police of the West Riding Constabulary had … made use of their powers in a most excessive manner'.[50]

An equally problematic figure was Sergeant Obed Caygill, who came to Upper Agbrigg having been demoted from the rank of inspector because of inefficiency. Although another Lancastrian, he had served nine years in the Bradford force. A long-standing teetotaller, Caygill was the epitome of Storch's 'domestic missionary'. The zeal with which he prosecuted innkeepers and beerhouse keepers, gamblers and 'nude' racers matched that of Heaton. As melodramatic in style as his superintendent, he dashed into a beerhouse in Scammonden, explaining that 'his suspicions were aroused by the mistress "swelling past him" through a dark passage towards the door of an inner room, at which she gave a peculiar knock'.[51] He followed, forced open the door and found eleven men playing cards. Even more dramatic was his arrest for gambling at the *Wool Pack Inn*, Deighton. Passing the inn between two and three in the morning, 'significant words and sounds greeted his ears – "hearts", "diamonds", "clubs" etc. were the words occasionally attuned; the chink of money relieved the monotony, and a shuffling as of cards filled up the interval'.[52] Unwilling to act alone, he obtained the assistance of another constable and

> together they set stealthily to work and removed the shutters; they next quietly opened the window, drew aside the curtain, and then contemplated the puzzled countenances of the party within, who until the change of scene was complete had been unaware of the pantomime part taken by the two blue-coated actors.[53]

In another case that gained local notoriety he and PC Manuel staked out the *Globe Inn* at Slaithwaite. At 10.30 p.m. they saw some thirty men 'drunk and creating a great noise'; returning at eleven-forty p.m. not only were they singing but also cursing and swearing. Unfortunately, the men concerned were members of the Slaithwaite hunt and had been attending their hunt supper. Such was the social standing of the men involved that the case was withdrawn. Caygill's unpopularity extended beyond the Slaithwaite hunt. He was the victim of several assaults and there were recurring accusations of his 'cruel, wanton and unnecessary … violence'.[54] And yet there appeared to be a positive end to an otherwise negative career. On the 13th of December 1862 the *Chronicle* reported on a presentation to Sergeant Obed Caygill at Linthwaite of a silver watch and a 'massive' silver chain, 'subscribed for by the inhabitants of that locality [as a] tribute to the high character and consistent discharge of duty which has marked Sergeant Caygill's residence in that locality.' In a reference to the Honley riot (discussed in chapter nine) the report saw 'the event [as] a pleasing contrast to what had transpired recently … and proves that there are men in the Force whose deserving conduct is deemed worthy of special recognition by the inhabitants amongst whom they are stationed'.[55] There was only one problem: the report had been made up by Caygill himself. He was required to resign.

William Corden was another active officer, involved in numerous prosecutions for licensing offences, gambling and the like in and around Golcar and Slaithwaite but, unlike Caygill, he was never attacked during his nine-years of service, notwithstanding the fact that he was as much involved in 'domestic missionary' policing as Caygill. Nonetheless, on his departure to become an inspector in Barnsley,

Corden was (genuinely) presented with a watch inscribed by 'a number of friends at Golcar' and at a presentation made at the *Rose & Crown Hotel*, Golcar Hill, he was praised for his 'straightforward and upright conduct' and 'a private life without blemish'.[56] It is not without significance that he was active as inspector of nuisances for Golcar and played an active role in enforcing the cattle plague regulations in 1866.[57] In a telling aside, a report on the fifth annual bowling match at Slaithwaite Bath Spa noted that 'Police-sergeant Corden [was] frequently applauded during the play'.[58] Here was living proof that involvement in community life need not involve 'going native' but, to the contrary, could strengthen the standing of the police.

Corden was not alone in winning support through his positive contribution to local life, both on and off duty. Sergeant Thomas Greenwood was a similar example of pragmatic policing. Greenwood had already served over five years in the police (mainly in Halifax) before joining the WRCC as a sergeant in late 1858. Probably because of his experience he was stationed at Slaithwaite and was responsible for policing in one of the more difficult areas. He had a reputation as 'an active officer' and was praised for his vigilance in a number of major cases (including horse theft and arson) but, like most officers, spent much of his time dealing with more banal incidents of out-of-hours drinking, gambling and clothes-line thefts – although his arrests had none of the flamboyance of Caygill's – and on a number of occasions, responded to requests from landlords or landladies to deal with obstreperous customers. His career was not without incident (he was attacked on a number of occasions) or blemish (he was criticised by magistrates for exceeding his duty in a poaching case) but he did not attract the opprobrium, let alone hatred, that surrounded some of his fellow officers. Quite why this was the case is not easy to explain from the limited evidence available but his handling of an out-of-hours drinking offence in 1864 provides some insight. The *Great Western Inn* at 'Top o'Stannedge' was located in one of the more remote parts of the district above Marsden. For many years the landlady was Hannah Rhodes, who was known for her cavalier attitude towards licensing hours. Affectionately known as 'Mother Rhodes' (in the 1850s) and 'Nanny Rhodes' (in the 1860s), her hospitality made the *Great Western Inn* a popular destination for day-trippers from Huddersfield, Sunday-school outings and even the occasional wedding party, but she was a serial offender with regard to the licensing laws. From a police perspective the problem was twofold. First, there was the question of resource allocation. There were enough public houses and beerhouses in Marsden and Slaithwaite to occupy the time of the police without worrying about Stannedge but the police could not totally ignore persistent flouting of the law. Second, any police action against a popular figure carried the risk of being counterproductive. When Greenwood acted in the summer of 1864 he proceeded with considerable tact. The evidence was clear-cut: over twenty people were drinking out of hours on Sunday afternoon when he visited but he made great play of his reluctance to take action – he told the court that he was 'personally unwilling to get the old lady into trouble [but was] compelled by duty to report what he saw' – and also stressed the generosity of 'Nanny Rhodes' – I have 'reason to believe that Nanny's accommodating disposition induces her occasionally to offer house-room to parties "turned out" at proper time on Sunday afternoon from the public houses in Marsden and the valley below,' he explained. As Greenwood well knew this was a fiction but it had the effect of defusing a potential problematic situation. Further, his general approach, as much reactive as proactive, also helped minimise hostility. In addition, he was another officer who took on wider responsibilities, for example as inspector of nuisances, which strengthened the welfare role of the police. Greenwood was not a paragon of virtue, nor could he avoid conflict, especially when breaking up prize fights, as he did on at least two occasions, but his career demonstrates that it was possible to be an active officer without antagonising large swathes of the local population. Unlike certain of his fellow-officers he was able to minimise and even marginalise opposition to police work, aspects of which inevitably impinged on popular leisure activities.

Sergeants such as Corden and Greenwood were important, not least in the example they set, in establishing the presence of the newly-formed WRCC. However, more important were the ordinary constables who were responsible for the bulk of interactions between the police and the public. Unfortunately, most of these interactions went unrecorded, and even where there is some evidence it is often so fragmentary that it is difficult to reconstruct a picture of the manner in which the new police went about their daily business. It is impossible to say how many constables were 'inoffensive and civil' like Constable Reuben Redmond.[59] Similarly, one does not know why members of the public came to the assistance of constables under attack – but they did. When Redmond was attacked by two men in the *Swan Inn*, Lockwood members of the public came to his aid, even taking him into a private house to await treatment.[60] Similarly when Constable William Holmes was attacked by the belligerent William Dyson, alias 'Bull Head', outside the *Star Inn*, Slaithwaite, three men helped him arrest his assailant.[61] Elsewhere, constables appear to have been viewed with something akin to affection. One such example is Robert Wardle, who served first in Berry Brow and finally in Kirkheaton in a career which lasted from the mid-1850s to the mid-1880s. Wardle was not a high flier but he soon established himself as a well-liked and respected figure, having 'a high character for vigilance and activity, although he was *neither a harsh nor a meddling officer*'.[62] However, soon after his appointment, his career almost ended in tragedy. Investigating suspicious noises in the wood above the *Grove Inn*, Steps Mill, he was set upon by two men who threw him over a wall into a quarry. He fell some twenty-five feet, landing on stones and fracturing his right thigh and elbow. Fortuitously, his groans were heard by two workmen returning home on the old turnpike road below. The viciousness of the attack appears to have won him sympathy.[63] It was not the last time he was assaulted. Called to the assistance of Constable Antrobus during the Honley riot, he was stoned by the angry crowd of villagers. On two other occasions he was violently attacked but both resulted from his intervention in cases of domestic violence.[64] However, for much of his long and unspectacular career, Wardle was 'a steady and efficient officer' but not one to assert himself in the manner of a Corden or a Greenwood. Although he made the occasional arrest for gaming in local beerhouses, many of his arrests were for careless driving, hawking without a license, sleeping rough or obstruction of the highway. He was known locally as 'Robert', a policeman who liked a drink, but one who tended to 'live and let live', exemplified by his somewhat dilatory approach to gambling in Kirkheaton. In that sense, his success came via low-intensity policing in which rigorous enforcement of the law was traded off against tolerance of the police. If Wardle struck an acceptable balance (and he was not criticised by his superiors for his inefficiency), not all men did. Exemplifying the fears that Colonel Cobbe had expressed from the outset, Constable William Booth was charged by Superintendent Heaton for neglect of duty, his conduct being 'very improper and unbecoming an officer.' As Heaton explained, Booth 'began to mix with the inhabitants instead of attending to his duty'.[65]

It would be simplistic to see the development of policing simply in terms of 'good cops' and 'bad cops'. Broader socio-economic inequalities, gender and class assumptions, the class orientation of the law and courts and the general expectations of the police created a context in which the individual constable operated and imposed constraints on his actions. Equally important were the practical realities of policing in a rural district characterised by scattered habitations and harsh landscapes. Nevertheless, the individual and his use of discretion was important and could have a critical impact on the relationship between police and policed, as will become even more apparent when the events of summer 1862 in Honley and Holmfirth are considered. Overall there was no Storchian 'open warfare', but there were signs that a new and enduring *modus vivendi* between police and policed was emerging, though yet to be fully established. Incidents of police violence still occurred but less often in the mid- to late-1860s; concerns remained about 'bad judgment' by the police but, again, fewer as time passed. The excessive use of handcuffs and other restraints on men and particularly on women as they were marched or carried by cart to the county police station in Huddersfield aroused popular anger in the late-1850s, less so in the late-1860s, not least because of the opening of new stations (or police houses with cells) that reduced the need to move the arrested long distances through the streets.[66] In broad terms, the police were becoming more disciplined but also more aware of the limits of their power in practice. They were also developing priorities that fitted better with popular concerns (most notably dealing with beggars and vagrants) and extending their role beyond narrow crime-fighting to broader 'welfare' concerns but, while progress was made towards a workable and working policed society, unresolved problems remained. There were still incidents of the police being openly insulted in the streets, their windows smashed and even their gardens vandalised. [67] More worryingly, there was also clear evidence of an unwillingness to cooperate with the police. As Heaton recognised, there was 'a great reluctance manifested by people to come forward to give evidence along with the police'.[68] Even when people appeared in court there was an ongoing problem of 'hardswearing' or giving false testimony, 'frequently resorted to by witnesses for the purpose of clearing their friends from the charges brought against them by the police'.[69] Further, notwithstanding the progress made in the early years of the WRCC, the relationship between police and public remained relatively shallow-rooted and fragile as the events in Honley and Holmfirth in 1862 were to demonstrate. These were the most serious challenges to the legitimacy of the WRCC that took place in the first generation of new policing, but before considering these events in detail it is necessary to conclude this chapter with a brief consideration of the relationship between the WRCC and the Huddersfield borough police force.

County and Borough: Conflict and Cooperation

The distinction between the Upper Agbrigg division of the county force and the borough force of Huddersfield might have made sense in administrative and legal terms but not in terms of practical policing. Many of the prize fights and dogfights that took place on Castle Hill were planned in the beerhouses of Castlegate, while highway robbers in Lindley fled for shelter in the pubs of Upperhead Row, and yet the writ of the town police ended at the boundary laid down by the Improvement Act and county officers, likewise, reached the end of their jurisdiction where borough and county met.

The relationship between borough and county at the highest level was tense. Prior to 1856 the situation had been complicated by the fact that the superintending constable for Upper Agbrigg was partly paid for by the rate-payers of Huddersfield and he could be called upon to assist within the 1848 boundaries. There was recurring concern that town constables were helping out 'over the boundary'. As late as 1855 there was confusion as to the relationship. Superintendent Thomas believed he 'was sworn in to act within a certain number of miles under Superintendent Heaton' but was told by the clerk to the Improvement Commissioners that 'Heaton could not call upon him [Thomas] to act without that boundary; yet Superintendent Heaton might be called upon to serve within the improvement limits for his emoluments partly arose from the payments of the ratepayers within those limits'.[70] The Improvement Commissioners had consistently defended jealously their force, most notably during the debates on the police bills in the mid-1850s. Although they were successful in retaining the independence of the borough force in the debates of 1855, the situation was not resolved. Indeed, matters worsened in the aftermath of the 1856 act when

Colonel Cobbe made it known that he wished to see the Huddersfield police incorporated into the county force. Cobbe's ambitions were effectively thwarted by Her Majesty's Inspector of Constabulary for the Northern Division who made it clear that he viewed the borough force as efficient and better able to offer protection to person and property than the county force. Nonetheless, minor territorial infringements continued to give rise to angry exchanges on more than one occasion. In August 1859 Cobbe, acting on a report from Heaton, complained of irregularities by the town police, notably Inspector Townend, who had sent men to investigate a robbery even though he knew well that the crime had been committed at Birkby swimming baths, outside the Improvement Commission boundary. Pedantically the Commissioners defended their police action on the grounds that the thief had fled into the town and that both victim and perpetrator lived within the HIC limits! Having asserted the correctness of their position, the commissioners expressed a wish that the two forces worked together 'harmoniously'.[71] Niggles continued. In September 1860 there was a spat over the attendance of three county officers at the opening of St. Thomas's church in Longroyd Bridge within the Huddersfield limits. Cobbe stressed that the two men were not present as officers on duty but as private individuals – and then complained, in tit-for-tat fashion, that two town officers had acted outside the limits. A tetchy exchange of letters did nothing to 'prevent misunderstanding' that both sides professed to want.[72] Thereafter, tensions diminished somewhat, but there was a further testy exchange of letters in early 1865 over the question of compensation for injured policemen, and matters were not helped by the fact that at incorporation an enlarged Huddersfield meant that police numbers in Upper Agbrigg were reduced as responsibility for places such as Lindley and Paddock changed hands. Relations were further soured by the arcane financial arrangements for the payment of county officers operating outside the HIC limits but within the township of Huddersfield. There was a sense of grievance that certain rate-payers were paying twice over because the payment towards the upkeep of the county officers came via the poor rates which were charged on the whole town, irrespective of the HIC limits. The issue festered on, becoming part of the argument for incorporation in 1862 and reappearing again in 1865.[73] Only after incorporation in 1868 was the matter resolved.

Relations between officers were somewhat different. From his appointment in 1848 Heaton had worked closely with the town constables, Sedgwick and Townend. Notwithstanding public spats over jurisdiction, there are several examples of town and county cooperating in a variety of way as criminals crossed police jurisdictions. As Heaton made clear because 'our districts are so closely connected and interwoven together it is indispensably necessary we [the police] should cooperate'.[74] Very rarely, there was not simply cooperation but coordination, organised from the top down. The policing of the 1865 election demonstrated that the two forces could work effectively together with no threat to their separate existence. The two superintendents worked well together, so much so that the town Watch Committee resolved to thank both Hannan and Heaton

> for the very efficient arrangements made by them for the preservation of the Peace during the Elections and for the manner in which they conducted themselves and directed the men under their command amid circumstances of great difficulty and danger.[75]

There was a double irony to the 'most excellent feeling [which] now exists ... between the County and Borough Police'.[76] In the short run, the handling of the election (including the evidence given to the subsequent parliamentary enquiry into allegations of bribery and corruption) played an important part in the downfall of Hannan. In the longer term, incorporation would render redundant any belated *rapprochement* between the Improvement Commissioners and Colonel Cobbe.

Endnotes

1. S H Palmer, *Police and Protest in England and Ireland, 1789–1850,* Cambridge University Press, 1990, chapter twelve.
2. *HEx,* 17 November 1855.
3. *Ibid.*
4. *HEx*, 16 February 1856. The paper was quite explicit in condemning the concentration of power, as it saw it, in the hands of the Secretary of State.
5. *Ibid.*
6. Much of this chapter is based on an analysis of the careers of the men who served in Upper Agbrigg from 1856 to 1868 as chronicled in Examination Books of the West Riding Police, housed at West Yorkshire Archive Service, Wakefield but also available online via Ancestry.

7 There were 65 applicants for the job, of whom twenty-four were army officers, five naval officers and five serving officers in other police forces.

8 Reports of Inspectors of Constabulary to Secretary of State, 1856/7, *Parliamentary Papers,* 1857/8 (20), p.39.

9 *HC*, 27 December 1862 and 17 September 1864.

10 There was a similar reliance on superintending constables in the newly-founded North Yorkshire County Constabulary. P Bramham. 'Parish Constables or Police Officers? The development of a county force in the West Riding', *Regional and Local Studies*, 1987, pp.68–80, is incorrect in stating that Cobbe refused to appoint previous superintending constables (p.72).

11 Bramham, 'Parish Constables', p.72.

12 Parker's subsequent career was chequered. In early 1869 he was promoted to the rank of superintendent, only to be demoted two years later for misconduct.

13 C Steedman, *Policing the Victorian Community: the Formation of English Provincial Police Forces, 1856–1880,* London, Routledge, Kegan & Paul, 1984, p.70.

14 W J Lowe, ''The Lancashire Constabulary 1845–1870: the Social and Occupational Function of a Victorian Police Force', *Criminal Justice History,* vol. 4, 1983, p.55 and Steedman, *Policing the Victorian Community*, pp.93 & 94.

15 Lowe, 'Lancashire Constabulary', p.57. Steedman's figures for the Buckinghamshire and Staffordshire forces are not directly comparable. Her figures relate to individual years and are sub-divided according to length of service of recruits in each year. Steedman, *Policing the Victorian Community,* pp.95–6.

16 There were a small number of widowers who have been included in with married men. Almost 60 per cent of married men had families of one to three children but 17 per cent had four or more.

17 The police background is quite diverse. There were men who had served in the county forces of Devon, Gloucester, Hampshire and Somerset as well as nearby Lincolnshire; and men from Roxborough, Sidmouth and the Irish Constabulary. There were, of course, Huddersfield-born men in other divisions of the WRCC.

18 Earnshaw's dismissal remains a mystery. The WRCC record simply notes his dismissal, giving no reason. Local press coverage shows that Earnshaw continued much as before in the months January to May 1857 (arrests for licensing offences, obstruction and gambling but one minor and one major theft case) at which point he is never mentioned again in either the local or regional press.

19 Reports of Inspectors of Constabulary to Secretary of State, 1865/6, *Parliamentary Papers,* 1867 (14), p.81. The maximum wage paid to a WRCC constable remained at 21s (£1.05) a week from 1858 to 1866 when it rose to 22*s* 2*d* (£1-12). The Lancashire County force, which had paid its men at the same level as the WRCC in the late-1850s and early-1860s began offering more (24*s* 6*d* or £1-22½)) from 1865.

20 *HEx,* 7 & 14 March and 30 May 1857. R Storch, 'The Policeman as Domestic Missionary', *Journal of Social History,* 9, 1976 at pp.482 & 487 misleadingly refers to 'unpoliced areas' around Huddersfield.
21 *HC,* 14 March, 5 September and 7 November 1857 & 23 October 1858.
22 R Storch, 'The Plague of Blue Locusts: Police Reforms and Popular Resistance in Northern England, 1840–1857',' *Int. Rev. Soc. Hist.,* xx, 61–90, at p.87. The example of 'resumed open warfare' quoted by Storch related to Lees, near Oldham, during the exceptional circumstances of the cotton famine. There are no references to the events in Honley and Holmfirth in 1862.
23 *HC,* 10 January 1857.
24 *HC,* 21 November 1857.
25 *HC,* 21 November 1857 and *HEx,* 14 November 1857 for opposition to the policing of 5th November celebrations.
26 *HC,* 9 July 1859.
27 *HC,* 7 & 14 March 1857. See similar comments after an attack in Kirkheaton, 21 June 1860.
28 *HEx,* 28 February, 1857.
29 *HEx,* 3 January, 7 & 28 February, 14 March, 13 June 1857 and *HC,* 17, 24 & 31 Jan., 7 February, 7 & 14 Mar., 4 & 11 Apr., 6 June, 4 Jul, 3 Oct., & 7 Nov. 1857.
30 The initial detachment (January 1857) was distributed across twelve villages. In half of these there are no reports of positive or negative responses to the new police in the local press.
31 *HEx,* 30 May 1857. Heaton's decision to prefer a charge against a man who had claimed to have beaten the police (the charge of drunk and disorderly behaviour brought by Heaton had been dismissed) was condemned as 'petty and malicious'. The *Examiner* shrewdly observed that a single action such as this would damage the reputation of the police and 'tend to aggravate the popular feeling of dislike to the county police'.
32 *HEx,* 7 March 1857, 'The glorious county police'. *HC,* 14 March & 7 November 1857.
33 *HC,* 5 June 1858.
34 *HC,* 1 December 1860, 21 November 1862, 6 October & 24 November 1866.
35 *HC,* 7 April 1860.
36 For local responses, including Honley see *HC,* 9 Jan., 3 Apr., 1 May, & 10 Jul. 1859, 16 Jun., 21 Jul., 1 Sep., 22 Oct., 1 Dec. 1860, 2 Feb., 16 Mar., 25 May, 23 Nov. 1861.
37 *HC,* 23 June 1866.
38 *HC,* 30 December 1865 & 4 January 1868.
39 *HC,* 16 March 1867.
40 *HC,* 22 October 1864.
41 *HC,* 18 May 1867.
42 *HC,* 3 October 1857 and 11 September 1858.
43 *HC,* 28 November 1863.
44 *HC,* 1 December 1860.
45 *HC,* 8 August 1857. James Garside, a handloom weaver in his late thirties, was hardly a paragon of virtue, appearing in the magistrates' court on a number of occasions for offences including poaching, assaulting the police and failing to support his wife and six children.

46 *HC*, 9 January 1858. Benjamin Garside, another handloom weaver in his late-thirties, was another who dabbled in criminal activities, not least the Castle Hill cockfight discussed in chapter ten.
47 *HC*, 28 April 1860.
48 *HC*, 2 April, 9 July and 20 August 1859.
49 *HC*, 30 June 1860.
50 *Ibid*, 30 June 1860. Later that year Manuel was again criticised for 'more uncalled interference'. *HC*, 20 October 1860.
51 *HC*, 6 April 1861.
52 *HC*, 19 February 1862.
53 *HC*, 19 June 1862.
54 *HC*, 10 July 1858.
55 *HC*, 13 December 1862.
56 *HC*, 24 & 27 February 1874.
57 Sergeant John Turner is another example of a man who played a very active role as inspector of nuisances, in his case, to the Newsome Local Board as well as enforcing cattle plague regulations in 1866/7.
58 *HC*, 1 August 1868.
59 *HC*, 16 June 1860.
60 *Ibid*.
61 *HC*, 11 November 1865. Dyson had eleven previous convictions for assault, three of which were against the police.
62 *LM*, 15 January 1859.
63 *HC*, 8 January 1859.
64 *HC*, 25 January 1864 & 15 August 1868.
65 *HC*, 21 May 1864.
66 *HC*, 7 Nov. 1857, 10 Jul., & 23 Oct. 1858.
67 *HC*, 7 Apr. 1860. See also 16 Apr., 24 Dec. 1859, & 3 Nov. 1860. The Golcar police constable had his celery uprooted in 1860, just before the annual village feast. *HC*, 29 Sep. 1860.
68 *HEx*, 28 May 1864 and *HC*, 16 June 1866.
69 *HC*, 8 December 1860.
70 *HC*, 6 January 1855.
71 Watch Committee Minutes, KMT 18/2/3/14/1, 29 August 1859.
72 Watch Committee Minutes, KMT 18/2/2/2, 5 September 1860.
73 *HC*, 14 March 1857, 6 August 1859, 10 March & 8 December 1860, 14 June 1862 & 5 August 1865.
74 *HEx*, 9 June 1855. Heaton also made reference to the frequency with which he had cooperated with John Thomas of the borough force.
75 Watch Committee Minutes, KMT 18/2/3/14/2, 24 July 1865.
76 *Ibid*.

Trouble in Honley and Holmfirth

THE INTRODUCTION OF the WRCC into the Upper Agbrigg district had been achieved with some difficulty but, after five years, there were encouraging signs that suggested that a *modus vivendi* was being established between the new police and the bulk of the population. Indeed, when, between the 24th of June and the 9th of July 1862, the men of the WRCC were inspected, it was the judgement of Lt. Col. J. Woodford, Her Majesty's Inspector for the Northern District, and formerly Chief Constable of the Lancashire County Constabulary, that they had 'been maintained in a highly satisfactory state of discipline and efficiency'.[1] Regarding Upper Agbrigg, he was 'satisfied with the state of the men, books and cells, everything being regular and satisfactory'.[2] Such positive and reassuring statements must have appeared very strange to many local people as the police inspection coincided, almost exactly, with two major demonstrations of anti-police sentiment in Honley and Holmfirth, which revealed a widespread antipathy towards the police and certain police methods and cast important light on problems facing the 'new' police in the 1860s.

On the 28th of June 1862 the *Leeds Mercury* carried a report under the eye-catching by-line: 'Desperate Attack On The Police By A Mob Near Huddersfield'. The riot came out of the blue and was avidly covered by the local and regional press and even gained mention in the national press.[3] The arrival of the 'new' police in Honley had been largely uncontroversial but matters changed with the transfer of PC Edward Antrobus to the village. Little is known of Antrobus's earlier career. His entry in the WRCC archive is sparse. Born in Stockport around 1830, he was appointed in February

1861, transferred to Upper Agbrigg in March 1861 and transferred out four months later, before being dismissed in October 1863 for unspecified reasons.[4] The local press is more informative. Antrobus's actions were first noted in April 1861, when he was faced with an angry crowd of thirty to forty people outside the *Butcher's Arms* in Deighton.[5] The significance of the event, apparent in hindsight, was less clear at the time as Deighton had a reputation as a trouble spot, where parish constables, as well as the new police, were periodically subject to attack. However, the fact that Antrobus was transferred out of Deighton suggests that the police authorities had reservations about his behaviour. He was next stationed in the small village of Farnley Tyas but a mere three weeks later was moved again, this time to Honley, where his career was nothing if not spectacular. In just over a year he was responsible for more prosecutions than had been brought by all constables in the village in the four years since the formation of the WRCC. He pursued his cases with zeal and pressed for heavy charges against men (mostly) and women, who were not well-paid as agricultural labourers or factory workers. Some of the most contentious cases involved public houses, beerhouses and the enforcement of the licensing laws. In October 1861 he brought a prosecution against a local landlord and his customers for the illegal sale of alcohol at the Honley Feast, only for the magistrates to throw it out on the grounds that the men involved were *bona fide* travellers and, as such, there had been no infringement of the law. Before the end of the year he was the alleged victim in three assault cases, two in Honley and one in Thurstonland. On at least one occasion, his evidence was flatly contradicted by witnesses who declared Antrobus to be the aggressor.[6] In January 1862 Antrobus brought another assault charge but was accused of throwing a man to the floor and attempting to throttle him.[7] Although the significance of the event was not obvious at the time, he also brought an unsuccessful assault charge against well-known local character, Johnny Moss. His activities did not abate. In the spring of 1862 Antrobus brought another charge of illegal Sunday drinking (this time involving a landlord and his customers, two churchwardens and a parish constable, in nearby Netherton) only for it to be thrown out by the magistrates. Finally, in the same month (May) he was involved in yet another fracas in the *George and Dragon*, Honley, in which he was accused of hitting a woman.[8] In addition, on numerous occasions Antrobus charged people with obstructing footpaths or highways; and when he was not bringing prosecutions he made frequent use of the now well-established 'move on' tactic.[9] 'Moving on' was always fraught with tension, even when implemented with moderation but when it was not (as in Honley), as one local writer noted, it was

> exceedingly galling in a manufacturing district, where the operatives are immured in factories during the day; and they surely should not, if, after work hours, they meet together to breathe the free air and exchange thoughts with each other, be taken 'for obstructing the road'.[10]

Such was Antrobus' zeal to ensure the free movement of pedestrians and vehicular traffic through Honley that he did not confine his activities to groups of twenty or thirty, which might reasonably have been seen as a potential obstruction, but to groups of two or three. Infringing 'a working man's privilege to saunter through the streets and lanes of our populous villages of the evening' was bad enough but, to make matters worse, the village was hardly a hot-bed of disorder. As the *Examiner* tartly observed: 'Town Gate Honley is not New Street Huddersfield'.[11]

Matters came to a head on Monday the 23rd of June when simmering ill-feeling 'found vent'.[12] Antrobus was on duty between 6 p.m. and 7 p.m. and was attempting to 'move on' three 'respectable' inhabitants of the village when Johnny Moss came up and cheeked the constable, calling out 'Come up, Antrobus! Roll up, Antrobus!' which was 'part of a pre-concerted signal to gather the rowdy populace'.[13] Moss was 'aided by a bell, a mule and a cart, together with a troupe of youngsters with penny whistles'.[14] A crowd of some 200 quickly gathered and the hostility towards Antrobus became more apparent. Surrounded by a 'mob' in Towngate, he was offered a drink by James Coldwell, one of the accused at the subsequent trial, who, coming from Dobson's beer house with a glass of ale in his hand, allegedly said: 'Here, sup old bugger; thou hasn't long to stop here; we'll warm thee before the neet's out'.[15] A crowd, by now as many as 300, ran Antrobus from the village, stoning him, knocking him senseless, albeit momentarily and, as 'the crowd disported around him', it was alleged, someone shouted: 'Give him more; kill the ----; he's only acting'.[16] Antrobus was able (or allowed) to escape over the fields and reach the safety of the house of the district police sergeant (Turner) who also lived in Honley. At 10 p.m. that evening, in the company of two other officers, he returned to find two fires blazing. One was at a bridge close to the village but the other was at his house. A crowd, now estimated at 400, fired the cottage and burnt in effigy both Antrobus and his wife. The stoning resumed and Antrobus was forced to flee to the main Honley/Holmfirth road where he found refuge, somewhat ironically, in an inn. The crowd surrounded *Jacob's Well,* threatening to burn it down. Some remained there, keeping Antrobus trapped until midnight; others returned to his cottage, broke its windows with stones and even threw 'burning straw besmeared with tar' at Mrs Antrobus.[17] No arrests were made that night but the police returned the following day with warrants for the (alleged) ring leaders. Six of the ten men who had been charged were arrested; an attempted mass rescue of the prisoners failed and the men were taken in handcuffs to the cells in Huddersfield. The anti-police rioting died down but a local defence committee was established to raise funds for the forthcoming trial; money flowed in from all quarters. Such was the ill-feeling towards Antrobus that 'many of the most respectable inhabitants ... subscribed liberally to the defence [fund]'.[18]

The composition of the defence committee cannot be determined but, Honley's radical tradition and earlier links with the Chartist movement might well explain the decision to seek the help of the well-known radical lawyer, 'Mr Roberts of Manchester' who was contacted to represent the arrested men. 'Mr Roberts' was the former Chartist and prominent radical lawyer William Prowting Roberts, widely known as the 'miners' attorney-general'.[19] Roberts had appeared for the defence in a number of industrial cases in the West Riding, not least the trial of men involved in the Thongsbridge Weavers' strike of 1860.[20] However, of greater relevance was Roberts's attitude towards the 'new police' and his involvement in cases relating to them. He had referred to the 'new police' as 'a plague of blue locusts' and created a stir when, in a case in Manchester, he was reported to have recommended 'the knocking down of a policeman if he interfered with innocent people'.[21] Roberts had appeared in a number of local cases involving the 'new police' and their forerunners. In May 1850 he crossed swords with Superintendent Heaton, who was seeking to restrict the opening hours of beerhouse keepers in Holmfirth and, almost a year later in April 1851, he appeared at a special session in the Guildhall, Huddersfield, representing those who objected to the continuation of a paid constable in nearby Kirkburton.[22] In late 1859 he represented a miner accused of assaulting a police constable during the Silkstone Colliery strike, but his most relevant and most recent involvement was in a case of alleged police brutality in Slaithwaite in 1860. In an eloquent defence, Roberts had highlighted the humiliating practice of parading handcuffed prisoners through the streets and the existence of a 'damp and loathsome [police] cellar' in which his client had been held overnight. He also castigated Heaton for failing to censure the police constable involved. Roberts, quite simply, was the obvious man to defend the Honley rioters.

In total thirty-four men were brought to trial – ten in the first trial, twenty-four in the second. Of these twenty-four have been positively identified in the 1861 census.[23] The oldest was over seventy but a third were under twenty years old and a further third aged between twenty and twenty-nine. 46 per cent of those positively identified were unmarried. Three-quarters of the remainder were family men. At least 54 per cent were employed in the woollen trades, though a quarter were labourers. Of the remainder there were two mechanics, a cordwainer, a butcher and the colourful figure of the hawker, Johnny Moss, who had been at the centre of the initial disturbance.

The arrested men appeared before magistrates at Huddersfield on the 28th of June. In a 'densely packed' court, the alleged ringleaders heard a prosecution case alleging 'wanton outrage', 'a determined spirit of rebellion and revolt against the authority and control of the police' and pressing the magistrates to agree to the serious charge of riot.[24] Roberts stressed that the accused were 'all decent respectable men' and laid great emphasis on the class bias of the police, specifically Antrobus, who 'had exercised a degree of surveillance, cruelty and tyranny towards them [the accused] which he would not have exercised towards gentlemen'.[25] There was, as Roberts argued, a pettiness about the police, prodding children with their sticks, but it was the combination of unwarranted use of 'moving on' and arrest practices that led to people being 'handcuffed and treated with every degradation which police malignity could invent' which resulted in a system of 'cruelty to the working classes … [and] servility to the rich'. The riot was 'the unfortunate result of a perfectly legal resistance' to the excessive and illegal behaviour of the police. Roberts sought to generalise his critique. He stressed the specific shortcomings of Antrobus but he represented him as part of a wider police system that was presided over by the 'large swelling pomposity of Mr.

Superintendent Heaton' – a comment that provoked loud laughter in the courtroom.[26] He was also aware of magisterial concern with unacceptable actions by the county police (most recently in the Slaithwaite case) and appealed to their paternalistic instincts: 'the people of Honley ... [he asserted] relied on the magistrates to protect them from Mr. Heaton and his myrmidons'.[27]

Roberts' speech was typically flamboyant but it would be misleading to dismiss it as rhetorical excess. His comments and questions struck a chord among the men and women of Honley who packed the court. Their responses provide an insight into the animosity towards Antrobus, whose evidence could not have been better calculated to inflame local feelings. Under questioning by Roberts, Antrobus openly admitted that 'he had brought more cases before the magistrates than any of his predecessors' and scarcely helped his case by claiming he was 'not aware that any complaints had been made against him from Honley'. Worse, he asserted that he never 'moved on' groups of two or three people, a response that created 'a sensation among the crowd' in the court. Similarly, his claim that the heavy fines (of £1 and even £3) that he had sought had not created any 'distress' because 'they could get drunk five or six times a week' was not well received.[28] Police actions had 'outraged public opinion' which enabled Roberts to make a telling point about their mean-spiritedness. He told the court that he struggled

> to characterise their conduct. Tyranny was too strong a word; but they evinced a spirit of interruption, a dislike of seeing people happy, a sort of envy and jealousy which led them to construe a race, a game of cricket, or any other form of amusement into an obstruction of the highway.[29]

The magistrates were not persuaded by the prosecution argument that the events constituted a riot and as such, triable in a higher court and carrying a higher penalty. The case was treated as a common assault and relatively lenient punishments in the form of fines ranging from £1 to 5*s* (25p) were handed down. The decision was well received by those in court and, when the prosecution counsel responded to the punishment with the hyperbolic claim that he would 'recommend the chief constable to let his men be killed off as fast as the mob could kill them', he was greeted with hoots of derision.[30] Although the magistrates had not explicitly accepted Robert's argument that poverty was being penalized, their decision to treat the case as one of common assault and the levels of fines that they imposed showed they had little sympathy with the actions of Antrobus and those like him.

Unfortunately, for the police at least, this was not the end of the matter. Tension increased as news spread that 'between twenty and thirty fresh summonses were being distributed in the village' and the defence committee was 'promptly reorganised' in response to the 'uncalled for intrusion upon the domestic quiet of so large a number of families upon such trifling pretences'.[31] Furthermore, this decision meant 'we are no longer dealing with Police-constable *Antrobus* but with Superintendent *Heaton*' who had replaced Antrobus at the centre of the stage. The *Examiner* was unequivocal in its condemnation of the 'vindictiveness...of his actions' and arguing that

> had it been Mr Heaton's intention to have proved the truth of the charges brought against the police generally ... that of "cruelty to the poor" he could not certainly have accomplished this more effectually than by taking the course he so unwisely adopted.[32]

Twenty-four more Honley men, charged with aiding and abetting the convicted 'ringleaders', were brought to court and the impact was, if anything, more sensational. Honley came to a halt. 'Work seemed to be suspended by common consent and groups of people stood at the street corners, talking over the events of the day in an excited manner'.[33] The trial started with a revelation about the strength and breadth of popular sentiment. Then, to the amazement of many in court, the trial was brought to a halt. Following discussions and agreement between the magistrates and the two counsels, Mr Learoyd, the prosecutor, explained that

> he had come to the conclusion to recommend the withdrawal of the charges against the defendants on the ground that such a course would serve more than any other to promote the restoration of kindly feeling in the village of Honley.[34]

The magistrates issued a statement that stressed their duty to both the police and the people but made clear that 'if a policeman exceeds his duty the Bench, *as in many previous cases*, would discountenance his proceedings'. Furthermore, through Learoyd, Heaton made it known that he had 'no desire to sanction in the officers any excess of duty on their part'.[35] The matter appeared to be over. The response in the village was unequivocal: 'Honley was "all alive" with such a display of popular feeling as, perhaps, never before manifested in a country village'.[36]

And it might have ended there had not Heaton, reportedly 'discouraged' by the magistrates' decision to call off the second trial, come to the decision – politely described at the time as 'very indiscreet' – to prosecute twenty-four boys, aged between ten and twelve, for their part in the riot 'for no other ostensible fault than playing their tin whistles &c at the riot'.[37] The impact in Honley was dramatic. The police decision was seen as vindictive and 'aroused public sympathy for the boys' and, according to the *Chronicle* 'did not abate the strong feeling manifested against the other side [the police]'.[38] Indeed, according to the *Examiner*:

> the indignation of the entire community was now fairly roused and the sixpences of the poorest joined with the guineas of the rich in attesting the unmistakable unanimity of feeling with which this oppressive supplementary proceeding was regarded.[39]

The public protest that took place on the next day (the 1st of July) when the boys were due in court was strikingly high-profile. 'The boys walked down to Huddersfield, two and two together, like scholars at a school-feast, accompanied by their mothers, and a host of other women'.[40] For just over an hour, this procession of women, not simply accompanying but protecting their children, made its way from Honley along one of the main roads into Huddersfield through 'crowds of sympathising friends and relatives'.[41] Once again the magistrates decided not to proceed with the charges; once again the people of Honley celebrated. A large crowd, estimated to be in excess of 3,000, turned out, and in a prominent position was Johnny Moss, on his mule, which had been renamed Antrobus for the occasion! A local band, from nearby Berry Brow, played 'Oh dear, what can the matter be' (and other unnamed 'lively airs') as the 'monster procession' made its way, 'most peaceable and orderly', through the village. There was a 'thrill of joy through the neighbourhood ... [and] demonstrations of joy and welcome'.[42] The celebrations ended at the village cricket ground, where, after some short speeches, there were 'three hearty cheers for Roberts the Defence Advocate and the [Honley] Defence Committee', followed by 'three times three cheers' for Princess Alice's marriage, which had taken place that day. 'Finally the whole of the large crowd sang the national anthem in good tune and with a violence that made the valley ring again.'[43] Significantly, 'the additional police force in the town [Honley] did not interfere at all, but wisely let the villagers have their frolic out in their own way'. It was a decision that eased tensions to such an extent that even the police were treated with 'due civility' and it also 'showed that Honley people can be quiet and peaceable when they are let alone'.[44] Reflecting on events, the *Chronicle* expressed its regret that 'some policemen do not act more in accordance with their general instructions, which are that "constables must be particularly cautious not to interfere idly or unnecessarily"'.[45] The *Examiner*, generally more critical of the police, took a similar position. It conceded that it would be 'ungenerous to overlook in any degree the onerous nature of a policeman's duties and the unpopularity which, in certain quarters their faithful discharge will almost necessarily entail' but was concerned with improper restrictions on personal liberty, arguing that 'the only guarantee for the legitimate use of [police power] is to be found in the possession of good nature, intelligence and common sense'. Sadly, it concluded, 'nothing seems clearer than the injudicious exercise of this, some discretionary power by the police of Honley'.[46]

This was not the end of the saga. A week later there was a well-attended meeting at Honley town hall at which it was decided to send a memorial to the Chief Constable of the WRCC, condemning, in general 'the irritating and insulting conduct of police' and specifically the 'indiscreet and injudicious, if not illegal conduct' of PC Antrobus. It warned that it was

> our strong opinion that the people of this village have in many cases been most improperly interfered with and that too, in spirit and conduct much more likely to irritate and provoke than to allay and soothe unpleasant feelings towards those who are put over us as guardians of the peace.[47]

and concluded that 'the peace of the district [of Honley] cannot be maintained because of the bitterness of the feeling which is entertained against [PC Antrobus] by the villagers.'[48] However, the signatories, described as '133 manufacturers, merchants, solicitors, tradesmen, &c', made it clear that it was the actions of the police generally, not just Antrobus alone, that was cause for concern. In saying this, they were not suggesting that the police should be removed but rather that the force should act properly.

> If the police of this district will thus try to discharge the duties imposed upon them, they will have the regard and support of all respectable men; but if they transgress proper limits and encroach upon the liberties and privileges of the people, all the prosecutions which may be threatened, cannot prevent that which we fear and deprecate – disorder, riot and crime.[49]

There could be no clearer statement of the desire for a properly policed society, in which laws were upheld but liberties protected. The memorial concluded with a specific request that Antrobus be removed. Cobbe, who had also received a letter from Antrobus asking to be moved, agreed and a new constable took his place. There was no trouble at that year's Honley Feast and the greatest disturbance in the village was caused by a tornado that hit in October.[50] An unpopular policeman had been run out of town but there was no rejection of the police *per se*. Honley was never an unpoliced village but when PC Grant was installed a new working relationship had to be established – and one which reflected the villagers' sense of the legitimate limits of police action. Grant, although not a local man – he had been born in Devon – was an experienced officer, who soon won the support of many of the people in Honley. The number of prosecutions, especially for minor offences, dropped dramatically and such was his success that he was promoted to first-class constable in April 1863 and sergeant in May 1864, at which point he moved to Kirkburton, where he served out the remaining fifteen years of his career. On his retirement he was described as a 'much respected sergeant of police' who had 'gained the just esteem of everybody' including 'the class with whom policemen chiefly come in contact'.[51] Although such a judgement needs to be viewed sceptically, there is clear evidence that Grant was successful in building bridges with local communities.

There was one final twist in the Honley saga, which reflected positively on Grant but also suggested that senior policemen had not properly learnt the lessons of the previous months. In the summer of 1863 the defence committee held its last meeting, a supper 'celebrating the popular triumph over a meddling and over-officious policeman' at the *Allied Tavern*. The supper would not have taken place had the senior police officers, Colonel Cobbe and Superintendent Heaton, not 'disapproved' of the defence committee's proposal to present '£2 to Police-constable Grant ... who had gained the respect and confidence of the inhabitants by his excellent conduct as a police officer'.[52] No reason was given for the refusal but the proposal, as well as the overt praise for Grant, was implicitly a criticism of Cobbe's decision to transfer Antrobus to Honley and Heaton's defence of him as 'a model officer'. Undoubtedly Honley after the summer of 1862 was much quieter. Far fewer cases were brought before the local magistrates, though press reporting of foot races and the like suggest no significant change in local behaviour. However, it was noted in the local press that there had been 'a very great change … in the public mind at Honley with regard to the police'. Unlike Antrobus, the new constable, Grant, was reported to have won 'entire approval'.[53] It is unlikely that village mores had changed dramatically. The police had learned to use their discretion in the implementation of the law rather than pushing it to the limit as had been the case with Antrobus.

Almost simultaneously, widespread public discontent with the new county police was showing itself, albeit in a significantly different form, in the nearby village of Holmfirth where there was 'considerable dissatisfaction … with the manner in which the [new county] police have interfered with the peaceable inhabitants' which 'rendered themselves obnoxious to many'.[54] Protest in Honley had been driven from the bottom up. The sense of injustice in the village created a cross-class sense of unity but middle-class involvement followed rather than led events. In contrast, in Holmfirth protest was coordinated by members of the middle classes, who took the initiative in calling a public protest meeting for Monday the 7th of June, 1862. Headed by the Rev. T James, twenty or more of the respectable male population of Holmfirth demanded a meeting to consider what action should be taken in light of 'the glaring encroachments of the police upon the rights and liberties of the peaceable inhabitants of these places'.[55] The roots of the problem went back to the introduction of the new county force. Unlike in Honley, in Holmfirth the new police, from the outset, had been 'very diligent', particularly in enforcing licensing laws and prosecuting cockfighting. In the summer of 1858 there were reports of 'dastardly attacks on the police-constables of the neighbourhood'.[56] However, police zeal was tempered to a significant degree by the attitude of the highly-regarded Inspector Haworth. His departure, in late 1859, removed an important force for conciliation between the police and respectable Holmfirth folk. At a special meeting he had been given a hearty vote of thanks and speakers praised the fact that 'his object ... [was] to carry out the law rather than to impose fines ... [and he] had frequently cautioned disturbers of the peace instead of taking them before the magistrates'. In particular, he was praised for being 'free from the overbearance and officiousness to which some officers are too prone'.[57] In the absence of his restraining presence matters began to worsen, with the conduct of certain constables being described as an 'intolerable nuisance'.[58] There was also a growing suspicion that the local magistrates were too willing to accept police evidence, so much so that 'gentlemen ... having heard the cases, say the decisions are against evidence'.[59]

The situation deteriorated rapidly in the late-1860s and 1861. Once again the attitude of individual officers was critical. One of the most assiduous men was Joseph Briers, who had been moved to Holmfirth, having been demoted from sergeant as the result of unspecified indiscipline. Briers was a high-profile and unpopular man. In February 1861 he was viciously beaten by a gang of seven men after he had (at the request of the landlord) cleared the *Rose and Crown*. Their trial caused 'considerable excitement in the district' and, though found guilty and fined £6 and costs each, the money was paid immediately.[60] Even more interest was aroused by the subsequent trial of Briers for perjury. Much depended on the notes taken by the local reporter, John Sanderson. The case was dismissed but this was 'evidently distasteful to the crowded court who manifested their dissatisfaction by their muted execrations'.[61] Three months later he was transferred out of the village but much damage had been done to police/public relations. Briers was not alone. The names of two other men appear time and again in the local press: PCs Linas Hancock and John Strange. Both men were outsiders – coincidentally both born in Gloucestershire – and both were later moved out of Holmfirth and subsequently dismissed. Their careers throw light on the difficulty faced by Cobbe and Heaton in recruiting good men. Hancock was serving his second term in the WRCC and never progressed beyond the third class; Strange was marginally more successful, though was demoted to the second class before being moved out of the district.

Matters in Holmfirth finally came to a head in 1862. Working men had borne the brunt of police zeal initially. After two sessions in which there had been no business for the magistrates, their session of May 1862 saw a sharp increase, mainly as the result of 'trivial' cases brought by the police, mainly for allegedly drunk and disorderly behaviour.[62] Within a few weeks the situation had deteriorated dramatically. The *Chronicle* editorialized about the need for the Holmfirth magistrates to consider other testimony, especially when police evidence was unsupported. Only in this way could 'a proper respect for authority' be restored.[63] Under the heading 'Frivolous Police Charges And Their Results', a correspondent detailed cases of men being charged with obstruction when making their way home or even standing on private property which gave rise to 'strong feelings against the police'. The case of Joseph Balmforth, a painter, epitomised the problem. He was charged with 'obstructing the road' as he made his way to his front door, through a crowd of people, including a police officer. The officer testified that Balmforth had taken him by the shoulder and deliberately caused an obstruction and, in the absence of any other witness in court, the magistrate, emphasising the fact that the police evidence was on oath, fined him 1*s* (5p) and costs.[64] Whereas once animosity towards the police had been confined largely to 'rougher' elements by the summer of 1862 anti-police anger 'now pervades every class in the community'. The nature of many of the cases brought before the local magistrates, the suspicion that a number of police cases were 'imagined or manufactured', and the willingness of the magistrates to accept uncorroborated police evidence united local sentiment against 'a persecuting force'.[65]

This was the context in which the meeting demanded by Rev. James took place. The organizers seriously underestimated the number of people who wished to attend. As the time for the start of the meeting approached,

> the road in front of the [Town] Hall was thronged with countless wearers of blue smocks, the hard working and aggrieved portion of the community who have especially been the subject of the harsh treatment of which they complain ... The thousands of people who had assembled consequently wended their way to [the cricket ground] to prevent obstruction of the road.[66]

The mass meeting was chaired by the chief constable of the graveship of Holme and the township of Netherthong but the initiative was taken by middle-class men who dominated the speech-making. The very visible presence of these middle-class figures, equally aggrieved at police high-handedness, helped direct local anger into the more respectable form of protest of petitioning the authorities. Nonetheless, there was real anger, not least at the stance of the chief constable who had written to the Rev. James claiming, not only that he had received no complaints, but that the police had acquitted themselves well. The first claim was denied by some of those present and the second dismissed as 'bosh and nonsense'.[67] There was further anger with the manner in which the village's grievance had been investigated. Cobbe simply asked the relevant Superintendent, Heaton, to look into matters and he, only interviewing the police involved and, totally ignoring the petitioners, had concluded that nothing was amiss.[68]

Two resolutions were put before the meeting and both were passed unanimously and accompanied by 'triumphant cheers' before being sent to both the Chief Constable and the Lord Lieutenant of the county. The first was proposed by Alfred Wood, a mill-owner, and seconded by the woollen manufacturer, James Holmes; the second proposed by a local shopkeeper, John Sanderson was seconded by James Schofield, a draper. The first resolution made clear the prevailing mood.

> [T]his meeting has viewed with feelings of intense disgust, the conduct of the police in this district; that the paltry and trivial cases which have been brought before the bench of magistrates at Holmfirth and the mode in which these cases have been dealt with have greatly excited universal indignation amongst the inhabitants of this neighbourhood.[69]

Wood spoke forcefully of the 'petty tyranny which has for some time past been exercised by the police towards the different classes of the community' and bemoaned the fact that 'in Holmfirth the police were not their servants; they were their tyrants'.[70] He was not alone in expressing such sentiments. The speeches were dominated by a rhetoric that stressed the liberties of the English, and their constitutional rights and references were made to the threat posed by the new county police which would reduce the people of Holmfirth to the level of 'the crawling serfs of a Russian or an Austrian despot.'[71] At the same time there were very specific criticisms made of the county police. Despite the cost of maintaining a force, it was seen to fail in its basic responsibility of protecting property and person. Wood damned the police for their incompetence in dealing with the robbery from his mill and for their insulting behaviour to respectable men of the town.[72] There was also sympathy for less respectable victims of police action.

> Notoriously too many of them [the police] now levy a species of black mark upon the doubtful persons who frequent the streets at night; often they extract fees from the 'unfortunates' [prostitutes] in their beat not to molest them in their vocation.[73]

Specific police practices, notably the humiliation of being handcuffed in public and of being moved on for no good reason, were also highlighted. Yet more serious accusations were made. Several speakers complained that the police effectively manufactured cases and gave false evidence even when under oath; only for the local magistrates to accept the uncorroborated evidence of the police, even in the face of contrary evidence from 'respectable' witnesses.

The 'policeman's meddling-malady' was a common complaint. One speaker, the weaver Benjamin Stanley, waxed eloquent on the 'petty tyranny and pomposity' of the police, and the paltriness of the cases that they brought. He cited a number of cases including one from his own experience when he and his wife

> happened to take the daring liberty of looking over the battlements [of Victoria Bridge in the centre of Holmfirth] at the water, when up came a man with very bright buttons and a very blue coat, and who, with that kind of mock dignity which I suppose he had borrowed or stolen from his superiors, ordered us to 'move on'[74]

They didn't and felt the full force of the law. He concluded his speech with a rhetorical question.

> What species of tyranny can be so hateful as that which presents its ugly face at the corner of every street, pokes its nose into the privacy of dwellings, domineering with low-bred surliness on every public occasion, and is borne with and upholden by the 'powers that be' [the magistrates] in spite of the testimony of most respectable witnesses?[75]

There was an element of social snobbery from middle-class men who resented being told what to do by men who were their social inferiors and 'comers-in'. However, it was clear from both the size and the response of the crowd that these criticisms struck a chord among 'the wearers of blue smocks' as well.[76]

There was further anger at the suggestion that there was a conspiracy against the police. As Holmes made clear that 'it is not that we want to do away with the police' but rather fewer and better policemen. Like Wood, he stressed 'the dictatorial and officious actions of the police' and quoted Roberts's claim at the recent trial of the Honley rioters that the police waged a war against the poor. The situation was not helped by the fact that the new policeman was 'a low-bred stranger with whose antecedents we have no acquaintance' and who acted in a manner that had more in common with 'John Moss's mule'.[77] To compound matters further, and quoting a recently retired policeman, Holmes argued that the police were told from the very top (Superintendent Heaton) not to be friendly with members of the local community. Despite the undoubted anger on display, the calls for moderation prevailed and, after the second resolution had been passed to resounding cheers, the crowd gave a further three cheers for the Queen and then dispersed quietly – but there was to be one final twist to the events of the day.

Superintendent Heaton had been aware that a mass meeting was scheduled to take place in Holmfirth and that local feelings were running high. By way of precaution, and not wishing for a repeat of the scenes in Honley, he arranged for thirty-six men, from three divisions of the West Riding, to be present under his leadership. Entraining from Huddersfield, they duly arrived in Holmfirth to be greeted more with mirth than anger. The 'most peaceable and orderly' conduct of the meeting (and its aftermath) was beyond reproach and the police had nothing to do and no-one to arrest. However, as a local eye witness (described as 'a gentleman in whose truthfulness we have entire confidence') told the *Examiner*, the police 'determined to make the best of the unfortunate occurrence by kicking up a shindy of their own'. Presumably in the absence of Heaton (though there is no mention of his whereabouts), fifteen or so drunken policemen 'sallied forth into the town and neighbourhood and ... suffered their usual surly dignity to melt down into swearing, leap frog and other antics much to the amusement of those who saw them'. Having spent much of the early morning of Tuesday drinking copiously in the *Rose & Crown*, Holmfirth, four or five policemen then 'perambulated the road from the end of Victoria Street to Upper Mill, rousing many of the peaceable inhabitants from their slumbers at 4 a.m. Two were seen 'performing the donkey's part between the shafts of a cart' while 'oaths and various kinds of ribaldry' were heard as the police roamed through Upper Mill. Perhaps the most amazing aspect of this drunken spree is that it was eleven-and-a-half miles from Holmfirth to Upper Mill.[78] Matters could scarcely get worse for the reputation of the police – but they did. On the following day,

> [o]n the platform at the Holmfirth station and during their ride to Huddersfield, they [the police] cheered themselves and others, by lustily singing 'Here's to the red, white and blue', emphasizing strongly the last word, and adding to it occasionally the word Antrobus.[79]

Cobbe's response to the Holmfirth resolutions was not reported in the local press but it is striking that by the end of August no cases had been brought by the police before the local magistrates.[80] There were also changes in police personnel in Holmfirth and whereas 'the last police acted on the system that if there was not a squabble in the street they would make one' but now there were no police cases – a change that was 'much the better'.[81] As in Honley, so in Holmfirth a *modus vivendi* was established through the restriction of police activities.

Standing back from the detail of the two disturbances, a number of broader questions and conclusions emerge. The first question centres on the typicality of Honley and Holmfirth. Both had traditions of liberal and radical politics, though both (Honley in particular) prided themselves on being law-abiding. There were undoubtedly 'rougher' communities to be found in Upper Agbrigg but by virtue of the trouble that erupted in these villages, they were unusual. There were differences between the two outbursts of anti-police sentiment but they were essentially one of degree, and the active involvement of middle-class critics of the police in both towns was significant. More generally, there was an ongoing, grumbling hostility that manifested itself in smaller scale attacks on the police in various parts of the area. During the trial of the ringleaders of the Honley riot, the prosecutor, Mr Learoyd, drew attention to how the 'revolt against the authority and control of the police ... had pervaded to an alarming extent some of the places surrounding this and neighbouring towns'.[82] This might be dismissed as courtroom hyperbole but the evidence suggests that there was a real problem for the new county police in some areas. The pages of the Huddersfield newspapers bear witness to continuing animosity towards the police, particularly in Lindley, Kirkheaton and Scammonden.[83] Furthermore, it was a problem that continued into the following decade. In 1873, Heaton conceded that there were places, such as Skelmanthorpe 'where the police were interfered with in the execution of their duty'.[84] In the autumn of the previous year the inhabitants of another nearby West Riding village, Emley, celebrated the departure of an unpopular constable in spectacular fashion. PC Suttle, a teetotaller, had made himself very unpopular during the two years that he spent there. His departure sparked a rousing send-off. Angry villagers in Honley had burnt an unpopular policeman in effigy; their counterparts in Emley indulged in a spectacular form of 'rough music' to express their disapproval.

> The local band was engaged, an irregular procession formed and a crowd of persons marched through the village. One man carried a beer-barrel on his back, another carried a loaf of bread, held aloft on a hay fork. A third carried a ham on his head, while others for want of better things, tied their handkerchiefs to the end of sticks and held them up to flutter in the breeze … beer was plentiful … and great was the rejoicing.[85]

PC Suttle could not escape unnoticed.

> As the policeman essayed to depart [members of the crowd] brayed discordant noises in his ears and in those of the horse drawing the cart full of goods, and not content with that, and with shouting uncomplimentary and coarse epithets, they stoned, jostled and knocked him down and otherwise insulted him.[86]

Such public shows of communal disapproval drew strength from traditions, firmly rooted in a pre-industrial, largely rural past, but still seen as relevant in an industrial and increasingly urban present. As Roberts had pointed out in the trial of the Honley rioters, 'the law might be in favour of the goaders [but] a goaded people [will] find means of showing their contempt for those who use the law with cruelty'.[87] PC Antrobus was not the only person to be burnt in effigy, nor was PC Suttle alone in being subjected to 'rough music' in the West Riding in the third quarter of the nineteenth century.[88]

Putting aside various industrial disputes in different parts of the country that gave rise to major anti-police disturbances, there are indicators that the problems experienced in the West Riding were to be found elsewhere. For example, in Hull popular concern with wrongful arrests and police brutality led to a major anti-police disturbance in January 1870 in Raywell Street, which itself gave rise of a police enquiry that revealed a 'tendency to over-authority, or an impatience of restraint … [and] apparent vindictiveness' that is reminiscent particularly of the complaints from Holmfirth.[89] Echoes of the events in Honley were to be found further afield, for example in the demonstration in the Essex village of Stebbing in 1888 when the inhabitants celebrated Guy Fawkes' day

> by making an effigy of a gentleman in Her Majesty's employment who has rendered himself unpopular by doing his duty. The effigy of Pc Enoch Raison was borne through the village in the afternoon and again at night in a torchlight procession before being hanged and burned at Bran End.[90]

Raison (and his family) was driven out of the village and almost immediately resigned from the Essex county force. In the absence of systematic research into the subject, it would be foolish to generalize from a small number of examples but the scattered evidence does suggest that the popular response to the 'new police' in the West Riding was not unique.

The third major question centres on the typicality of men such as Antrobus. The magistrates at the trial of the Honley rioters certainly suggested that 'there might be three or four men … that might bring the whole [force] into disrepute'.[91] There can be no doubt that PC Antrobus was highly unpopular. He was variously described as 'peculiarly obnoxious' and 'officious and overbearing' and some contemporary commentators focused on the *ad hominem* anger manifest in Honley but, as at least one writer pointed out, the riot was a 'fire [that] only wanted igniting' and Antrobus was the spark. In other words, there was a 'dislike of the police generally' as well as animosity towards Antrobus that came to a head on that Monday in June 1862.[92] Few, if any, officers had a record of indiscipline to compare with his. Having been found guilty of assault on more than one occasion and having been twice dismissed from police forces before he joined the West Riding constabulary, he was hardly a typical policeman. He was also extremely zealous in his work while at Honley. However, if his past record (about which he kept quiet) was unusual, his approach to police work was less so. Indeed, as became clear at the Honley trial, he was closely connected with Superintendent Heaton. Antrobus, of whom Heaton spoke in positive terms as a 'model officer', had a prosecution rate was undoubtedly above average but it would be misleading to see him as wholly untypical. He was not alone. The evidence from Holmfirth points in the same direction. Although not as officious as PC Antrobus, PCs Briers, Hancock, Strange and Taylor, as well as the newly-appointed Inspector Parkin, showed a degree of zeal in prosecuting landlords and their clients that brought them into conflict (sometimes literally) with some inhabitants of Holmfirth.[93] Elsewhere, there were many ordinary men and women who would have recognised Roberts's claim, made when defending the Honley rioters that some members of the police showed 'servility to the rich' and 'cruelty to the working classes'.[94] However, as the evidence in chapter eight demonstrated, there were also other officers whose actions were less antagonistic.

The final question relates to the notion of policing by consent, which will be discussed more fully in the final chapter. Suffice it to say here that the Honley riot and the Holmfirth mass protest of 1862 revealed a scale of ongoing mistrust, which could rapidly turn to outright opposition, which had been played down by defenders of the 'new' police. More importantly, these events highlight the very real limitations of police power and authority and the need for the police to accommodate themselves to their community, rather than simply imposing their authority.

Endnotes

1. *Report of Her Majesty's Inspectors of Constabulary, 1861–2, Parliamentary Papers* 1863 (20), p.74. Much of this chapter is based on D Taylor, 'Protest and Consent in the Policing of the Wild West Riding ofYorkshire, c.1850-1875: The Police v the People, Northern History', II (2), 2014, pp.290-310.
2. *HEx,* 12 July 1862.
3. See for example, *Daily News*, 26 June 1862. On the same page as a lengthy report on a major fracture of the Fleet sewer that threatened underground railway works in London there was reference to 'a most disgraceful riot … at a village near Huddersfield'.
4. *West Riding Police Records*, Examination Book D, 1858–61, accessed via Ancestry.co.uk, 30 August 2015. Antrobus also lied about his previous police disciplinary record. It is impossible to say how many other men gave false information to the police authorities.
5. *HC*, 6 April 1861.
6. *HC*, 19 October & 28 December 1861.
7. *HC*, 25 January 1862.
8. *HC*, 5 & 19 October 1861, 25 January, 3 May 1862. For other reported cases see *HC*, 28 December 1861, 10 May, 14 June 1862.
9. Concern with obstruction was nothing new but, as the General Orders for the Metropolitan Police clearly demonstrate, senior police officers were

acutely aware of the need for sensitivity in enforcing the relevant laws. Likewise, moving on had emerged as (from a police perspective) a sensible tactic to prevent large groups assembling but again required the careful use of discretion to avoid being counter-productive.

10 *HC*, 5 July 1862.
11 *HEx*, 5 July 1862.
12 *HEx*, 28 June 1862.
13 *Ibid.*
14 *Ibid.*
15 *LM*, 30 June 1862.
16 *Ibid.*
17 *LM*, 28 June 1862.
18 *LM*, 2 July 1862.
19 For details of Roberts's varied career see R. Challinor, *A Radical Lawyer in Victorian England: W. P. Roberts and the Struggle for Workers' Rights*, Farnham, Tauris (1990). Although discussing police action on a number of occasions, C. Frank, *Master and Servant Law: Chartists, Trade Unions, Radical Lawyers and the Magistracy in England, 1840–1865*, Farnham, Tauris, 2010 has a more specific focus.
20 *HC*, 24 March 1860. See also *HC*, 16 November 1850, 15 August 1857 for examples of Roberts defending workmen charged with embezzling woollen waste under the Worsted Acts.
21 *HC*, 14 May 1853. The case involved a beerseller who had been charged with having disorderly people on his premises. The 'plague of blue locusts' quotation is cited in Challinor, *Radical Lawyer*, p.81.
22 *HC*, 11 May 1850, 12 April 1851. The Holmfirth case provides a very good example of Heaton's pedantic determination to enforce laws that might restrict licensing hours. In this case the debate centred on whether Holmfirth existed 'under the construction of the words of 15th section of 3 & 4 Victoria'. The local magistrates refused to adjudicate on the matter and recommended that Heaton apply to the Court of Queen's Bench for a definitive ruling.
23 Of the remaining ten, three cannot be traced at all and seven cannot be unequivocally identified. For example, there were five George Boothroyds in the village. Two were aged forty-one, married and woollen weavers; two were aged thirty-one, married and woollen weavers; and one was a fifteen-year-old mule piecer.
24 *LM*, 2 July 1862.
25 *LM*, 30 June 1862.
26 *LM*, 5 July 1862.
27 *Ibid.*
28 *HC*, 5 July 1862. It was alleged that the fines amounted to more than £100.
29 *LM*, 30 June 1862. The reference to public opinion is in *HEx*, 5 July 1862.
30 *LM*, 30 June 1862.
31 *HEx*, 5 July 1862.
32 *HEx*, 28 June 1862.
33 *HEx*, 5 July 1862.
34 *LM*, 2 July 1862.

35 *Ibid*. Italics added.
36 *HC*, 5 July 1862.
37 *Ibid*.
38 *Ibid*.
39 *HEx*, 28 June 1862.
40 *HC*, 5 July 1862.
41 *HEx*, 5 July 1862.
42 *HEx*, 28 June 1862.
43 *HEx*, 5 July 1862.
44 *HC*, 5 July 1862 and *HEx*, 5 July 1862.
45 *HC*, 5 July 1862.
46 *HEx*, 28 June 1862.The paper also criticised the Holmfirth police for the same failings.
47 *HC*, 12 July 1862.
48 *HEx*, 12 July 1862.
49 *Ibid*.
50 *HC*, 25 October 1862.
51 *HC*, 15 March 1879.
52 *HEx*, 29 August 1863.The sum was the difference between the £41 subscribed for the defence of the Honley rioters and the £39 than had actually been spent.
53 *HC*, 28 May 1864. Grant may have been helped by the sudden and unfortunate death of his thirteen-year old son in the December of 1862. Antrobus later confessed to having been dismissed from two police forces before joining the West Riding constabulary and having been convicted for assault on more than one occasion, though he had lied about this to gain re-employment as a police officer. *LM*, 22 Oct. 1863.
54 *HEx*, 5 July 1862.
55 *HEx*, 12 July 1862.
56 *HC*, 5 June 1858. See also 1 December, 1858, 24 December 1859 & 1 September 1860.
57 *HC*, 5 November 1859.
58 *HC*, 1 October 1859.
59 *HC*, 1 September 1860.The paper concluded that 'these cases are almost becoming a nuisance'.The actions of the Holmfirth magistrates contrasted with those of their counterparts in Huddersfield, where most of the Honley cases were heard, who were more sceptical of the police and openly criticized them on occasion.
60 *HEx*, 9 March 1861.
61 *HEx*, 16 March 1861.
62 *LM*, 5 May 1862.The reasons for this upsurge in police activities are not given.
63 *HC*, 21 June 1862.
64 *Ibid*.
65 *HC*, 17 August 18611 & 21 June 1862.
66 *HC*, 12 July 1862.
67 *LM*, 10 July 1862 & *HC*, 12 July 1862.
68 *HEx*, 12 July 1862.

69 *HC*, 12 July 1862.
70 *HEx*, 12 July 1862.
71 *HC*, 12 July 1862.
72 Wood claimed that he had informed the police of the likely perpetrators (seen spending freely in town) but that they had failed to prevent the robbers from leaving with the stolen goods from Holmfirth and nearby Brockholes railway stations. *HC*, 12 July 1862.
73 *Ibid.*
74 *Ibid.*
75 *Ibid.*
76 The unity of sentiment in 1862 contrasts with the hostility between Chartists and Anti-Corn Law Leaguers in Holmfirth in the 1840s.
77 *HC*, 12 July 1862.
78 *HEx*, 12 July 1862.
79 *Ibid.*
80 *HC*, 30 August 1862.
81 *HC*, 28 March 1863.
82 *HC*, 5 July 1862.
83 Responsibility for the policing of Lindley switched to the Huddersfield borough force following incorporation of the town in 1868.
84 *HC*, 12 July 1873. Heaton appears to have overstated his case. There were some disturbances involving navvies, briefly staying in the village, but local press coverage reveals far fewer anti-police incidents than in places such as Scammonden or Kirkheaton. Conflict between miners and colliers, on the one hand, and the police on the other, was reported on numerous occasions in the last quarter of the nineteenth century, See for example *HC*, 16 May 1879, 1 & 5 June 1880, 18 October 1888, 20 January 1894.
85 *LM*, 2 October 1872.
86 *Ibid.* The following year saw the inhabitants of Ossett complaining that 'instead of being a protection to the people they [the police] were positively a terror'; so much so that 'the feeling ... is so strong that the police have been turned out of their lodgings and ... compelled to live in the police cells' in the town. *LM,* 31 December 1873.
87 *HC*, 5 July 1862.
88 For local examples of burning in effigy see *HC*, 24 November 1860, 20 June 1863, 1 July 1865, 19 June 1869, 22 June 1872, 30 June 1874, 22 October 1879, & 21 August 1890. For examples of rough music see *HC*, 20 June 1863, 2 July 1864, 1 July and 23 September 1865, 1 September 1866, 30 March 1867, 6 April 1878, 26 August 1884, 23 June 1890; *LM*, 16 February 1863, 12 June 1866, 22 August 1866, 21 December 1866, 30 June 1874, & 17 October 1893. The custom was undoubtedly less common by the end of the century and the *Leeds Mercury*, not entirely accurately, consigned 'stang-riding', as it was often termed, to the category of bygone punishments in the 1880s. See for example 2 February 1884.
89 *Hull Packet*, 11 March 1870.
90 *Essex Weekly News,* 9 November 1888 cited in M. Scolan, *Sworn to Serve: Police in Essex, 1840–1990,* Chichester, Phillimore, 1993, p.43.
91 *HEx*, 5 July 1862.

92 *HC*, 28 June 1862.

93 See for example *HC*, 27 June, 12 September 1857, 12 & 30 October, 13 November 1858, 8 January, 2 April 1859, 21 July, 4 & 18 August, 27 October, 10 & 24 November, 8 December 1860, 9 February, 25 May, 22 June, 17 August, 28 September & 26 October 1861.

94 *LM*, 30 June 1862.

Crime, Custom and Culture

SUPERINTENDENT HEATON'S ANNUAL report for 1868–69 detailed the incidence of crime in Upper Agbrigg. Only nineteen people had been committed for trial and over 50 per cent of these were for simple larceny. There was a single case of cutting and wounding and one of burglary. In the same year 173 people were dealt with summarily. In the more eventful year of 1866–67 there had been three cases of manslaughter, two of cutting and wounding and two of rape but even then indictable offences accounted for only 15 per cent of all cases which were (as in every year) dominated by simple larceny. Over 50 per cent of summary offences were accounted for by three offences: drunkenness (17 per cent of the total), assaults (21 per cent) and vagrancy and begging (24 per cent).[1] However, there were other offences – notably poaching, vagrancy and offences against the Worsted Acts – that exercised the minds of local law-enforcers, even though they did not figure large in the statistics. Many of the major offences – assaults and drunkenness – were not dissimilar in character to their urban counterparts and have been discussed earlier.[2] Instead, the focus of this chapter will be on a number of crimes that were of particular concern in the countryside. Contrary to popular fears, the WRCC in Upper Agbrigg often chose to minimise their role, for example regarding poaching and even embezzlement, and even where they attempted a more interventionist approach, their impact was limited.

Embezzlement

Protection of property was a central aspect of the development of the law in the eighteenth and nineteenth century. Property rights were a major concern for employers in a wide range of industries and their views brought them into conflict with their employees and their notion of customary rights or trade perquisites. The clearest statement of the new protection afforded to local employers came in the form of the 1777 Worsted Acts, which made it an offence to possess woollen or worsted material that had been embezzled or whose ownership was disputed. The acts also provided for both the buying and selling of embezzled goods with a sliding scale of penalties for first and subsequent offences. To enforce the acts, a Worsted Committee was established and inspectors employed. Over the course of time there were significant changes in the personnel of the Worsted Committee. By the 1840s the dominant force came from larger-scale manufacturers, particularly from Bradford and Halifax.[3] There was also a fundamental change in the focus of activity as factory production expanded and domestic production declined, though the practical approach of the inspectors, checking on the persons and property of workers, did not change in essence.[4] Although the inspectors did not have the right of arrest, they had the power of entry and search that gave them considerable powers of surveillance. Further, the burden of proof was such that it was relatively easy (in comparison with other property offences), to bring a successful prosecution, especially if the case was prosecuted summarily. The Worsted Committee was at its peak in the second quarter of the nineteenth century. By the mid-nineteenth century, the composition of the West Riding magistracy was such that employers often heard cases brought under the Worsted Acts. A major change in funding in 1853 resulted in a reduction in the level of activity for much of the period under consideration in this book. Godfrey and Cox make only passing reference to the Huddersfield district and its inspector, R H Kaye, but the local experience throws some interesting light on the implementation of the law in the 1850s and 1860s. In Upper Agbrigg, the old domestic system remained strong in several villages, while the development locally of the trade in recovered wool added to the urgency of the question of the ownership of waste.

The joint Huddersfield and Holmfirth Manufacturers' Protection Association was formed by an amalgamation of two organizations in 1846 and employed two inspectors – Richard Henry Kaye and John Earnshaw – at Huddersfield and Holmfirth respectively, until

1856 when it was decided not to pay for a Holmfirth inspector. The inspectors took a clear and firm line, requesting the committee

> to insert in the annual circular a desire on their part that all manufacturers be very particular in demanding from their Weavers or other Persons they may employ, all Gears, Tools, Spare Weft or Warp of every description, on completing the work they have in hand.[5]

The Association operated until 1866 at least but its annual reports show a significant drop in the volume of activity from the mid-1850s onwards. Between 1850 and 1854 the number of prosecutions averaged thirty-five per annum; between 1856 and 1866 the number fell to eleven.[6] The majority of cases involved the embezzlement of woollen and worsted material, not always as waste. However, there were also prosecutions for the embezzlement of looms, gears and dyestuffs.[7] Newspaper reports show a number of very straightforward cases. Heaton and Kaye searched Joseph Crowther's house in Linthwaite and 'found in the attic and other parts of the building several parcels containing quantities of various waste – carding and scribbling wool, billy ends, nippings and slubbings' – to a total of 424lbs, which he claimed he had bought from Messrs. Haigh of Honley. Heaton demonstrated that the material 'was of a quality such as the Messrs. Haigh would not have in their possession as they merely did "country work"'.[8] Crowther was fined the maximum of £20. John Taylor of Meltham was fined £20 for 'failing to give a proper account of how he became possessed of the pieces of cloth'.[9] Richard Varley, a shopkeeper of Marsden, was also fined £20 because, as the magistrates' explained 'he might have had no intention of doing contrary to the law [but] he had done so in purchasing [a quantity of linsey woolsey] of a party not duly authorised to dispose of the material'.[10] A similar fate befell John Norton, a 'highly respectable merchant'.[11] In this case the magistrates at Huddersfield, conscious of the importance of the case, deliberated for two hours before returning a guilty verdict.[12] Eli Taylor, in contrast, was unable to produce an invoice and was fined £20 and forfeited the waste material while Joseph Crowther (again) produced invoices but they matched neither the quantity nor the quality of the 424lbs of woollen waste which he was accused of embezzling.[13] More ingenious but equally unsuccessful was the farmer-cum-weaver, William Kenworthy, of Moor Edge. He first claimed that the disputed cloth had been woven on his loom but Kaye demonstrated that 'different gears to that then in his loom' would have been needed. Kenworthy then fell back on the defence that the cloth had been legitimately purchased and produced an invoice to that effect. Unfortunately, the invoice was ten years' old and related to a different piece of material. He was fined £20.[14] In contrast, despite being accused by Inspector Kaye of obtaining forty-five lbs of woollen and twenty-two lbs of worsted waste 'under suspicious circumstances', Abraham Waterhouse was able to produce invoices and 'left the court without the slightest imputation upon his character'.[15] Finally, there were a number of repeat offenders for whom the penalty (£30 in the case of a second offence) was the price to pay in ongoing criminality.[16]

Other cases were less straightforward, not least because of the varying attitudes and practices of local employers. Some, such as Taylors of Newsome, paid their out-weavers a monetary wage and expected all waste to be returned to the mill.[17] Others still permitted perquisites. In a case involving Honley Mill, James Brook conceded that they turned a blind eye to 'some portion of waste which it was not necessary to return'.[18] Others did not require their weavers to return waste but, somewhat jesuitically, claimed not to have given 'the authority to sell the waste'.[19] Worse still, in the eyes of inspectors and magistrates, some employers still implemented 'the exceedingly dangerous practice' of a mixed-wage, 'allowing perquisites to workmen in lieu of money'.[20] To what extent workers saw perks as a right in the mid-nineteenth century is open to question. Godfrey and Cox argue that it was no longer a live issue. However, in Upper Agbrigg there were some for whom it was. Henry Swallow's defence counsel argued that 'it was customary for weavers to have the waste and to dispose of it'.[21] Similarly, John Waite, a spinner of Moldgreen, who rented two mules at Firths' Mill, 'considered himself entitled to the sweepings from the floor'.[22] Further, not all employers decided to prosecute, though the reasons for doing so are not recorded.[23]

Of greater interest are the decisions arrived at by the local magistrates, many of whom were manufacturers. At times, concerns about bias were expressed and very occasionally individual magistrates chose not to be involved in embezzlement cases.[24] However, the presence of a manufacturer on the bench did not necessarily ensure a conviction. The Worsted Committee Registers shows an overall conviction rate of 82 per cent. When both magistrates were textile manufacturers the figure rose to 88 per cent, whereas when neither magistrate was a textile manufacturer, the figure fell to 70 per cent.[25] The figures for the Huddersfield district are somewhat different. In the years 1850–54 the conviction rate was 90 per cent but only 74 per cent in the years 1856–66. Further, there were a number of local magistrates who were critical of the Worsted Acts themselves and of the activity of Inspector Kaye.

In some instances, a case was dismissed because of the ignorance of the law on the part of the individual charged. Jonathan Moorhouse, a weaver from Castle Hill End, was charged by Kaye with selling twenty-one ounces of thrums and yarns to a local shopkeeper. The magistrates accepted his claim that 'he did not know he was doing wrong' and dismissed the case, 'nothing being known against his character', and simply cautioned the man.[26] When a conviction was achieved the Worsted Acts laid down clear penalties: a maximum fine of £20 for a first offence and £30 for a second offence, but in practice inspectors and magistrates exercised discretion. Edmund Bottomley, 'a sickly looking man', pleaded guilty but also his illness as extenuating circumstances. The Association agreed not to press the case, the defendant was nominally ordered to pay expenses and forfeit the disputed goods but 'as a mere matter of form a conviction was entered with the distinct understanding that it should not be enforced'.[27] In some cases, expenses had to be paid and goods forfeit, in others expenses only were paid, and in yet others only the goods were seized. John Heward, an old man, was charged with embezzlement but the offence had been committed by his wife and daughter without his knowledge. The Association, after discussion with the magistrates, agreed not to press the case as long as the stolen goods (nineteen lbs of woollen waste) were forfeit and the costs – the not inconsiderable sum of 9*s* 6*d* (47½p) – were paid.[28] Mary Brayshaw, 'a decrepit old woman', living in Holmfirth 'similar to a hermit', faced seventy-seven charges but 'pleaded guilty with tears in her eyes'. A conviction was recorded but the magistrates ordered that the expenses of 8*s* 6*d* (42½p) were not to be paid.[29] John Haigh was found guilty of embezzlement. The goods were forfeit but it was agreed that 'in consideration of his extreme age ... the fine would remain in abeyance'.[30] Joseph Wood was also found guilty of embezzling over 100lbs of woollen waste but Kaye drew attention to the fact that he 'had a large family and was very poor'. After a discussion with the chair of the Association, the magistrates accepted their suggestion that 'the conviction should not be put into execution, unless the man again offended'.[31] Not all poverty pleas succeeded. Joseph Ainley, a Golcar weaver, told the court he had 'a family and four children at home, and nothing to eat' but was sentenced to two months in Wakefield House of Correction.[32] Similarly, Sarah Shaw, 'a poor feeble woman of great age' (she was seventy-seven years old) was sentenced to one month in Wakefield as she had no money or goods to pay the fine.[33] In some cases the magistrates saw prison as a positive outcome. George Berry, a poor man, living in 'a filthy hovel' was found guilty and, being unable to pay the fine, was sentenced to one month in prison. The magistrate expressed the hope that 'considering the state he was in, prison treatment might have a good effect upon him'.[34]

Very occasionally, prosecutor and accused could strike a compromise. In a complex and serious case in 1858, the clothes-dealer Absalom Lockwood was charged with embezzling 360 yards of woollen and cloth material in the process of manufacture and of 730lbs of woollen warp, weft and listing. Thirty witnesses had been called with more to come when the magistrates called a break in proceedings. While the magistrates were away a compromise was agreed, despite 'the tenacity of Mr Kaye', whereby Lockwood paid a fine of £20 and forfeited 'all unwrought material seized' but was allowed to keep some of the disputed material. The magistrates agreed to save the case from continuing to midnight.[35] In a similar case eight years later Levi Sykes came to a prior agreement with the Association which was accepted in court. Having already paid the Association £10, he pleaded guilty and was let off the remaining £10.[36]

In a number of occasions, individual magistrates did not take part in the discussion of embezzlement cases because of their vested interest but a majority did not feel that their membership of the Manufacturers' Protection Association compromised their position as a magistrate.[37] However, they were not necessarily totally supportive of the legislation and its implementation. Kaye's actions were criticised and doubts were expressed about the harshness of the law.[38] When James Weaver, a Dalton weaver, escaped prosecution in 1861 (he produced the necessary invoices) the bench commented that 'the act was an exceedingly oppressive one'.[39] In 1866 the magistrates at Upper Mill were even more outspoken. According to one 'it was a highly penal statute' and the other 'it was an act under which a man had scarcely any chance of escape'.[40]

A further, though related matter, was concern with popular responses, though again there was not a single or simple point of view. Although the acts were seen to protect employer interests, not all employees dismissed them out of hand. Catherine Hanley was convicted in January 1853. There was criticism of the local constable for his intrusive actions but 'by far the greater number approved of what he did' because in Thurstonland, 'a village of weavers', illegal behaviour 'weaken[ed] the confidence which masters ought to have in workmen'.[41] More often, the popular response was hostile and the cases bitterly fought. Mr Roberts of Manchester, who had defended the Honley rioters, appeared for the defence in a number of cases, not always successfully.[42] Successful defences evoked popular support. The case against Joseph Senior (a respectable figure who did 'country work') aroused considerable interest in and around Holmfirth in 1862. When it was dismissed there was 'evident satisfaction' in the crowded courtroom.[43] Even greater were the 'demonstrations of satisfaction' in court at Huddersfield later that year when another of Kaye's prosecutions failed but the authorities were so worried at the response that it was 'immediately suppressed'.[44] Perhaps the most telling case was the prosecution of William Bottomley who was accused by Kaye of embezzling tools. The proceedings started with a challenge to the jurisdiction of the magistrates – several of whom were members of the Manufacturers' Protection Association – which was turned down, to the evident disappointment of the defendants and their supporters in court. However, the case was dismissed and 'the decision was hailed with applause by a court crowded with operatives amongst whom the case appeared to excite great interest'.[45] The impact of popular animosity is impossible to determine but it is likely that the decisions of manufacturers and magistrates were influenced by consideration of the wider repercussions of enforcing this law.

Enforcing the Worsted Acts necessarily involved cooperation between inspectors and the police. Godfrey and Cox argue that there was no enthusiasm among police chiefs to pour resources into this aspect of work. The local evidence partly supports this view.[46] Even in the heyday of the Worsted Committee the number of prosecutions was limited and the initiative lay with the inspectors who called upon the police when an arrest was needed. Prior to 1854, when the Association was well-funded, Kaye was the central figure in bringing charges for embezzlement. He worked with a number of parochial constables, most notably John Earnshaw, who for a period combined the roles of sub-inspector and constable of Holmfirth, as well as with Heaton. For a brief period in the mid-1850s as many cases were brought by the police (mainly Heaton and Earnshaw) as by Inspector Kaye but by the advent of the WRCC, there is very little evidence of Heaton taking the initiative, suggesting that woollen and worsted embezzlement was not a priority for him or Colonel Cobbe.[47]

Kaye also participated in wider policing activities. As noted in chapter six, Kaye worked with Heaton on a number of raids on beerhouses. He also assisted the police in their ordinary business, coming to the assistance of a borough constable when arresting the troublesome correspondent of the *Halifax Courier*, William Hulke. As the funding crisis hit the Manufacturers' Association, Kaye, remained as the only inspector, but took on the role of inspector of weights and measures. In several years, especially in the mid-1860s, he appears to have spent more time charging shopkeepers and the like than prosecuting embezzlers.

Vagrancy

The Worsted Acts was not a major police priority but there was one point at which it intersected with a more mainstream concern. Although not entirely borne out by the facts, there was a concern among manufacturers that 'tramps and vagabonds' were at heart of petty embezzlement.[48] Concern with the threat posed by vagrants was nothing new. The Elizabethan fear of 'sturdy beggars' resurfaced time and again over the centuries. The 1824 vagrancy act formalised the distinction between the 'idle and disorderly', 'rogues and vagabonds' and 'incorrigible rogues', thereby adding to the common belief that there was a slippery slope through degrees of vagrancy to criminality. Opinion in early-Victorian Britain, strengthened by the conviction of prominent figures such as Edwin Chadwick, swung increasingly against the itinerant and indigent. The vagrant was seen as a thief in waiting. 'Vagrancy', explained PC Thomas Woollaston, '[is] very nearly allied to crime'.[49] The elision of vagrant and criminal masked a fundamental dilemma for the Victorians: was the vagrant a pauper or a criminal? The answer would determine how best to deal with the problem. There was never unanimity but opinion, expert and lay, tended more to the latter (a criminal) than the former in the mid-nineteenth century. As Lord Kimberley told his fellow peers, vagrants 'more properly styled rogues and vagabonds ... [were] a class which had hitherto escaped being regarded in the eyes of the law as criminal'.[50] In fact, particularly after the 1856 County & Borough Police Act, vagrants were subject to increasing police surveillance. From a police perspective the focus on vagrancy was a mixed blessing. It was very time-consuming in sprawling, rural areas like the West Riding, but, more importantly, it could have an important impact on perceptions of the police. Where vagrants were seen clearly as threats – be they imposters or criminals – firm police action could enhance the standing of the local constabulary; where they were seen as pitiable individuals, as victims rather than perpetrators, police action could be seen as insensitive or heavy-handed. Not surprisingly, enforcement of the law against vagrancy was highly erratic across the country.

Opinion in Upper Agbrigg tended towards the sceptical, if not outright hostile. During a discussion of the Marsden lodging house, the belief in the 'undeserving poor' was very evident: '[I]t is notorious that as a body the patronisers of public lodgings are the idle and dissolute, who will do anything but work'.[51] They were believed to be scroungers, enjoying a good life at the expense of others. 'Many [of them] could pay for their lodgings, and numbers of whom smoke and drink each night ... [and] have as comfortable or even better lodging procured than many an honest, hard-working man can obtain'.[52] Good facilities were seen as an inducement to laziness and strong action required to deter the undeserving. The Marsden assistant overseer of the poor was praised for driving away 'more than a score of applicants ... by threatening to handcuff them and take them to Huddersfield'.[53] The public discourse hardened in the 1860s. Holmfirth was 'much infested' with 'a batch of vagrants and tramps.' Wandering Irish men and women, augmented by desperate Lancastrians, looking for work during the Cotton Famine, aroused fear. Heaton looked to the magistrates for firm action, otherwise it would be 'impossible to protect people's property if such men were allowed to go about without restriction'.[54] In 1866, shocked by the revelation in the recently-published *Judicial Statistics* that there were 33,000 'sturdy rogues' in the country, the *Chronicle* ran a lengthy and highly critical article entitled 'The Sturdy Vagrant And Beggar Class', which castigated both vagrants and those who encouraged them through 'indiscriminate alms-giving.' Vagrants were 'as loathsome specimens of humanity as can be found in the worst parts of Africa or the South Sea Islands.' Further,

> [t]heir persons are in a condition too horrible to be precisely described. Their habits and language are even more filthy than their clothes. Their highest aspiration is to carry off some valuable from a closely-watched kitchen. Their highest enjoyment is to drink themselves insensible.

To make matters even worse, 'vagrancy, as is well known is an hereditary curse … Paupers breed paupers, vagrants breed vagrants and habitual law-breakers have, for the most part, been bred in criminal homes'.[55]

Even before this scathing critique the local press ran several accounts of fraudulent vagrants, such as 'Grandfather Whitehead' who exploited 'poor widows' in Honley and Lockwood, or Henry Hall, 'a systematic tramp'.[56] In fact, many of the cases that came before the courts were pathetic rather than threatening people. Ann and Maria Ferguson were charged with being 'idle and disorderly persons', having been found sleeping in a barn in Linthwaite. They were making their way to Liverpool but were found 'in a very distressed state'.[57] Joseph Garner, 'a poor wretch – dirt begrimed, ragged and houseless' was found sleeping on the roadside in Kirkburton, almost frozen to death. Found guilty of vagrancy, he was sentenced to three months in Wakefield – a verdict that guaranteed him some physical protection.[58] Robert Jones, 'a respectably-dressed working man' was 'entirely destitute' having lost his job. Twice he threw himself into the canal but failed to kill himself. He was arrested for vagrancy and attempted suicide and was paraded through the streets in handcuffs.[59] The desperation of many vagrants in the late-1850s led the *Examiner* to criticise both the police and the magistrates for criminalising poverty.[60] Others, if not poor, clearly suffered from mental problems. George Clegg, arrested as a vagrant, was 'a young man of deficient mental capacity and wandering disposition'.[61] In this case the magistrates deemed prison to be 'useless' and gave him back to his father with instructions to seek admittance to the workhouse for his son. Despite the dominant faith in the beneficial impact of prison, with its 'habits of regularity and cleanliness', many vagrants were persistent offenders. James Jackson was convicted for the fifth time in little over three months. Heaton, somewhat bemusedly, informed the court that 'the past two years of his life appeared to have been wholly spent in prison'.[62]

It is difficult to determine the scale of vagrancy in Upper Agbrigg, not least because of the difficulty of determining who was a vagrant and who was an itinerant workman/woman. Nonetheless, there appears to be a mismatch between the exaggerated language of the *Chronicle* and the numbers of vagrants in the district. Similarly, determining the importance of vagrancy as a policing priority is problematic. On a number of occasions Superintendent Heaton expressed his concerns but when the divisional criminal statistics are inspected the number of vagrants brought to court in the mid- and late-1860s averaged about one a week – hardly an indication of a perceived threat from a marauding horde of 'sturdy beggars'. Unlike the hard-line adopted by the Lancashire County Constabulary, the WRCC appear to have been more relaxed in its approach to this particular problem. Statistics drawn from the annual *Judicial Statistics*, summarised in Table 10.1, bear out this conclusion.

Table 10.1: Proceedings under Vagrancy Acts in Lancashire and the West Riding of Yorkshire

YEAR	VAGRANCY	ACT CASES		VAGRANCY	ACT CASES	
	Per 100,000	*Population 1861 census*		*Per 100*	*constables*	
	Lancashire County Constabulary	*West Riding County Constabulary*	*WRCC as % LCC*	*Lancashire County Constabulary*	*West Riding County Constabulary*	*WRCC as % LCC*
1860	*59.3*	*38.0*	*64*	*86*	*63*	*73*
1864	*73.4*	*46.9*	*64*	*106*	*70*	*66*
1867	*78.9*	*43.7*	*55*	*105*	*61*	*58*

Source: *Judicial Statistics*

The figures show clearly the greater emphasis on vagrancy in Lancashire. The likelihood of being prosecuted under the Vagrancy Acts was almost twice as high in Lancashire as in the West Riding. Correspondingly, greater police time was devoted to the problem west of the Pennines. The figures for prosecutions are the more remarkable because the respective police authorities reckoned there were more appreciably more tramps and vagrants in the West Riding than in Lancashire.[63] A maximalist approach on one side of the Pennines contrasted with a minimalist approach on the other.[64]

Poaching

WRCC adopted a minimalist approach to another potential contentious issue – poaching – though in this respect it was more in line with the majority of forces. The Games Law had long been a source of bitter conflict. The worst excesses of the early nineteenth century were past but the 'poaching wars' continued well into the third quarter of the century.[65] Traditionally poaching has been seen as a night-time activity and the preserve of the agricultural labourer in the south and east of the country. This 'Lincolnshire Poacher' view is trebly misleading. First, the increase in prosecutions in the 1860s and 1870s was driven by an upsurge of activity in the northern counties; second, the poacher was more likely to be an industrial worker than an agricultural labourer; and third, 90 per cent of prosecutions were for daytime poaching. There has also been dispute about the motives behind poaching. In some, mainly older, histories the emphasis has been on necessity and protest, but recent works have painted a more complex picture in which commercial concerns have a significant role to play.[66]

The extent of poaching is also not easy to establish. Figures for prosecutions give some indication but may tell more about changes in prosecution rather than fluctuations in the incidence of poaching itself. The total number of poaching offences in England rose from around 10,000 per annum in the early 1860s to about 12,000 by the end of the decade and peaked in the mid/late-1870s. The bulk of these cases were for trespassing in daytime in pursuit of game but more attention (then and now) was given to night poaching, especially after the 1862 Poaching Act, while the illegal buying and selling of game attracted limited comment.

Within the West Riding Upper Agbrigg accounted for 9 per cent of all game law prosecutions in the years 1857–62, exceeded only by Lower Agbrigg (11 per cent), while somewhat surprisingly, the Sheffield district accounted for only 7 per cent.[67] The 1864 returns also contained details at a parochial level. These figures (Table 10.3) need to be interpreted with care. It is unlikely that they give an accurate indication of the level and distribution of poaching across the district. The low number of cases in the parishes of Almondbury and Kirkburton is more likely a reflection of non-detection/ non-prosecution, whereas the figures for Huddersfield suggest a greater determination to prosecute, which in turn might reflect the determination of certain individuals.

Table 10.2: Game Law Prosecutions in the 1860s

YEAR	TRESPASSING IN DAYTIME IN PURSUIT OF GAME	NIGHT POACHING AND DESTROYING GAME	ILLEGALLY SELLING OR BUYING GAME	1862 POACHING ACT	TOTAL
1862	*9,138*	*887*	*47*	*17*	*10,089*
1863	*8,174*	*685*	*32*	*724*	*9,615*
1864	*8,522*	*673*	*22*	*877*	*10,094*
1865	*9,003*	*554*	*31*	*783*	*10,371*
1866	*9,285*	*637*	*29*	*855*	*10,806*
1867	*9,760*	*662*	*54*	*939*	*11,415*
1868	*9,668*	*674*	*47*	*1,007*	*12,253*
1869	*10,821*	*628*	*82*	*1,144*	*12,075*

Source: *Parliamentary Papers*, 1872, x, Select Committee on Game Laws, pp.438-9

Table 10.3 Poaching prosecutions in Upper Agbrigg by parish, 1857–62

YEAR	HUDDERSFIELD	ALMONDBURY	KIRKBURTON	KIRKHEATON	TOTAL
1857	*22*	*2*	*2*	*3*	*29*
1858	*7*	*7*	*0*	*6*	*20*
1859	*6*	*7*	*7*	*14*	*34*
1860	*10*	*7*	*2*	*5*	*24*
1861	*14*	*4*	*3*	*12*	*33*
Total	*59*	*27*	*14*	*40*	*140*
% overall total	*42*	*19*	*10*	*29*	*100*

Source: *Parliamentary Papers,* 1864 (9) Game Returns, pp.388–90

The local press provides a number of insights. The majority of poachers went out with nets and dogs (and maybe ferrets) in search of ground (rather than winged) game.[68] Poaching gangs were rare, though there was a major affray near Castle Hill in the autumn of 1850.[69] Poachers generally came from within (or close to) the district, though some came from Sheffield, and several were repeat offenders. Scattered evidence suggests that some poaching was done for commercial reasons. As with stolen woollens and worsteds, there were occasional prosecutions of beerhouse keepers for selling on stolen goods.[70] Police involvement was rare, certainly before the 1862 Poaching Act, which gave police the power of search of men and carts on the highway. As the poaching bill passed through parliament, several chief constables wrote to the Home Office, making clear their opposition to the direct involvement in the preservation of game, which they feared would add to the unpopularity of the police. There is little evidence of police-led actions against poachers in Upper Agbrigg. As a consequence of this police reluctance much depended on the determination of gamekeepers to take action.[71] Two men stand out in Upper Agbrigg: Abner Hill and Samuel Newsome.

Abner Hill, known locally as 'the Admiral', was a determined figure with a reputation for his physical strength and courage. For two decades, from the early 1850s to the early 1870s, he appeared regularly in court as he sought to protect the land of S W Haigh Esq., of Colne-bridge at Bradley Woods, on the edge of Huddersfield, from poachers from the town and nearby Brighouse. In the 1850s Hill worked with a number of under-keepers (as many as seven, according to one report) in a series of carefully organised ploys to capture those responsible for the 'frequent recent depredations'.[72] Most incidents took place during the day, but there were a number of night-poaching cases brought to court'.[73] Such was the frequency of his appearances that one magistrate (somewhat tongue in cheek) asked two poachers to 'let poor Abner have a bit of rest, for you lead him a weary life'.[74] 'Poor Abner' found the energy to pursue poachers for another decade. There were obvious dangers. He was assaulted on a number of occasions and threatened with a gun at least once but appeared undeterred, even though he received little help from the police.[75] Hill's career as a keeper was straightforward. Consistently over the years he pursued poachers. Samuel Newsome was an altogether different man – a poacher who turned gamekeeper before reverting to a life as a poacher. Having been prosecuted several times for poaching in Lepton Woods in the 1850s, he appeared in court in September 1859 giving evidence against a local poacher.[76] Variously described as a 'watcher' and 'under-keeper', over the course of the next eighteen months he gained a reputation as a 'vigilant gamekeeper' in Lepton Woods, an area he knew well.[77] His employment with Major Beaumont came to an end in the summer of 1861 and he reverted to 'his inveterate poaching habits'. Newsome was one of the first people in the district to be prosecuted under the new game law and by 1863 was seen as 'a confirmed poacher and vagabond'.[78] Newsome was an unusual figure but his career – on both sides of the divide – highlights the largely self-contained world of the poacher/gamekeeper into which the police rarely intruded.

Popular Leisure

There was one area in which the police played a very active role. Plebeian leisure – in its various guises – was seen to be problematic with a widespread belief that 'the devil makes work for idle hands'. Public houses and, even more so, beerhouses were obvious sites of immorality and criminality. Heaton's attempts to enforce the licensing laws, including the curtailment of gambling, have already been discussed in some detail. This section will focus on a number of other leisure-related problems and the success with which the police dealt with them.

Heaton's obituarist made great play of his success in prosecuting those involved in blood sports. He 'took great pains to follow the cockfighters ... to various parts of the petty sessional division and other divisions in the riding, as well as to places beyond the Yorkshire borders'.[79] Although cockfighting had been made illegal in 1835 it remained a popular blood sport across many parts of the country, not least the West Riding.[80] Support cut across class lines and police attitudes also varied from place to place. Woolnough's recent study of blood sports in Cumbria shows how, in an area where cockfighting retained its popularity throughout the nineteenth century, the magistrates at quarter session, chief constables and members of watch committees showed little interest in suppressing it. [81] In contrast, the magistrates in Upper Agbrigg made clear their detestation of 'the degrading spectacle ... [and] barbarous sport of cockfighting'.[82] However, many weavers, especially around Kirkburton and Holmfirth, were noted for being 'fond of visiting local cockpits' and the police view was that cockfighting was 'greatly on the increase' in the mid-1850s and remained popular well into the late-nineteenth century. It was not just local weavers who frequented the cockpits. Local gentleman patronised the 'sport' and, perhaps more importantly, men came from other parts of the riding and from other counties to bet on the fights. Improvements in transportation, especially rail transport, made it much easier for organisers to bring people together. Trains from Manchester, Sheffield, Leeds and Hull, for example, could drop passengers at Holmfirth or Marsden stations, where they were met by carts and gigs to be taken to the chosen fight venue. Given the nature of the terrain in these locations, this was a major logistical problem for the police.

In the late-1840s and early 1850s cockfights took place close to Huddersfield – in Dalton, Farnley Tyas and, above all, on Castle Hill. The latter was an ideal site, within walking distance of the town station, and easy to set watches to give warning of approaching police.[83] By the late-1850s the local press was lavish in its praise of Heaton's success in driving cockfighting increasingly into the remoter areas in the moors and thinly-populated districts on the borders with Lancashire and Cheshire.[84] One such thinly-populated place was Upper Maythorn. The police handling of the fight gives an indication of the difficulties they faced and their determination to overcome them. Acting on a tip-off, Heaton 'started for the scene on which the brutal sport was to take place, about 2 a.m. on Monday morning' accompanied by two other officers. To avoid detection, the three men hid themselves – to the surprise of a sow – in a pigsty, where they remained for almost three hours. The cockfighters began to assemble around 6 a.m. and such was the cold tried to find shelter in the sty but were prevented by parochial constable Earnshaw firmly grasping the door handle. Contenting themselves with making comments on the pig, they were soon joined by others, including 'two gentlemen ... in a gig' who oversaw the clipping and spurring of the cocks ready for the fight. At about 8 a.m. the fight commenced, at which point 'the officers left their concealment, jumped into the ring and each secured a prisoner'. Having identified several members of the crowd, a total of twenty-five men were subsequently arrested, brought to trial and fined for their part in the illegal cockfight.[85]

This was a considerable success for Heaton and the two parochial constables who accompanied him, but it is easy to exaggerate the extent of police success. In 1857 Heaton and his men were unable to prevent a cockfight at Brockholes, where a crowd of about 200 people had gathered.[86] The *Leeds Mercury* felt that such fights 'were becoming of late of frequent occurrence'.[87] The following year saw an incident take place that clearly highlighted the limitations of police power. Heaton, once again, had received information of a cockfight to take place on Castle Hill. With five other officers, he set off and enjoyed initial success. The cockfighters, estimated to be at least 200 strong, were unable to set the ring but, determined that the fight should take place, retreated a mile or so to Farnley Hey, where a second attempt was made and thwarted by the police. Retreating further down the Honley road the cockfighters, now 300 to 400 in number, succeeded in setting a ring at Sandbeds, Nettleton. The police were kept at bay by continual fusillades of stones while the fight took place. The only success for the police was the identification and subsequent arrest and trial of twenty participants.[88] It is impossible to establish the full extent of cockfighting in the 1850s but the local press carried reports of incidents, not just in noted 'cocking' districts such as Holmfirth and Kirkburton, but also in Almondbury, Kirkheaton, Marsden, Meltham and even Honley. Further, well-attended fights were reported throughout the 1860s. In May 1868, for example, crowds of 200 or more were reported at Farnley Tyas and Kirkheaton. At the latter, the police dispersed the original crowd, only for the fight to be resumed not far away in the village.[89] There was one further problem for the police, namely the interpretation of the law regarding cruelty to animals, under which many prosecutions were brought. A judicial ruling that cockfighting *per se* was not illegal greatly hampered the work of the police.[90] Thus, Heaton's success was qualified both in terms of the size and location of cockfights and this gave rise to criticism. The *Chronicle*, incandescent at the 'diabolical practice of cockfighting' felt that matters had got worse rather than better since the creation of the county force.[91] What the paper failed to appreciate was that police vigilance was insufficient to eradicate 'barbarous' recreations, as long as popular support for them continued. Popular support gradually waned and newer, alternative forms of popular leisure emerged. Thus, cock fighting declined from within, rather than being suppressed from without.

The same was true of dogfighting, though the demise of this 'disgraceful pastime' may have come somewhat earlier. Dogfights were not the monopoly of the countryside. Fights took place in the beerhouses (and even the cellars of houses) in Castlegate in the 1850s.[92] Further, many of the fights that took place in Lindley or on Castle Hill were between dogs bred and trained in the town. Once again, the local press praised the work of Heaton and the parochial constables with whom he worked. 'Through the instrumentality of our active county police superintendent, Mr Heaton,' the *Chronicle* told its readers, 'several convictions have been obtained against parties arranging and indulging in these brutalizing and disgusting exhibitions'.[93] His determination (and indeed courage) is beyond doubt. At one dogfight, scheduled for 5 a.m. on Castle Hill, the participants had 'sentinels stationed on the hill … [so he] took a circuitous route but followed the direction indicated by the hooting and raving of a large number of excited voices [amongst a crowd of some 100] … [he] stealthily peeped over the embankment … after taking off his hat'. The sentry raised the cry: "There's Tommy Yeaton" and Heaton 'made a gallant sortie into the midst of the routed and flying "fancy" more certainly to mark his men'.[94] Amazingly, Heaton was eventually able to arrest thirteen men, including the notorious local criminal, 'Slasher' Wilson but the extent of his success is revealed in an unusual piece of evidence. Six months after the trial of the Castle Hill dogfighters, Heaton received a letter, informing him that

> [w]e had some fine sport on Monday at a place near Peniston, for £25 a side. The dogs fought for 3 hours and 20 minutes. We was short of you as referree [*sic*]. We was 3 verry particular friends short; that is you, Slasher and Broadbent. (signed) 'One fond of the game'.[95]

As with cockfighting, gambling was an important part of the dogfighting scene and dogfights attracted large crowds from outside the district. The scale of these events can be seen from one that also took place in 1855. Advertised as a Yorkshire v Lancashire clash, the fight had been arranged to take place near Marsden. Local supporters came from Huddersfield but also men from Sheffield, Oldham and Stalybridge. A crowd estimated at 500 gathered less than 400 yards from turnpike road behind *Shepherd's Boy Inn*, 'near the Spa', Marsden. There ensued a pitched battle as Heaton with 'several constables … [with] previous instructions what to do' charged into the crowd. Eventually forty-two men were charged under the Cruelty to Animals Act.[96] The number of reported cases fell off in the 1860s but dogfighting was not eradicated.[97] However, in comparison with the Sheffield/Rotherham district (and even Barnsley) dogfighting was a rarer occurrence in Upper Agbrigg in the 1860s.

Although not illegal, prize fighting was increasingly condemned by respectable opinion. The police were used to prevent fights but, unlike in Cumbria, popular support ensured that it survived. Most fights were relatively small-scale affairs, though some attracted crowds of 100 or more. Most participants were local – Squire Sutcliffe of Deighton was a local fight celebrity – but bigger fights, involving men from outside the region, attracted larger crowds. When George Potts of Sheffield fought James Larvin of Dewsbury in February 1868 near Holmfirth, the crowd was estimated to be over 1,000.[98] Most (recorded) fights took place in remoter parts of the district, around Scammonden and outside Holmfirth and Marsden, but Castle Hill, for all its proximity to Huddersfield, remained a popular venue.[99] Although prize fighting was condemned for its brutality and associated gambling, police activity was largely directed at preventing, or at least disrupting fights and prosecutions for obstructing the highway or public disorder. The problems facing the police were considerable. The patrons of prize fights were well-organised and wily. Even when the police received evidence of a planned fight, there was no guarantee that it was not a false trail. Heaton clearly spent time planning his operations, which were resource-intensive, but it is difficult to see clear evidence of success. In April 1866 he appeared to have thwarted a fight scheduled to take place on Castle Hill, when he prevented a 'mill', even though some of his men had been lured downhill to Hall Bower. The spectators 'wended their way to Castlegate with the men in blue in the rear'.[100] Not for the first time the fight was rescheduled and not for the first time Heaton obtained intelligence that the chosen location was just outside Marsden. Taking advantage of the local train, he and his men set out confident of success. Unfortunately, it was false information and, as Heaton set off on a wild-goose chase up into the Pennines, some 200 people gathered on the edge of town at Fixby to watch the fight.[101] This was a particularly humiliating defeat for the local police, but not every venture ended in failure. The local press carried positive stories of fights thwarted, for example at Honley (October 1862), Scammonden (June 1864) and Marsden Moor (8 June 1867).[102] However, at the same time, there were more reports of fights taking place at a variety of local venues including not only Scammonden and Marsden – both remote locations – but also at Honley and on Castle Hill.[103] The Castle Hill fight of August 1863 was particularly galling for the local police. The fight between two well-known local pugilists – Smith and Mills – for a stake of £25 was scheduled for an early morning start but the police were initially able to thwart it. Their success was illusory. Within minutes (at 4.25 a.m. to be precise) the first of fourteen rounds commenced. Some forty to fifty 'roughs' in attendance provided a guard and 'the police much to their chagrin found that they had been completely baulked'.[104] To add insult to injury, Heaton's attempt to have the men charged with a breach of the peace failed. Amid allegations of perjury, several witnesses, including the landlord of the *Castle Hill Hotel*, near which the fight took place, strongly denied that there had been a fight. All he had seen was two men 'quavering their neives' [shaking their fists] at each other![105]

Police intervention, unsurprisingly, was unpopular but the extent of hostility in Upper Agbrigg was probably less than in the southern parts of the West Riding, where large-scale assaults on the police occurred, particularly around Barnsley and Sheffield.[106] The one exception was the affray at Dunford Bridge, outside Holmfirth, in 1868 that followed a fight, for a £25 stake, between two well-known pugilists, Potts and Larvin. The police were well organised, sending several officers under Inspector Nunn to lie in wait overnight and to liaise with men from the Cheshire and Derbyshire forces. The crowd, estimated at 1,000, at first fled towards the Cheshire/Derbyshire border but when they found other police present, they turned on the West Yorkshire contingent in 'a desperate affray' which saw 'volleys of stones and other missiles showered upon the constables who had to beat a retreat'.[107] Inspector Nunn received 'a severe scalp wound' but worst injured was Sergeant Turner who had 'two or three ribs broken and now lies in a dangerous state'.[108] Some arrests were made but the fight, which lasted for forty-one rounds and took over an hour, was staged at an alternative venue. Once again, the determination of magistrates and police is evident but so too is their limited success in the face of popular support for traditional pastimes.

Other forms of popular leisure also presented problems to the police. The mid-nineteenth century saw the increased commercialization of older forms and the emergence of new. Foot-racing was not new. Aristocrats in the eighteenth century wagered large sums on the sporting prowess of their men as well as sponsoring local events in a sense of *noblesse oblige*. The practice continued into the nineteenth century. In 1852, to celebrate Sir J W Ramsden Esq., attaining his majority, the family sponsored a series of prize races, including foot races, a sack race and a blindfold wheelbarrow race, 'in the Fields below Longley Hall'.[109] There were also more plebeian street races, including racing in clogs as well as 'novelty' events involving picking up eggs or stones during the course of a race, and even walking backwards.[110] Many of the races took place on the open roads. For the magistrates and police this posed a threefold problem. First, there was the shocking immorality of 'nude racing,' that is men in shorts and vests; second, there was the attendant gambling; and third, there was the obstruction to the highway. John Smith, a local miner, was arrested by Superintendent Heaton for running on the turnpike road between Birchincliffe and Lindley 'in the open day, in a state of nudity, to the disgust and annoyance of several passengers of both sexes'.[111] John Sykes, the local road inspector, charged two boys with obstruction as they raced on the turnpike road between Lockwood and Meltham, while Heaton and the Longwood constable (Taylor) charged five men with gambling on a foot race. One of the local magistrates, B N R Battye, made clear 'the determination of the Bench to put down such 'gambling and racing' in the district.[112]

While several of these events were little more than interpersonal challenges, there was a growing commercialisation of foot-racing. There was clear potential. A race on the turnpike between Marsden and Slaithwaite attracted a crowd of several hundred but also caught the attention of the police, who arrested eight men.[113] Entrepreneurs of leisure provided facilities, including refreshments, so that crowds could watch local and national professional athletes compete. Nowhere was this more apparent than in Honley where, to the disgust of the *Chronicle*, '[r]acing seems the only thing for which the working classes of Honley pay attention to, and to indulge in which they never seem fast for money'.[114] The potential was considerable. In May 1853 there assembled 'a great concourse of persons' despite 'Mr. Abbey, the surveyor, offering a £2 reward for the prosecution of races on the turnpike road'.[115] Seizing on the opportunity, a 440-yard circular race track was built behind the *George and Dragon*. In September 1862, on 'the most exciting day ever remembered in the annals of the Honley race course', almost 4,000 people paid 3*d* (1p) each to watch the local favourite, Boothroyd, race against 'Nerry of Manchester'. Even local events attracted crowds of around 2,000.[116] And Honley was not alone. A race ground was attached to the *Warren House Inn* on Lindley Moor while the Windsor Grounds at Blackmoorfoot had been built by the landlord of the *Star Inn*, Slaithwaite. Once again, most events were between locals and before moderately sized crowds but celebrities also appeared. In April 1862 the 'renowned Native American, Deerfoot', took part in a six-mile race at Lindley for a prize of £50. 'Some thousands of people assembled to watch the race on the race ground adjoining the *Warren House Inn*.'[117]

'Race running mania' was soon perceived as a major problem, exercising a 'demoralising influence ... [that] counteracted the labour of the Sunday School teacher and of the Mechanics' Institutions'.[118] The race grounds, especially the one at Honley, became 'the centre of attraction to all the loose characters in the county ... [creating] an intolerable nuisance'.[119] According to the *Chronicle*, 'young men and even families [were] ruined by a species of reckless gambling to which this racing gives rise to'.[120] To make matters worse, there was corruption in the form of race-fixing: 'Tom Firth, a Honley man, managed to lose by a dozen yards, amid the most terrific shouting by the Holmfirth party'.[121] Firth, an able athlete, was a notorious figure who did 'more to bring racing into disrepute' through race-fixing. Further, his blatant cheating also gave rise to a number of vicious fights between those who had gained from his dishonesty and those who had been cheated.[122] These incidents undoubtedly created problems for the local constables. In Honley in late 1862, with memories of the anti-police riot in the village still very fresh, this was a serious matter. However, there was a wider animosity towards the police for interfering in what were perceived to be as legitimate leisure activities. As early as 1852 'A Worker' had written to the editor of the *Chronicle* asking 'when did pedestrianism become criminal?'.[123] The letter continued with another rhetorical question – 'Is a foot-race with men immoral, or degrading or debasing? – on which it based a stout defence of this popular plebeian sport.

New sports also presented similar problems. Pigeon-racing attracted crowds of several hundred on footpaths and the highways. There were prosecutions for obstruction in Almondbury, Kirkburton, Lindley, Lockwood, Meltham, Marsh and Moldgreen.[124] Middle-class opinion was appalled by the 'intolerable nuisance' created by men 'going about the village [Marsden] howling worse than a tribe of wild Indians'.[125] The Reverend Robert Bruce preached a sermon in Huddersfield condemning 'the lower classes who delight in pigeon-flying, dogfighting and pitch and toss', deeming that such 'cruel and barbarous amusements ... may do for Spanish ladies but not for English men'.[126] More moderate voices welcomed the work of the new police but it did not escape the notice of senior police officers that a number of their men had been assaulted as they sought to move on crowds of pigeon racers.[127]

Cockfights and pigeon races were public and often large-scale events but perhaps most police time was devoted to the more unspectacular but ubiquitous issue of gambling. Gambling in beerhouses and gaming houses was undoubtedly a problem for the police in town and countryside – and one not effectively addressed by mid-nineteenth century legislation – but gambling took place in a wide variety of locations and took many different forms. Across the district mainly young men, and most commonly on a Sunday, met together to gamble – on the roadside, in fields, in stone quarries and at the local feasts – and week after week the local magistrates heard cases of men playing pitch and toss, dominoes and the like. In the eyes of both police and magistrates, gambling was the route to a life of crime but for all their efforts the 'crusade' against gambling enjoyed little success. It is not clear whether the incidence of gambling increased during the period or whether tolerance decreased but there was growing criticism of the police for failing to deal with the problem. An irate 'Ratepayer' complained to the *Chronicle* about 'the gangs of rough men and lads, swearing and shouting as they pass through the villages on their way to Castle Hill, where they resort for gambling purposes'.[128] Although critical of police failures, the correspondent unwittingly highlighted some of the difficulties they faced. This was 'a regularly organised system … [that included] scouts posted at the most prominent points of the hill in order to give the alarm should a policeman be seen approaching'.[129] Heaton was not a man to give in easily but in October 1866 he drew the attention of the magistrates to 'the great evil attendant on Sunday gambling' and conceded that 'cases were becoming so numerous and gambling so extensive' that 'the police found themselves inadequate to its repression'.[130] Here was the rub. Gambling was immensely popular with many working-class men. They did not see it as 'a great social evil' but rather as an opportunity for excitement with the hope of making some money. As the more perceptive critics began to grasp, many working men, being 'cooped up in mills and workshops during the week days … are prone to indulge in pastimes and games which are improper for the Sabbath'.[131] This posed real dilemmas for the police. Under pressure to stamp out gambling and other leisure activities deemed to be inappropriate and criminal, (by many in the upper echelons of society, at least) and subscribing to these views, the police found themselves in an unwinnable position. They lacked the resources to eradicate practices which had considerable popular support, but also their very actions – doomed though they were to failure – added to police unpopularity, precisely because of the legitimacy that such sports and pastimes had in the eyes of many working-class people.

Conclusion

This chapter has considered in detail a wide range of activities which were deemed to be illegal, at least by law-enforcers in the country. Some general points need to be made. At a time when the mid-Victorians were creating a cultural idyll of the English countryside –exemplified by the clear sense of *gemeinschaft* in John Frederick Herring's 1857 painting *Harvest* – rural districts were sites of social tension and criminal behaviour. Although the contrast between urban and rural crime has often been overstated by historians, there were certain crimes which, if not uniquely rural, had particular resonance in the countryside. Embezzlement, specifically offences against the Worsted Acts, was a common problem across the West Riding. The importance of the woollen and worsted industries – in both old and new forms – in Upper Agbrigg ensured that it was a source of tension that could add to the unpopularity of the police as they helped enforce laws that were seen to favour employers. Similarly, poaching, even when the poacher was more commonly an industrial worker, was a fraught arena into which the police were very reluctant to enter. Reluctance to become involved was also characteristic of the police approach to vagrancy. In contrast, the members of the WRCC in Upper Agbrigg took a more positive approach in their dealing with popular leisure. This cannot be explained simply in terms of pressure from magistrates and 'respectable' middle-class opinion-formers. Senior police figures, notably Superintendent Heaton, were convinced that there was an intimate (and causal) link between gambling, popular recreations and crime. Yet this approach was doubly problematic. First, attempts to curb, let alone eradicate, many popular leisure activities were doomed to failure – as Heaton himself recognised, not least with regard to gambling. Second, the interventions into aspects of working-class life which had popular legitimacy increased the unpopularity of the new police at a time when they were seeking to establish themselves and develop an effective but acceptable way of policing. It is to the question of 'policing by consent' that we turn in the final chapter.

Endnotes

1 Heaton's annual reports were reproduced in *HC*, 26 October 1867 and 16 October 1869.
2 There were some exceptions, such as the practice of 'pitchering', once to be found in many places on the Lancashire/Yorkshire border but largely confined to the Holmfirth district by the mid-nineteenth century. It was described as 'a form of "Lynch Law" practiced upon any unfortunate stranger whose affections may have become centred upon any of the fair daughters of the neighbourhood'. *HEx*, 17 April 1852. Few cases were reported in the local press but in a 'brutal outrage' at Paddock a youth was left for dead following a 'pitchering' attack. *HC*, 23 February 1861.
3 B Godfrey & D J Cox, *Policing the Factory: Theft, Private Policing and the Law in Modern England*, London, Bloomsbury, 2014, p.109.
4 Godfrey and Cox, *Policing the Factory*, pp.109–110.
5 *HC*, 27 July 1850.
6 Figures taken from the annual reports of the Huddersfield & Holmfirth Manufacturers' Protective Association as reproduced in the *Huddersfield Chronicle.*
7 *LM*, 9 June 1849, *HC*, 10 March & 13 October 1855 and 19 January 1861. There were also a small number of cases, often involving beerhouse keepers, for being in possession of embezzled goods. *HC*, 1 March 1851, 18 April 1857 and 19 April 1862.
8 *HC*, 13 March 1852.
9 *LM*, 5 September 1846. See also *HEx*, 13 December 1851 and 12 June 1852.
10 *LM*, 21 June 1851.
11 *B.Obs*, 28 May 1846.
12 *Ibid.*
13 *HC*, 5 October 1850 and *HEx*, 13 March 1852.
14 *LM*, 16 April 1862.
15 *HC*, 1 March 1851.
16 George Littlewood of Castle Hill, a well-known embezzler, was fined £30 in November 1862 for his second offence. Six months later he was fined a further £30. *HC*, 8 November 1862 and 23 May 1863.
17 *LM*, 2 November 1864 and *HC*, 16 June 1855 & 5 November 1864.
18 *HC*, 16 November 1850.
19 *HC*, 8 October 1859.
20 *HC*, 1 March 1851 and 23 October 1852.
21 *HC*, 14 May 1853. The magistrates took 'the opinion of several manufacturers … who stated it was not customary'.
22 *HC*, 6 February 1864. Waite's defence failed as Kaye showed that 'the sheet of woollen waste … was not of the character of sweepings'.
23 The annual reports of the Huddersfield and Holmfirth Association for 1860/1 and 1863/4 baldly record three and two cases not prosecuted at the request of the owners of the embezzled material. *HC*, 3 August 1861 and 3 September 1864.
24 *HC*, 31 March 1860 and 19 January 1861.
25 Godfrey and Cox Figure 7.3, p.159. Perplexingly, when both magistrates were members of the Worsted Committee the figure falls to 73 per cent.

26 *HC*, 8 April 1865.
27 *HC*, 28 September 1850.
28 *HC*, 1 March 1851.
29 *HC* 15 September 1855.
30 *HC*, 13 September 1851. See also 14 June 1851 for a similar case where expenses only were imposed.
31 *HC*, 4 October 1855. See also 20 March 1858 for a similar case and decision.
32 *HC*, 1 February 1868.
33 *HC*, 6 July 1861. Strangely, the report claimed the magistrates had no choice but imprison her. This was clearly not so.
34 *HC*, 3 September 1862.
35 *HC*, 22 November 1856.
36 *HC*, 14 April 1866.
37 *HC*, 19 January 1861.
38 *HC*, 22 March 1862, 3 January 1863 & 12 May 1866 for examples of magisterial criticisms of Kaye.
39 *HC*, 30 March 1861.
40 *HC*, 12 May 1866. See also 19 April 1862.
41 *HC*, 1 January 1853.
42 *HC*, 16 November 1850 Roberts lost a high-profile case in which five men, all from Honley Mill, were prosecuted for large-scale theft of waste. He was more successful in 1864 when he was able to argue that the alleged crime fell outside the purview of the acts. *HC*, 9 April 1864.
43 *HC*, 30 March 1861.
44 *HC*, 30 October 1861.
45 *HC*, 19 January 1861.
46 According to the annual reports of The Huddersfield and Holmfirth Manufacturers' Protective Association 228 cases were brought to court, of which 122 have been traced in the local press. The whole of the discrepancy is due to the under-reporting of cases in the years 1850–4.
47 See for example, *B.Obs*, 11 October 1855, *HC*, 19 April and 14 June 1856. Only two cases involving alleged stolen woollen waste have been found after 1857. *HC*, 10 August 1861 and 14 December 1867.
48 *HC*, 16 October 1852.
49 Quoted in C Emsley, *The Great British Bobby*, London, Quercus, 2009, p.77
50 Quoted in M J Weiner, *Reconstructing the Criminal*, Cambridge University Press, 1990, p.150.
51 *HC*, 18 January 1851.
52 *Ibid.*
53 *HC*, 13 February 1858.
54 *HC*, 23 May 1863.
55 *HC*, 24 November 1866.
56 *HC*, 12 April and 22 November 1862. See also 17 September and 3 December 1864 and 4 March and 1 April 1865 for similar references to 'professional cadger' and 'professional beggar'.
57 *HC*, 15 February 1851.
58 *HC*, 19 January 1861.
59 *HC*, 19 July 1851.

60 *HEx*, 17 October 1857.
61 *HC*, 14 February 1857.
62 *HC*, 23 June 1860.
63 The figures for tramps and vagrants in the Judicial Statistics should not be taken as an accurate measure but in conjunction with the figures for summary prosecution they do provide an insight into the priority accorded to the perceived problem in the two counties. In 1867 the number of tramps and vagrants in Lancashire was given as 1,096 but in the West Riding the figure was 1,343.
64 A policy similar to that adopted in Lancashire was followed in Cumberland and Westmorland, particularly after the appointment of chief constable John Dunne. G Woolnough, 'Policing Vagrancy in South Westmorland in the Nineteenth Century', unpublished M.A. dissertation, University of Lancaster, 2008.
65 *Parliamentary Papers*, 1872, x, *Select Committee on Game Laws, Statutory Provision for Preservation of Game*, pp.444–51.
66 H Hopkins, *The Long Affray: The Poaching Wars in Britain*, London, Macmillan, 1986, J E Archer, 'Sheep Rustling in Yorkshire in the Age of the Industrial and Agricultural Revolutions', *Northern History*, 1984, pp.127–145 and *"By A Flash and a Scare": Arson, Animal Maiming and Poaching in East Anglia, 1815–1870*, Oxford, Oxford University Press, 1990 and H Osborne and M Winstanley, 'Rural and Urban Poaching in Victorian England', *Rural History*, 17 (2), 2006, pp.187–212.
67 *Parliamentary Papers*, 1864, xxx, *Game Law Returns.*
68 *HC*, 30 November 1850, 4 January 1851, 15 May & 3 July 1852, 17 June & 4 November 1854, 29 September 1859, 25 July 1855, 16 April & 21 May, 25 June, and 13 August 1859, 31 October12 April, 6 September, 18 October, 8 & 15 November 1862, 27 June & 4 July 1863; 30 April, 9 July, 24 September & 12 November 1864, 21 January and 11 February 1865, 1 December 1866 & 31 August 1867.
69 *HC*, 14 September, 19 & 26 October 1850. See also six men arrested for poaching at Gledholt, *HC*, 15 November 1856.
70 *HC*, 2 December 1856, 21 August 1858, 19 April 1862 & 30 June 1866.
71 Only twelve cases of direct police action have been traced in the local press.
72 *HC*, 27 May 1854.
73 *HC*, 20 May, 24 June and 30 December 1854.
74 *HC*, 3 October 1857.
75 *HC*, 23 July 1853, 27 March 1854, 7 November 1863.
76 *HC*, 2 January 1858 and 26 March 1859 for prosecutions for poaching. He is first noted as a keeper *HC*, 3 September 1859.
77 *HC*, 3 March 1860, 11 August 1860 and 2 February 1861.
78 *HC*, 6 June 1863.
79 *HEx*, 10 April 1883.
80 Cruelty to Animals Act, 1835, 5 & 6 Wm. IV, c.59. See also the 1849 Cruelty to Animals Act, 12 & 13 Vict., c.92.
81 G Woolnough, 'Blood Sports in Victorian Cumbria: Policing Cultural Change', *Journal of Victorian Culture*, 19 (3), 2014, pp. 278–94, esp. p.286.
82 *HC*, 13 & 20 June 1863 and 28 April 1873.

83 *HC*, 27 April, 1850, 31 July 1852 and 17 June 1854.
84 *HEx*, 19 April 1856.
85 *HC*, 19 April 1856. That was not the end of the morning work. 'There was also a "main" being fought out, at the [nearby] *Flouch Inn* the same morning; Mr Heaton and the other officers proceeded there ... The fight was over when the officers arrived – consequently the could do no more than disperse the party.'
86 *HEx*, 18 April 1857. See also *HEx*, 11 April 1857 (Kirkheaton) & *HEx*, 25 April 1857, (Dalton).
87 *HC*, 18 April 1857 and *LM*, 12 May 1857.
88 *HC*, 5 July 1858.
89 *HC*, 23 & 30 May 1868.
90 *HEx*, 6 & 13 June 1863 and *HC*, 13 June 1863.
91 *HC*, 11 April 1857. The paper had hoped the suppression of cockfighting would be 'compensation for the additional rates' to be paid.
92 *HC*, 18 January 1851 and *HEx*, 21 November 1863.
93 *HC*, 14 Sept. 1850.
94 *HC*, 5 May 1855. See also 17 August 1850 for dogfight in which Heaton and Inspector Thomas single-handedly seized the two dog-handlers (and their dogs) at a fight on Lindley Moor.
95 *HC*, 1 Dec. 1855.
96 *HEx*, 15 September 1855 and *HC*, 1 Dec. 1855.
97 *HC*, 27 February and 1 March 1862, 11 & 18 June 1864 20 May 1865, and 23 March 1867 and *HEx*, 21 November 1863 and 18 June 1864.
98 *Sheff.I*, 13 February 1868.
99 *HEx*, 30 January 1858 (Holmfirth), 2 February 1861 (Isle of Sky), 18 January 1864 (Scammonden) and *HC*, 18 June & 8 October 1864 and 3 January 1865.
100 *HC*, 7 April 1866.
101 *Ibid.*
102 *LM*, 28 October 1862, *HEx*, 8 June 1867, *HC*, 8 June 1867.
103 *HC*, 18 June 1864 (Scammonden),3 January & 3 June 1865 & 7 April 1866 (Castle Hill), 8 June 1867 (Marsden), 20 July 1867 & 29 February 1868 (Honley).
104 *HC*, 1 August 1863.
105 *Ibid.*
106 *Sheff.I*, 14 & 28 September 1850, 15 July 1854, 28 September 1861 11 January and 15 November 1864.
107 *HC*, 15 February 1868.
108 *Ibid.*
109 *HC*, 4 September 1852.
110 For example, Joshua Longbottom of Berry Brow wagered & won 50*s* (£2-50) for walking blindfold from Big Valley, Armitage Bridge to the top of Castle Hill in less than 30 minutes. He achieved the feat in 23½ minutes. *HC*, 17 Dec. 1870. Other novelty races included a 100-yard dash outside the *Shoulder of Mutton*, Lockwood, between a man of ten stone and a nineteen-stone rival, carrying a fourteen-stone man on his back. Those betting on the lightweight lost their money. *HC*, 18 August 1868.

111 *LM*, 22 June 1850. Smith claimed that he was 'very fresh' [drunk] but the magistrates were unimpressed and fined him £2 with 19s (95p) costs.
112 *HC*, 25 May 1850, 25 January & 3 May 1851.
113 *HC*, 25 June 1859.
114 *HC*, 17 Jan. 1863.
115 *HC*, 28 May 1853.See also 13 May 1851.
116 *HC*, 24 September 1864.The 2,000 crowd assembled during Honley Feast and the main race, for £25 a side, was for local men over 300 yards. *HC*, 27 September 1862.
117 *HC*, 19 April 1862.
118 *HC*, 25 January 1862.
119 *HC*, 21 December 1862 and *HEx*, 12 October 1861 for a reports of the 'race-running mania' in Honley that brought hundreds of spectators to the village race course.
120 *HC*, 21 December 1862.
121 *HC*, 21 December 1862.
122 *HC*, 26 April 1862.
123 *HC*, 2September 1852.
124 *HC*, 2 February 1856, 24 January 1857, 2 & 30 June 1860, 5 January 1861, 30 September 1865 and 26 October 1867.
125 *HC*, 10 June 1852. Similar complaints were made in Kirkheaton (19 May 1855), Meltham (16 March 1867) and Almondbury (26 October 1867).
126 *HC*, 10 November 1855.
127 *HC*, 10 November 1860 & 30 September 1865.
128 *HC*, 20 October 1866.
129 *Ibid*.
130 *Ibid* & 23 May 1868.
131 *HEx*, 8 May 1852.

Conclusions and the Contentious Question of 'Policing by Consent'

THIS HAS BEEN a detailed study of policing in a relatively small area of Britain made in the belief that such local case-studies throw up important complexities that are necessarily lost in more general accounts. However, the significance of local developments for broader interpretations of the advent and impact of the 'new police' has to be considered. It is time to consider the three broad strands and the over-arching question of policing by consent.

The first strand is essentially institutional, focusing on the key features of the development of the borough and county forces. In both cases the contrast between existing policing arrangements and the 'new' forces that were created (in 1848/9 in Huddersfield and 1856/7 in Upper Agbrigg) was modest, though significant. The new Huddersfield borough force showed clear elements of continuity in personnel, albeit with consolidated and new leadership. This contrasted with both Halifax and Hull, where the introduction of the 'new police' was marked by a clean break with the past, but had more in common with the experiences of Leeds and Sheffield. Given the criticism of pre-1848 policing in Huddersfield (and the perceived superiority of Halifax), this is surprising. However, the newly-appointed Improvement Commissioners thought that improved 'new' policing could be achieved through a significant degree of continuity and experience from the past. A greater and unresolved problem in Huddersfield was the relationship between the Improvement Commissioners, who employed and dismissed all members of the force, and their senior police officers. Members of the Watch Committee (and the Improvement Commission in general) involved themselves in the detail of day-to-day policing. Although there were differences in approach over the course of the 1850s and 1860s, the political leaders of the town had a clear view of their responsibility and relationship with the police and also of the way in which the force should be organised and run. This led to ongoing conflict with successive police superintendents, all of whom left (with the exception of the first superintendent, who was forced to resign through ill-health soon after his appointment), having clashed with local politicians. Unlike in Hull (and even Halifax and Middlesbrough) local politicians in Huddersfield did not view their police chiefs as professionals and were not willing to give them the space to implement operational matters. This was understandable in light of the inexperience of superintendents Thomas and Beaumont but less so with regard to superintendent Hannan, who had demonstrated his ability in Middlesbrough. For whatever reason, and it was never made explicit, members of the town's Watch Committee thought, firmly and persistently, in terms of masters and servants as far as the police were concerned.

The situation in Upper Agbrigg was different, not least because this was but one division within the larger entity of the WRCC and many key decisions were taken in Wakefield. Unlike the borough force, most of the men who first came to police the division had no previous police experience and even more had no local experience. This was deliberate policy as the chief constable, Colonel Cobbe, firmly believed that policemen should be apart from the communities they served for fear of them 'going native'.[1] In fact, very few county men did so and the same was true for men in the borough force, even though appreciably more of them were born locally. In many villages there was a suspicion of outsiders, especially men from the Lancashire County Constabulary, and lack of local knowledge hampered police action. On the other hand, there were policemen who appeared to be part of their local community without their independence of action being compromised. There was an important element of leadership in Upper Agbrigg and other districts. The new superintendents, almost without exception, had previously been the superintending constables for petty sessional divisions in the county. In Upper Agbrigg, the dominant figure was the indefatigable and experienced Thomas Heaton. His knowledge of the area around Huddersfield, his policing priorities and his training role in the first months and years of the county force locally made him the most important single figure in local policing. Heaton's experience highlights another significant point: Upper Agbrigg was not unpoliced before 1857. From his appointment in 1848 Heaton effectively created a proto-police force, comprising some parochial and paid constables, and working with other law enforcement agencies, most notably the Woollen and Worsted Inspectorate.

The two 'new' forces both faced unsurprising problems of retention and, to a lesser extent, recruitment. Applications for the borough force were good (in quantitative terms, at least) but there is evidence that in the mid-1860s the county force faced recruitment problems. Retention was a major problem and in this regard Huddersfield fared worse than other local towns and cities. On several occasions the Improvement Commissioners adopted a lenient policy towards ill-disciplined policemen but with mixed results. The sources are less complete for the WRCC but it remains clear that many recruits lacked the necessary discipline to become constables, succumbing to the temptation to snatch a nap or a drink while on duty. The policy of recruiting married men to bring about a greater degree of stability in the force had a limited impact. The situation was further complicated by the policy of transferring men between divisions either as punishment or reward. The persistence of these problems casts doubt on the ability of these forces to achieve the 'constant surveillance' of working-class life as argued by an earlier generation of revisionist historians, influenced by Robert Storch.[2] Despite these problems, in both forces a core of longer-serving, more experienced men emerged, which brought a degree of stability that had not been experienced in the earliest years. There were several positives that flowed from this. These men had a greater degree of local knowledge and they had developed some understanding of how best to police the local communities. Selective enforcement of the law was central to police success. Rigid enforcement of a range of laws that impinged most heavily on working-class life would have overwhelmed the courts but, more importantly, would have alienated the communities whose support, however qualified, was essential to the success of the police. Further, in the absence of meaningful formal induction for new recruits, these men were able to train up new recruits who learnt on the job. However, there was also a downside. The arduous nature of routine policing meant that the job took a physical (and psychological) toll which reduced the effectiveness of older men. The trade-off between experience and effectiveness, impossible to measure with any precision, was nonetheless real.

Finally, in institutional terms, the relationship between the borough and county forces was, at best, uneasy. Huddersfield's political leaders were jealous of their powers and position and resented any encroachment from central government or the WRCC. Cobbe's openly-expressed desire to see the town force incorporated into the county police was hardly a recipe for cordial relations, and so it proved. The Huddersfield force was not small by mid-nineteenth century standards and there were stronger grounds for maintaining its independence. Its force of over thirty men compared favourably with the five-man strong Doncaster police formed in 1837, or the two-man Ripon force, formed in 1848 but incorporated into the WRCC in 1887. Indeed, as towns grew the WRCC lost control of Dewsbury (in 1863 when a nine-man force was created) and later Barnsley. The incorporation and enlargement of Huddersfield in 1868 also created some friction. Thus, at times quite petty incidents provoked a flurry of angry letters between the aggrieved parties, which did little for harmony and cooperation. Such political pride and posturing, however, was partly undercut by practicalities. Criminals, petty or serious, did not attach great significance to the boundary between town and county forces, except insofar as moving from one jurisdiction into another *increased* their likelihood of evading the law. This was not lost on the local police and throughout the 1850s and 1860s there were examples of informal cooperation between officers and, in 1865, formal cooperation during the election of that year proved highly successful.

The second strand is concerned with the social history of the police. The problems of adopting a 'bottom-up' approach have been well-documented by Klein in her study of city forces in the early twentieth century and there is no English equivalent to Wilson's study of the policing of nineteenth-century Melbourne.[3] Despite the limitations of the local primary sources, certain observations about the ordinary working-life of the police can be made. Perhaps the most obvious starting point is the *inappropriateness* of policing for many of the men recruited in the 1850s and 1860s. Whether it was the excessive demands of the job that led to dismissal, or better opportunities elsewhere, which led to resignation, large numbers of men simply did not last beyond a few months and in some cases weeks or days. For those that remained there was the security of regular employment/wages throughout the year and the possibility of some pension, albeit discretionary, for many mid-century policemen. There were periodic requests for pay increases but there was nothing to compare with the 1853 pay strike by the Hull police, which led to the dismissal of six men and the enforced resignation of a further forty officers.[4] In addition, there was that sense of belonging and self-worth that developed as police forces matured and policing itself was no longer seen as a stop-gap form of employment but rather as an occupation in its own right. The point must not be overstated: in part, because the evidence is scant, often indirect or inferential, in part because even in the late-1860s recruits with previous police experience still identified themselves in terms of earlier trades and occupations.

Much play has been made – not least by senior police figures – of the promotional opportunities held out to the ordinary constable and there were examples of men who had risen through the ranks to the very top, at least in a few boroughs. The realities in Huddersfield and Upper Agbrigg were less rosy. The opportunities for a single promotion, let alone a second, were limited, especially in the borough force. As a consequence, a large percentage of career policemen did not escape the drudgery and tedium of beat work and even those who did gain promotion had to spend time (often several years) on the beat. The unspectacular realities of routine policing, therefore, are central to an understanding of the experience of mid-Victorian policing. It is difficult to capture effectively the numbing effects – both physical and mental – of night-time patrolling, particularly in the winter months, with little happening on the beat. In addition, there were more occasional dangers associated with vicious dogs, runaway horses and belligerent members of the public, some drunk, some sober. It is clear, not least from the physical record, that long years on patrol led to a range of problems from flat feet and arthritis to recurrent colds and even pneumonia. Fuller records from other forces give a better picture than the local records. In Hull, the police surgeon, Dr Henry Munro, kept very detailed records for two years, 1857/8 and 1858/9 from which he concluded that 'for each Policeman in the Force, according to his age, I find that the sickness experienced by the Police Force is double the amount of that experienced by operatives living in large towns'.[5] Only 15 per cent of the force was unaffected by accident or illness, of one form or another, in these years. The number of days per year lost amounted to just over three weeks per man for the force as a whole. If the figure is recalculated to include only those who were injured or ill, it rises from three to four weeks. The reasons for time off work are illuminating. Only 13 per cent of days lost were due to injuries or wounds, almost the same figure for time lost to diarrhoea and just less than that for rheumatism. 28 per cent of days lost were due to colds and coughs and 33 per cent to fever.[6] Huddersfield was not the same as Hull but it is unlikely that the local experience differed significantly from the pattern seen in Hull.

The physical harshness of policing is well-known, but less attention has been given to the psychological pressures. There are a number of interrelated points to be made. First, there was the uncertainty of the job, which was particularly acute for new recruits, to all intents and purposes untrained, and expected (and expecting) to learn by experience 'on the job'. Even for the more experienced men, there was always the possibility, even on the quietest of nights, that they might be called to a fire or to a drunken brawl. Closely related to this was the problematic issue of discretion. Contrary to Steedman's emphasis on the importance of police obedience, policemen in and around Huddersfield appeared to have made judgements on a regular basis. Often in a heated situation and with little time for reflection, but always with the knowledge that a misjudgement could make a bad situation worse and result in threats to life and limb for the individual constable and any colleague he might have with him.[7]

This in turn was linked to the more general question of the relationship of the police (and their families) with the public – being in a community but not of that community. This was particularly true of the county constable, who could easily find himself the only constable in a small village, such as Farnley Tyas, and his nearest fellow-officer two or three miles away, in this instance in Honley or Berry Brow. Even in that idealised rural setting of Candleford Green, 'nobody seemed to like [the local bobby] ... despite being 'a kindly good-tempered man ... and he and his wife led a somewhat isolated life, in the village but not entirely of the village'.[8] To make matters worse, according to Flora Thompson, even law-abiding people with 'no reason for fearing the police [viewed] the village constable as a potential enemy, set to spy upon them by the authorities'.[9] Matters were probably worse in Kirkburton or Kirkheaton and Marsden and Meltham. One should not overlook the public demonstrations of respect for a small number of long-serving officers and it is also clear that some men were able to make some links with their local community, via the annual flower and vegetable show or the local bowls club, but this was not easy when men were routinely transferred from place to place, not least to stop them 'going native'. Such difficulties for policemen were considerable, but for their families they could be worse. It is impossible to estimate the intra-family tensions created by repeated moves, continuing semi-isolation and community suspicion, if not outright dislike, but they constituted a real problem.

Finally, there were the psychological pressures of the job itself. Policemen were called upon to drag drowned men and women from local canals; to cut down the unfortunates who hanged (or tried to hang) themselves in cellars and barns; to tend to pedestrians, often young children, who had been run down and mangled by 'furious' drivers; to attempt to rescue people from fires or to deal with dead children who had fallen into the domestic hearth; to sort out the emaciated, penniless beggars, the rough-sleepers at Aspley kilns and the abandoned children begging at the roadside. The list could be extended with ease – what impact did the discovery of the Shelley lunatic, in his contorted position, tied to a squalid bed in an equally squalid room, have on the men sent to the scene? – but the point hardly needs reinforcing. It is easy to assume that the greater frequency of death, accident and illness meant that Victorians were hardened to suffering. There is an element of truth in this but it is also a comforting myth, perpetrated at the time and repeated later. Working-class sensibilities are poorly recorded but there is clear evidence that working-class men and women were as much grief-stricken by the death of a child (especially if in an accident) or shocked by the poverty and desperation of those on the fringes of society as any sensitive and refined middle-class observer, then or now. Grief, sorrow and suffering were burdens hard to bear, irrespective of class. For the constable facing such incidents as an inescapable part of his job, there was an emotional/psychological price to pay. 'Burn out' is not exclusively a twenty-first century social problem, though it may be better recorded and better understood now than in the mid-nineteenth century.

The third strand is concerned with the social history of Huddersfield and its surrounding district through the prism of policing. By the nature of the perspective adopted this gives a partial picture of local society. It excludes much that is important, not least the growing prosperity of the local economy and the material and cultural benefits that this brought, particularly to the middle-classes of the town but also to sections of working-class society. The expansion and development of retailing was indicative of an emerging mass market for foodstuffs and, to a lesser extent in the mid-nineteenth century, for clothing and footwear. Similarly, the opening of singing-saloons and music-halls and the expansion of commercialised sport was further evidence of growing effective demand that included many working-class men and, to a lesser extent, women. However, such developments, which figure large in the social histories of the period, are themselves only part of the picture. It is a picture of progress, albeit marginal and halting for many, of winners in a world that was becoming somewhat less harsh and insecure. There was, however, another picture of the less fortunate in society – the unskilled, the sick and disabled, the unfortunate, thrown from relative prosperity to penury due to a slump in trade, the accident of illness or injury, or other factors well beyond their control. These were the people who struggled to make a living in a society with limited welfare provision beyond a harsh and unpopular poor law, and charity often as cold as it was uncaring. This was the world of the makeshift economy in which men and, especially, women struggled to survive, devising strategies to keep themselves and their families alive, fed and clothed. This was the pick-and-mix world of casual and irregular employment, begging, occasional recourse to the workhouse or a local charity, involvement in (largely petty) criminal behaviour and, in some cases prostitution and, in the most desperate of circumstances, suicide. The marginalized, the misfortunate, the non-beneficiaries of mid-Victorian progress – these were the people most likely to come into contact with the local bobby and the local magistrates' court. Their evidence casts light on the grim underbelly of mid-Victorian society, even in a relatively thriving town and district like Huddersfield. Respectable and caring members of society in the town were genuinely concerned (as well as feeling threatened) by the squalor and immorality they saw before them and they tried to alleviate these problems. However, there was much that they scarcely saw, even though it was there before their eyes. There was a growing concern with 'wife-beating' as definitions of masculinity changed but little was said about the equally (if not more) pervasive male-on-male violence. It was as if such behaviour was only to be expected given the nature of the 'rough' elements of working-class society. Self-harm was seen but often rationalised in terms of the accident of illness or personal misfortune that rendered the victim of 'unsound mind' at the time he or she killed themselves. There was little awareness (and less willingness to address) structural problems in the economic and social organization of society at the time, which provide a deeper understanding of events which would otherwise be no more than individual tragedies. Similarly, abject poverty was seen but all too often explained away in terms of feckless outsiders (especially from Ireland or Lancashire), bogus alms-seekers or ill-disciplined, work-shy skivers. Mid-Victorian policemen shared the preconceptions and prejudices of their fellows but their work brought them into contact with sections of society that were all too often marginalized and ignored; and such experience could bring a different, more sympathetic perspective. The reporting of these cases was also flawed. Caricatures of Irish men and women were commonplace and cheap witticisms were made at the expense of often inarticulate individuals but the very details of the cases in the magistrates' courts, week on week, bear testimony, albeit unwittingly, to the harsh realities of mid-Victorian life for many working-class men and women.

In addition to these three themes there is an overarching concern about the nature of the policed society that was emerging in these years. Put simply, could it be described as 'policing by consent'? The term, 'policing by consent', has been and continues to be widely used as if it reflects a fundamental and unproblematic reality that demonstrates the unique nature of British policing.[10] Few historians or social scientists have attempted to provide a rigorous definition.[11] For many Victorian politicians, as well as senior police figures, 'policing by consent' was a powerful but self-serving argument. Implicitly, it carried the connotations of a Lockean 'social compact' whereby people voluntarily gave up some of their individual rights and powers in the interest of a greater, societal good.[12] It conveniently glossed over the fact that the new police were imposed from above, via a variety of parliamentary acts, upon a populace that had no direct say in their formulation. It conjured up a more comforting picture of the police, a protective line of blue, ensuring that the law-abiding majority, irrespective of class, gender or ethnicity, did not fall foul of the threat posed by a law-breaking minority. Such has been the power of the concept that in certain important quarters it is still treated as being straightforward and reassuring. *Blackstone's Student Police Officer Handbook*, for example, treats the term as largely unproblematic, describing it as 'the active cooperation and tolerance of a majority of the populace'.[13] Others, such as Tim Newburn, see it as a problem in the present but persist in the belief that it was fundamentally different fifty years ago.[14] Such views have not gone unchallenged. Reiner and Wilson have referred to the myth of policing by consent, while Crowther and Campling draw attention to 'the popular misconception in police history that the police have won the consent of the entire population' – a sentiment expressed by an earlier generation of radical criminologists, not least Scraton, who spoke of the 'controversial tradition of the police'.[15] Police historians have discussed key issues, such as the inter-action between police and public, including the contentious issue of police brutality, but there is no sustained examination of policing by consent, including such critical considerations as the nature of police legitimacy or the use of minimal force.[16] Indeed, it is the distinguished criminologist, Robert Reiner, influenced by the American historian Wilbur Miller, who has provided the most thorough analysis of the rise and fall of police legitimacy in Britain since the early nineteenth century.[17]

Reiner rejects naïve maximalist positions – consent will never be total – but argues that policing by consent is an ideal to aspire to but in the knowledge that it is unattainable. The most that can be achieved – and Reiner believes this had been achieved by the 1950s – is 'the wholehearted approval of the majority of the population who do not experience the coercive exercise of police powers to any significant extent, and *de facto* acceptance of the legitimacy of the institution by those that do.[18] There are a number of general points that need to be made, not least the recognition that police powers could be and were used coercively. The first set of observations focus on the key concept of legitimacy. There is a growing body of contemporary evidence that suggests strongly that compliance with the law owes more to the perceived legitimacy of an institution, such as the police, than to instrumental calculations based on the deterrent effect of the law.[19] Legitimacy, in turn, derives from the 'public belief that institutions have the right to exist, the right to undertake the functions assigned to them, and the right to dictate appropriate behaviour'.[20] Building on Tyler's procedural justice model, the 'most powerful factors' in establishing and maintaining police legitimacy are the ways in which the police use their authority in myriad interactions with members of the public.[21] Further, as Jackson *et al.*, argue 'conferring legitimacy on an institution, such as the police, is an 'act based on the expression of shared values: a sense of moral alignment'.[22] Valuable as such insights are, it is important not to lose sight of the complexities and contradictions that might be subsumed under these broad observations. The functions assigned to the police, then and now, are varied and not seen as equally legitimate; similarly, 'appropriate behaviour' raises thorny questions of what constitutes 'appropriate' behaviour and who determines that it is so; and, finally, the notion of 'shared values' should not obscure the reality of alternative values, also seen to be legitimate.

The second set of observations relate to the policed. Overwhelmingly, though not exclusively working-class, the policed comprised a heterogeneous group in mid-Victorian England. The commonly-made distinction between 'rough' and 'respectable' is at best a convenient shorthand. In reality, the line between the two was often blurred and, more importantly, a 'respectable' figure in one aspect of life could become 'rough' in another.[23] The experience of women differed from that of men; likewise, of the Irish from the English. Further, such was the range of police activities that an individual's experience of the police could vary widely.[24] Finally, Reiner's reference to '*de facto* acceptance' should be emphasized. Even in the early years of the new police, there was a strong sense of pragmatism in the popular response. The police were no more likely to disappear or be forcibly removed from the landscape than were the mills of the West Riding. However, there was also an important degree of pragmatism on the part of the police. The law – or more accurately, the panoply of laws and by-laws – was not enforced to the full. In part, this was a reflection of practicalities. In Upper Agbrigg, and even in Huddersfield, police resources were simply insufficient to proceed against every law-breaking beerhouse keeper, beggar or drunk; and even if the police had had the necessary resources to do so, the court system would have been swamped and brought to a grinding halt. More importantly, such a 'maximalist' stance would have alienated a wide swathe of the population and thereby made an already difficult challenge – developing an effective working relationship with the largely working-class population at large – all but impossible. There were principled reasons for police discretion but also powerful practical ones. Heavily outnumbered in town and countryside, the police needed to neutralise potential opposition as much as they needed to win positive support. Discretion was crucial in a number of important ways. The police needed to know when to turn a blind eye to an infringement of the law; to know when to give a second chance via a friendly 'move on' or even to help a drunk home; to know which groups, such as travellers, or locally unpopular individual men or women could be 'targeted' without alienating the wider community; even to know when simply to look for costs, rather than the full penalty of the law, when a case came to court. Contrary to the claims that have been about the limited scope for individual action in rural forces, the evidence of constabulary action (or inaction) from Upper Agbrigg demonstrates that, even in the same village, there was often considerable variation in the assiduousness of individual constables, which, in turn strongly suggests that decisions about the implementation of the law were being made at this level.[25] However, there was a balance to be struck. Too much policing could undermine legitimacy in the eyes of the policed, but too little policing could equally undermine credibility.

In light of Reiner's definition of policing by consent, there would appear to be widespread support for the police from the local authorities (magistrates and Watch Committee members) and from the largely unpoliced middle (and upper) classes. There was criticism – at various times of police violence, of police ineffectiveness, of the cost of policing and even the appropriate size of the force – but no challenge to the legitimacy of the police.[26] The evidence of popular responses to the police in Huddersfield and Upper Agbrigg – incomplete though it is in a number of important respects – does not point to simple conclusions. In Huddersfield the transition from old to new police was characterised as much by continuity as change and was not accompanied by an upsurge of hostility in the town. Further, there was a clear recognition by the police of acting appropriately to gain and retain the support of the public. However, police/public relations could (and did) fluctuate over the course of time. There was no simple linear pattern of improvement. Indeed, the most sustained and aggressive outburst of anti-police behaviour came in the mid- and late-1860s in the form of the Irish Small Gang. Their hostility towards the police was proclaimed in words and deeds, but determining the significance of their actions is less clear cut. The leading figures, the M'Cabes, were driven by a very real sense of injustice that went back to the mishandling of the 1847 Mirfield murders case and its aftermath. The gang itself was not widely popular in all working-class districts of Huddersfield, not least because of the 'turf wars' it fought. Indeed, such was their unpopularity that, on occasion, members of the public went to the assistance of the police who were attempting to arrest members of the gang. The particular circumstances surrounding the Irish Small Gang, however, should not obscure the fact that relations between the police and the town's Irish communities were characterised by recurrent outbreaks of violence, some individual, others communal. The ferocity of some of the verbal abuse hurled at the police indicates a depth of dislike verging on hatred. Similarly, the physical violence inflicted on the police, as well as asserting the strength of opposition, often involved very visible humiliation. Many of the incidents took place in yards, which were contested areas – public to the police but private to the inhabitants – and were associated with familial events (weddings and wakes). This suggests that there was a very real popular sense of the limits of policing, which justified resisting the police to protect geographical spaces and activities that were not seen as legitimate areas for police involvement. Other disturbances, however, took place in indisputably public spaces and there is something problematic about these incidents. Heavily outnumbered constables were able to make arrests and (in many cases) resist rescue attempts and bring their prisoners to the police station. There was something ritualistic or carnivalesque about such disturbances that involved the pragmatic recognition of the existence (and continuing existence) of the police as well as a statement that excessive behaviour would not be tolerated, but little to suggest a fundamental rejection of the police, or even of their role in arresting drunk and disorderly individuals. Less dramatically, police officers lived in and around the Irish-dominated districts of Castlegate and Upperhead Row but did not see their houses attacked, nor were they driven out. In the one occasion that PC Wilson had his windows smashed his assailant, Mary Curtis, did so to be sent to Wakefield House of Correction, not because she hated the police.

Such complex responses were to be found elsewhere. There were beerhouse keepers across the town who were part of a wider illegal, 'black' economy as well as being repeated offenders against the licensing laws, and yet even these men and women made use of the police and the courts when they felt it appropriate. Constables were called in to clear out obstreperous drunks or to arrest petty thieves. There was an element of calculative accommodation that extended to pawnbrokers and general dealers who cooperated with the police on some occasions while still operating semi-legal, even illegal, transactions. Almost certainly, not all incidences of the pawning of stolen goods were reported to the police, though the actual percentage is impossible to determine. More generally, working-class men and women also made use of the local criminal justice system which indicates not simply a recognition of the *de facto* existence of the police in particular, but an awareness that there was a legitimate role for the law (and its enforcement agencies) in the everyday lives of ordinary men and women. Victims of thefts and also victims of washing-line quarrels called the police to their assistance and looked to the local magistrates for redress. Across the socio-economic spectrum certain actions were seen as simply 'wrong' and enforcing the law 'the right thing to do'. Calculative accommodation also extended to the police who, for reasons already given, were selective in their enforcement of the law. Such an interpretation raises other questions, not least relating to the oft-quoted working-class suspicion of the outsider in general and authority figures in particular.[27] It seems self-evident that the policeman was an outsider, literally set apart by his uniform but, in towns at least, the situation was more complex. Routine policing brought regular contact with various members of the public. The concerns of senior police officers that constables gossiped and fraternised inappropriately bears witness to the extent of interaction that took place. Further, it is by no means clear that the majority of policemen renounced their working-class backgrounds.[28] There was a greater degree of sympathy with working-class values and activities among many ordinary policemen. Indeed, it could be argued that 'moral alignment' between police and public in the mid-nineteenth century manifested itself in a belief that certain actions were not unequivocally illegal or that certain laws were biased and unjust. Further, though the evidence is scanty, the Huddersfield police, for the most part, acted with a sufficient degree of fairness and respect to avoid the troubles that befell their counterparts in Honley and Holmfirth in 1862. The argument must not be pushed too far. The fact that police chiefs had to warn repeatedly of the need to behave properly at all times is indicative of an ongoing and unresolved problem of police/public relations. Further, there is clear evidence of an unwillingness to cooperate with the police that sits uncomfortably with later perceptions of policing by consent.

In cases from the early 1850s to the late 1860s witnesses perjured themselves, while informers were hissed and booed; and in incidents similarly spread across the two decades, members of the public were unwilling to come forward to give evidence, let alone assist the police in the streets, in all but a handful of cases.

The situation in Upper Agbrigg was different in a number of important ways. The advent of the new police was more dramatic than in Huddersfield, even though the district was not unpoliced before 1857, and the employment of non-local men made them more 'outsiders' than their urban counterparts, while their relative isolation limited the opportunities for fraternisation.[29] Contrary to earlier interpretations the initial response to the county police was more patchy and less hostile in Upper Agbrigg, at least. There is virtually no evidence of any broad-based desire to drive out the new policemen. That said, in some villages (Golcar, for example) there were determined campaigns to annoy the police and in others (notably Jackson Bridge) attacks on the police led to a number of resignations. Nonetheless, in the first five years of its existence, the WRCC in Upper Agbrigg, taken as a whole, developed a working relationship with the local communities, albeit in a tentative manner and with no guarantee of longer-term success. 1862 was a critical year. The incidents in Honley and Holmfirth demonstrated, in dramatic fashion, that without broad-based popular support, policing could become all but impossible. They also revealed the persistence of arguments regarding freedom and liberty that had been aired earlier in the century – and which historians have suggested had been abandoned by the mid-1850s. The breadth of support in both villages – as evidenced by financial contributions to the defence fund in Honley and attendance at the open-air protest meeting in Holmfirth – is important to note, though one must be cautious about the extent of shared attitudes and values. In both villages unpopular policemen, exercising their authority in an excessive and officious manner, provoked a strong reaction. Whatever prior calculative assumptions had been made, there was widespread feeling that the police had not acted fairly or with respect. The trial of the Honley rioters revealed considerable anger not simply at individual policemen but at the police as a whole, though some of this owed more to the rhetoric of 'Mr Roberts of Manchester' than to the testimony of witnesses. However, there was no suggestion that the WRCC should be disbanded or the district be unpoliced.

Indeed, in the letter sent to chief constable Cobbe in the aftermath of the Honley riot trial, the emphasis was on the desirability of a policed society but the need for appropriate policing. Similarly, the memorialists of Holmfirth stressed that they were not opposed to the police *per se* – indeed, they felt this was an unjust accusation that had been levelled against them – but strongly objected to the unfair and disrespectful way in which local policemen had acted. In both instances the solution was seen to be the removal of inappropriate policemen and an insistence on appropriate behaviour by their replacements. In other words, the men and women of Honley and Holmfirth were effectively removing their consent from the local police, denying the right of *individual* policemen to be there and challenging their right to enforce certain laws in a petty-minded and mean-spirited manner. Their challenge was to specific officers and their particular enforcement of specific laws. In so far as 'policing by consent' implied a contract between police and policed, whereby the policed obeyed the law in return for its proper enforcement, the contract had been broken and consent withdrawn. However, action was taken, most notably the transfer of the highly unpopular PC Antrobus, and a working relationship re-established in both villages, albeit one which witnessed reduced police action. The events of 1862 clearly demonstrate the limitations of police power and the extent to which they were constrained by the policed. The events after 1862, however, demonstrate that a viable working relationship could be (re-) established. If there is meaning to the term 'policing by consent' in this, the first generation of new policing, this is where it is to be found.

The spectacular nature of the events of 1862 command attention but they need to be placed in context. The drama was confined to two villages in one year. It would be naïve to suggest that similar tensions did not exist elsewhere in the period under review. They most certainly did but they were contained. As in Huddersfield, the local police provided a range of services that were viewed positively. Prosecutions for theft and arrests of vagrants from outside were generally well received; welfare activities made them a more valued and accepted part of the community; and some men were able to integrate themselves into local society without 'going native' in a way that worried their superiors. Nonetheless, certain tensions remained unresolved. Enforcement of the licensing laws could be counterproductive and it is no coincidence that even Heaton adopted a less confrontational role, insisting upon prosecution to show that the law was being upheld but pressing for costs only, especially where there were mitigating circumstances. Similarly, intervention in popular leisure activities – old and new – was problematic. To some extent changes in attitude towards violence and cruel sports worked in favour of the police, but there were still numbers of people who resented the encroachment of the police on their favoured and time-honoured pastimes. Here there was no moral alignment but there was an element of calculative accommodation. On several occasions, Heaton and his men were able to break up various fights and arrest and bring to trial the principal offenders. The police were able to argue that they were upholding the law, the main protagonists saw the occasional fine as the price to pay for their sport, and the bulk of spectators escaped scot-free. Again, the argument must not be pushed too far. As the Huddersfield police failed to eradicate the beerhouse-brothels found across the town, so the county police were unable to stamp out cockfighting, dogfighting and prize fighting. There were common problems of witnesses unwilling to come forward in the first place as well as being unreliable, if not outright dishonest, later. If widespread and active cooperation with the police is seen as a key component of policing by consent, it was conspicuous by its absence in this part of the West Riding in the mid-nineteenth century.

In view of the difficulty of finding a realistic definition of the term and of the complex, even contradictory, nature of police/public relations at this time, there is a strong case for abandoning the use of the notion of policing by consent. However, such is its ubiquity and seductive (if superficial) attractiveness, that this cannot be done. What, then, did policing by consent mean in the context of the first generation of new policing in Huddersfield and Upper Agbrigg? There is no simple answer, not least because of the limitations of surviving primary source material, but a number of 'factual' observations can be made from this study. First, in certain quarters, there was a suspicion of the new police – most notable of the county force – that drew on an earlier radical critique and which expressed itself most dramatically in 1862. However, it is less clear that this was this was the only, or even predominant, popular sentiment, particularly in that part of Huddersfield that fell under the 1848 Improvement Act. Second, there were ongoing incidences of verbal and physical violence towards the police in town and country, though mass protests were limited to the villages of Honley and Holmfirth in 1862. Much of this antagonism grew out of police interventions in a range of popular recreational activities, ranging from carousing to cockfights. Third, there was a degree of involvement, even cooperation, with the police and the courts. Working-class men and women called upon the police in a variety of circumstances – as victims of theft or assault – and, in cases impossible to number, provided information to assist the police. However, there were very real limits to this cooperation. On occasion the police bemoaned the fact that no witnesses were forthcoming from a large crowd that had witnessed a crime, or if they did so, gave false evidence in court. The significance of these facts, however, is more problematic. Should the Honley riot be seen as the tip of the iceberg of popular hostility or a one-off event? Were assaults on the police, particularly in the context of popular recreation, a response to insensitive policing or a more fundamental rejection of the police as an institution? Indeed, is there a clear-cut polarity: conflict or consent? The argument advanced here is that police/public relations were complex (even contradictory) and were shaped as much by pragmatism as by ideology on the part of the police and those they policed. There was, or so it appears, an acceptance of the permanence of the new police, on the one hand, but also an acceptance of the strength of popular feeling regarding a range of activities that extended beyond popular recreation, on the other. While the police could and did constrain the actions of the public, the policed could and did constrain the police. Both police and policed needed to find a *modus vivendi* but the process was very much one of trial and error, particularly on the part of the police. The critical issues were the extent of the police's legitimate role – which activities, and which areas, should be subject to police intervention? – and also the manner in which they carried out their duties. There were contested activities and contested sites but also areas of common ground. Put in somewhat simplistic terms, there was broad acceptance of the police's crime-fighting role and approval of a range of welfare functions carried out by the police, but there were important differences of opinion of the more 'domestic missionary' role of the police. Moreover, these differences of opinion were not simply between police and policed but also within these two broad groups. Cockfighting, for example, was not universally popular among the working classes; anti-gambling laws were not universally supported by ordinary policemen. As neo-revisionists, such as Churchill, acknowledge, 'antagonistic encounters ... coexisted with more moderate views'.[30] More contentious, is the claim that 'insults, abuse and violence' constituted a rejection of police legitimacy.[31] The evidence from Huddersfield and Upper Agbrigg gives, at best, partial support to this argument. Certain communities – in which mining was generally the major occupation – and certain sections of working-class society may well have rejected the legitimacy of the police but even they accepted the *de facto* existence of the police, even to the extent of using them as a resource at times. Undoubtedly, for some working-class men anti-police violence (verbal or physical) was a means of asserting a threatened masculinity, but there is also a very real sense in which many of the confrontations were effectively ritualised in a manner reminiscent of later confrontations between police and strikers during the period of 'push and shove' picketing. There was also an element of winning by appearing to lose, again on both sides. Large numbers of cockfighters fled the scene at the appearance of three or four policemen but regrouped to fight another day; policemen failed to make mass arrests among those attending such fights but apprehended the principal offenders, thereby demonstrating that the law was being upheld. Overall, the period witnessed a process of calculative accommodation but this did not take place in a value-free context. The myriad contacts between police and policed were mediated through a complex set of popular values. The events of 1862, exceptional in their scale, nonetheless provide a clear insight into this process and the accompanying mentalities. In both Honley and Holmfirth, overzealous and officious constables, enforcing the law in a manner that was seen as unfair, petty-minded and lacking in respect, aroused considerable opposition across a wide swathe of local society, which was given form in a language of radicalism, emphasising the threat to time-honoured individual liberties. Policing *per se* was not rejected – to the contrary – but the local communities made clear the acceptable limits of policing. The removal of unpopular individual policemen and a rowing back of certain police activities resolved the conflict and resulted in an acceptable and peaceable relationship. To that extent policing by consent also meant consent gained through non-policing. Anti-police sentiment did not disappear, no more did concerns for liberties; consent was often given begrudgingly and conditionally, and in some quarters not given at all. Furthermore, the relationship between police and public changed significantly in subsequent decades, as Klein's work on the twentieth century demonstrates. Nonetheless, in this part of the West Riding at least, the first generation of new policing was characterised not simply by suspicion and conflict but also by a degree of cooperation that went beyond simple self-interested calculation. Thus, realistically defined and subject to the important qualifications detailed above, there was a meaningful sense in which policing by consent existed. Police/public relations were never as positive and broadly-based as Victorian police chiefs and 'Whiggish' police historians argued but neither were they as confrontational and conflict-ridden as some revisionist historians have claimed.

But behind this general conclusion – important though it is for our general understanding of the development of Victorian policing – were thousands of interactions, most unrecorded, between the small minority who donned police uniform in Huddersfield and Upper Agbrigg and the majority who, to a greater or lesser extent, conformed with the law. However, in a diverse population there were many whose attitude towards the law (or at least certain specific laws) and those who enforced it was often ambivalent. The police operated in a broad context characterised by socio-economic inequalities and gender and racial assumptions as well as the class orientation of the law itself and the workings of the courts. Thus, to a degree beyond their control, their actions were constrained but much depended upon the actions or inactions of a variety of policemen who displayed varying degrees of commitment, ability and experience. As these pages have demonstrated, there were certain men who stand out as crucial figures in the evolution of local policing, most notably the long-serving William Townsend, whose career started as a parochial constable and finished with him a venerable inspector, the stalwart of the borough force, and Thomas Heaton, who, as superintending constable and later as superintendent of the Upper Agbrigg division of the WRCC, was the most influential single figure in local county policing. But more important than these high-profile individuals were the less well-known figures, glimpsed in the minutes of the Watch Committee or in pages of the local press. Many did not stay in the force long enough to have a major individual impact, but collectively their misdemeanours or lack of commitment are unlikely to have had a positive effect. Others stayed longer but had a negative impact on police/public relations – none more so than PC

Antrobus in Honley, Sergeant Briers and PCs Hancock and Strange in Holmfirth, and Sergeant Caygill and PC Manuel in Lindley. Other longer-serving men such as PCs Boler, Hirst and Wardle were the work-horses of the 'new police'. All faced popular hostility at one time or another during their careers but their approach to policing was often minimalist. They arrested a sufficient number of furious drivers, vagrants and gamblers to satisfy their superiors but did not adopt a proactive stance. Wardle (and he was not alone) became an accepted part of the local community – living in it, if not wholly part of it. Yet others, such as Sergeant Mellor, were more proactive but managed to live in Dock Street, just off troublesome Castlegate, among the very people he arrested for disorderly behaviour in its many forms. Abraham Sedgwick, as a member of both the borough force and the WRCC, was a similar, though more divisive figure – at times antagonistic to his superiors as well as to the public at large. Detective Nathaniel Partridge was a more contradictory figure, a successful 'thief-taker' but also a man prone to gambling, which brought him into compromising situations with local landlords. And then there were men like PC Grant, who succeeded Antrobus in Honley and re-established good relations in the village, or Sergeants Corden and Greenwood who were active officers but capable of winning local respect. The careers of these men – and others like them – are of central importance in the wider story. Their varying interactions with members of the public created the dynamic in and from which one of the more significant developments of the nineteenth century – the evolution of a policed society – took place.

Endnotes

1 The extent to which policemen were instructed to hold aloof from their communities is impossible to determine, but the comment attributed to an unnamed ex-policeman during the Holmfirth protest meeting, if true, shows that Heaton discouraged 'fraternization'.

2 R Storch, 'The Policeman as Domestic Missionary', *Journal of Social History,* 9, 1976, p.487. C Steedman makes a similar point, *Policing the Victorian Community: The formation of English provincial police forces. 1856–80,* London, Routledge & Kegan Paul, 1984, p.96.

3 J Klein, *Invisible Men: The Secret Lives of Police Constables in Liverpool, Manchester and Birmingham, 1900–1939,* Liverpool, Liverpool University Press, 2010 and D Wilson, *The Beat: Policing a Victorian City,* Beaconsfield, Victoria, Melbourne Publishing Group, 2006.

4 D R Welsh, 'The Reform of Urban Policing in Victorian England: A Study of Kingston upon Hull from 1836 to 1866, unpublished Ph.D., University of

Hull, 1997, pp.299–316.

5 Dr H Munro, *Medical Statistics*, p.11 cited in Walsh, 'Reform of Urban Policing', p.360.

6 Calculated from Munroe, *Medical Statistics*, pp.8–9, cited in Walsh, 'Reform of Urban Policing', p.359.

7 Steedman, *Policing the Victorian Community,* p.147.

8 Flora Thompson, *Lark Rise to Candleford*, 1943, reprinted London, Penguin, 1974, p.484. The same point was made by Richard Jervis, recounting his early experiences of policing in Lancashire. R Jervis, *Chronicles of a Victorian Detective, 1907*, reprinted Runcorn, P and D Riley, 1995, p.84.

9 Thompson, *Lark Rise,* p.484.

10 The Home Office, in a freedom of information release, detailed 'Robert Peel's 9 Principles of Policing' and quoted with approval Charles Reith's description of this philosophy of policing as 'unique in history and throughout the world because it derived not from fear but almost exclusively from public cooperation' that resulted from police behaviour that won them 'the approval, respect and affection of the public'. https://www.gov.uk/government/publications/policing-by-consent, accessed 16 October 2015.

11 See for example, G Slapper and D Kelly, *The English Legal System,* London, Cavendish, 2001, referring to 'British policing … based on consent rather than sheer strength' p.36; or A Crawford, 'Plural Policing in the United Kingdom', in T Newburn, *ed., Handbook of Policing,* Cullumpton, Willan, talking of 'the legitimacy of modern policing through consent', p.160.

12 It is less obvious that the founders of 'policing by consent', Rowan and Mayne (or their successors) accepted the corollary that popular support could be withdrawn if the social compact were broken.

13 *Blackstone's Student Police Officer Handbook, Oxford,* Oxford University Press, 2006, p.161.

14 T Newburn, 'Policing since 1945' in Newburn, *Handbook of Policing,* p.109. A similar point is made by N Tilly, 'Modern approaches to policing: community, problem-oriented and intelligence-led' in Newburn, *Handbook of Policing, p.373* and M Rowe, *Policing Race and Racism,* Cullumpton, Willan, 2004, pp.144–5.

15 R Reiner, 'The Organization and Accountability of the Police' in M McConville and C Wilson, eds., *Handbook of Criminal Justice Process,* Oxford, Oxford University Press, 2002, p.23; D Wilson, *What Everyone in Britain Should Know About the Police, London,* Blackstone, 2001, p.230; C Crowther and J Campling, *'Policing Urban Poverty,* Basingstoke, Macmillan, 2000, p.127; P Scraton, *The State of the Police: Is Law and Order Out of Control?*, London, Pluto, esp. chapter two. See also J Lea and J Young, *What Is To Be Done About Law and Order?, London,* Pluto, 1993 and M Brogden, 'The Myth of Policing by Consent', *Police Review*, 22 April 1983.

16 See for example, C Emsley, *The English Police: A Political and Social History,* 2nd edition, Harlow, Longman, 1996, (esp. chapters 4 and 8, though 'policing by consent' does not appear in the index) and P Rawlings, *Policing a Short History,* Cullumpton, Willan, 2002. W R Miller, *Cops and Bobbies: Police Authority in New York and London,* Columbus, Ohio State University Press, 1999 (1st published 1973), chapter five explores the strategies drawn up

and implemented by the first Metropolitan police commissioners, Rowan and Mayne, and seeks to 'assess the degree of police legitimacy among the working classes' without defining the term 'policing by consent'. The present author is guilty of using, but not examining rigorously, the notion of policing by consent in a number of his earlier writings, as noted by D Churchill, '" I am just the man for Upsetting you Bloody Bobbies": popular animosity towards the police in late nineteenth-century Leeds'. *Social History*, 39 (2), 2014, pp.248–266 at p.249.

17 R Reiner, *The Politics of the Police,* 4th edition, Oxford, Oxford University Press, 2010. Reiner identifies specific policies crucial for the engineering of consent including organizational issues (bureaucratization, accountability), operational tactics (preventative policing, minimal force), image (impartiality, rule of law) and impact (crime fighting, service role) to which he also adds the changing socio-economic context in which new policing developed.

18 Reiner, *Politics*, p.60.

19 J Jackson, M Hough, B Bradford, K Hohl and J Kuha, 'Policing by Consent: Understanding the dynamics of police power and legitimacy', *Topline Results (UK) from Round 5 of the European Social Survey,* 2012.

20 Jackson, et.al., 'Policing by consent', p.4.

21 Jackson, et.al., 'Policing by consent', p.5 and J Jackson, B Bradford, M Hough and K H Murray, 'Compliance with the Law and Policing by Consent: Notes on Police and Legal Legitimacy', in A Crawford and A Hucklesby, eds., *Legitimacy and Compliance in Criminal Justice* accessed 16 October 2015 at http://ssrn.com/abstract=1717812.

22 Jackson, et.al., 'Compliance with the Law', p.5.

23 See the seminal article by Peter Bailey, '"Will the real Bill Banks please stand up?": Towards a role analysis of mid-Victorian working class respectability', *Journal of Social History, 1979.*

24 D Taylor, *The new police in nineteenth-century England,* Manchester, Manchester University Press, 1997, p.127.

25 Steedman, *Policing the Victorian Community,* p.146, argues that 'policeman watched, they waited'.

26 The *Examiner* opposed the introduction of a county force in 1856 and was concerned with the threat to English liberty but, after the passing of the 1856 Act, it never sought to have the force disbanded.

27 See for example Churchill's quoting Richard Hoggart, 'I am just the man', p.266.

28 A similar argument is put forward by Klein, *Invisible Men,* especially chapter seven.

29 There were clear examples of outright opposition to the proto-new police before 1857. The fact that parochial and paid constables were appointed on an annual basis made it easier to reject unpopular constables.

30 Churchill, 'I am just the man', p.265.

31 *Ibid.*

Author Biography

DAVID TAYLOR IS emeritus professor of history at the University of Huddersfield and former dean of the School of Music, Humanities & Media. As well as lecturing on the subject for over twenty-five years, he has written numerous books and articles on the history of crime and policing in the nineteenth and twentieth centuries. His books include *Policing the Victorian Town: the Development of the Police in Middlesbrough, c.1840–1914,* (2002), *Hooligans, Harlots and Hangmen: Crime and Punishment in Victorian Britain,* (2010),and (with Keith Laybourn), *Policing in England and Wales, 1918–39: the Fed, Flying Squads and Forensics,* (2011) and *The Battle for the Roads of Britain* (2015).

Index

C

D

Q

R

Y